# BUTTERUA A MANGY DOG!

# BUTTERUA
# A MANGY DOG!

O.C. Sharma

KALPAZ

ISBN : 978-93-5128-017-0

Price: ₹180

First Published 2014

*Published by*

**Kalpaz Publications**
C-30, Satyawati Nagar,
Delhi-110052
Ph. : 9212142040
E-mail: kalpaz@hotmail.com

*Laser Typesetting* : Awadhesh Computer, Delhi
*Printed at* : G. Print Process, Delhi

**Cataloging in Publication Data--DK**
Courtesy: D.K. Agencies (P) Ltd. <docinfo@dkagencies.com>

**Sharma, O. C.,** 1991-
Butterua a mangy dog! / O.C. Sharma.
p. cm.
Novel.
ISBN 9789351280170

1. Adult students--Fiction. 2. Indic fiction (English). I. Title.

DDC 823.92 23

*DEDICATIONS*

*For my parents and all teachers*

*For my friends and pupils*

*For IIT*

*For American Institute*

*For every student of my country*

# Preface

*'Butterua A Mangy Dog'* is his first novel. The story of the book is about an amazing teen age middle class student named Butterua who deals in any impossible work without thinking. And very surprisingly becomes successful as well. As a student his life is full of romance, comedy and srangeness.he gets passed in 12th as the second topper of the state. Like his other friends he also wishes to any technical course. However much he tries, but he can't move for his further step. Thus, the storm of bad time visits to his life. And then he becomes very serious. He leaves his family and everything else. He reaches Mumbai a no purpose boy, completely flat broke, hungry and extremely sad boy. He is nearly to die but ....

O.C. Sharma is a sort of sentimental author. In this novel, due to some emotional reasons he has used *broyee* for brother's wife; and *Mani7ha for Manisha*. The story of the novel is somewhat motivated with his own life. Many poems are used, supporting the story.

Accordingly, in his own practical life O.C. Sharma is quite like *Butterua*, the main character of the novel. He belongs to a middle class Brahmin family of a village in U.P. But very soon he is going to shift himself in Mumbai.

He is very simple, kind hearted and serious. To be the most impressive author of the country is his soul desire.

You can know more about him by visiting— www.oc sharma.com or emailing him at info@ocsharma.com

**O.C. Sharma**

Acknowledgements

To write this book has been remained a great experience of my life. Actually, I didn't write this book on the contrary I had to write. Because it is said that in life do something that other must write or write something that other must read. I could not be anything. So it was my compulsion to write something.

You know writing this novel has definitely been quite a challenge not just once, but a number of times. I tore the manuscript of this book three times and could complete it in eighteen months. Well I could not have reached this far without the blessing and love of god and my parents. So the first thank to god and to my parents.

I'm into the co-operation and faith that my friends have had in me.

During my lows, I always would be inspired by the doings of Shri Abhitabh Bachchan, a great Bollywood actor. So, a short note of thanks to him also.

A special bunch of thanks to American Institute where I got an essential experience of life from.

I'm thankful to my elder brother Shri Deshraj Sharma for his great economical support and to my cousin Shri Jitendra Sharma for his great comments on the manuscript.

A thank to my dear students and to my younger brother Manoj Kumar Sharma who held me in my bad days.

There is a remarkable thank to Kalpaz Publications, for publishing my Novel.

And lastly, I'm thankful to you all for struggling in your life for getting success.

With that, I would like to welcome you to 'Butterua A Mangy Dog'. I promise after reading this novel you would be a great fan of mine. Remember, it is my soul desire to be the most loving author of INDIA.

# Prologue

"Still, I'm alive, not died. You give up being worried. Study hard and be merry. I would handle all. Nothing can harm you in my presence– be sure!" I cooled him; spoke with all heart." And get me the cell no. of your Upadhayaya sir– I would talk."

"Nine seven five six two seven seven nine four nine." He recited his cell phone number in two minutes– and I memorised it already.

"*Okay* now don't worry. Hold fast to my words. I'm here, there is nothing you to fear," I said. I would fain handle everything, cheer up!" Bhaiya, one more thing. "He spoke when he felt I was going to disconnect the call.

"What?" I said, was more worried at this.

"Where are you speaking from?"

"From mouth" I laughed.

"That I know . . ."

"So?"

"I mean, where are you nowadays?" he showed his cunningness.

"It's none of your business!" I said and disconnected the call. *Bhaiya-bhaiya. ..., as* expected he was crying and crying. I could feel he kept crying all the time.

My dream got broken. I arose suddenly, a lot of sweat on my face. *Nine seven five six two seven eight no not eight seven. . . . . . .* I tried to remember the digits, I asked *Manoj* in dream.

Banke Bihari also got disturbed; he woke up with a sudden jerk, murmuring.

"Hey, brother! Would you kill me? What is this? Nine seven five-fix and blah-blah?" Amit looked at me with surprise. He was noting me for a long time— he would sleep near me, you know better.

"My Manoj is in danger! I must go" I spoke childishly; was excited in worried manner all the time.

"Who Manoj? And where are you talking to go?"

"My brother!"

"You have any family?" he asked, startling and waited for a pause so that he could get his answer.

"...Listen, I tell you all that, happened to me." I whispered with delirious expression after half a minute, he had asked that he was never interested in.

He came close to me, noting if not curious about my story words. He straightened himself and nudged me to be on.

Pronto, I had a stormy look at the stored up past of mine and started the story.

# 1

***Dumo Arihantdam***
***Dumo Sidddam***
***Dumo Aayriyadam***
***Dumo Uvaj-jhay dam***
***Dumo loy Sabb Sahudam***

It is the shalok of Jain religious people which was engraved on the wall in front of me while I sat on a 'bench by the office and was trying hard just to recite that tongue twisting mantra. Actually, it was a sort of trusty college and was being run by all the Jains of Rampur. So, there in a niche, some up wards the shalok, was a graven image of Mahaveer Swami also.

Yes I was at Jain inter college, the best college of the whole district and this was the first choice of toppers. Here, I had come to get admission. It was more than that I ever heard. A triple storey building, a large play ground and a team of 34 experts, moreover, the principal experienced with 99 marks is physics in $12^{th}$, enough to arrest my sort of student.

All the college was stuffed with new students, seniors and some students' leaders. I was very silent in myself; could watch them wandering here and there. They all were in fly dress. I evaluated myself. I was clinically clocked with a grimy old pink shirt and a rough nevy blue pants swelled along and torn black polythene, with the computerized marks-sheet of $10^{th}$ in it.

I was actually very shy boy, but very confident too. There on the bench, I was waiting for my chance just to get in the office.

Trrrr. . . . . . . . ., the bell rang. A peon, somewhat dark complexioned, a fatty 'dhole' around forty went inside the office. He came out two minutes later with some cobra files in his lap.

I thought for twenty seconds and all of a sudden stood up.

I followed that peon— I had an idea in my mind. I was not a bad mixer whether it was the first time. I entered any big college in the city alone but my confidence and attitude was not weak even then; I, without any hesitation, followed him.

"Good morning, Sir!" I offered him the sort of bidding as I caught him.

He became mad. As expected, he raised his eyebrows in surprise unable to digest the fact that I had dumped GOOD MORNING for him. Actually in big colleges, peons or any other fourth class employees are not given any sort of respect. So to be wished is beyond!

"Good morning, sir!" I wished him again when I received no answer from him.

"Good morning!" he vibrated. He noticed me deeply and did not take more time to guess about me. "From country?" he gave me a puzzled look.

"Yea. . . "

"Any work?"

"Yea, admission . . . . !" I shook.

"Then meet principal; office is there"

"There is a lot of gathering and noise as well."

"So what? It is a college; noise resounds here always." He smiled.

I became a bee buzzing in the clove, "Sir, would you do something?" I said.

He smiled again. "Okay, just wait for few seconds; I would try!" He said and in thirty minutes, he made me talk to the principal K.K. Arya, a serious and valued looking person– his personality imposing and age 34. On his fair complexion, I noticed blue suspenders, its sleeve rolled-up, *coco cola tie,* and rest hidden by the long glass table– my eyes itched for being unable to see them.

"Sir.....!" The peon said and paused.

"What?" He whispered being busy with his any work.

"Sir, he wants to take admission in eleventh–B." He mediated, "He has very good marks."

"Marks sheet; have you carried?" Principal Sir said, looking at me.

"Yea", I took out my $10^{th}$ class marks-sheet from the polythene, hung in my left hand and la it on the table.

He got shocked as he went through my marks. "Where were you so far?" He scolded me.

"Sir, I'm a farmer; and was busy with paddy-crop–it is its session."

"Then, why are you standing here? Go and be busy with your wheat-crop." He said and pushed away my marks-sheet.

Today, he made me remember the lesson, THE ANT AND THE GRASSHOPPER, I read any time.

"Sir, there is no season going on for the wheat-crop, now." I said innocently.

"Shut up! Shut up!" He cried fumbling, "70 per cent marks is a tough task in U. P. Board! But you people have no value of your study– so indolent!"

I stood silent looking around the room, this college must be in the hands of this sort of principal, I thought inwardly—his ownity worth touching his feet— my mind, a roistering insect in his words.

The peon left the room as he noticed his anger high.

"Sir, we are villagers; we have to face many problems. If I didn't see the farms, my study would have been nowhere."

"Then, why are you studying? Who says? Leave it, be a farmer!" He threw a hotchpotch voice with acting; both laugh and anger in it, *"Jai Javan, Jai Kisan!"*

I could control hard to stop my laugh due to the effect of his words on me.

"You are laughing?"

"Sorry, sir!" I cut my tongue. I kept standing there for seven minutes while he busied himself in his work again and ignored me at all.

"Why are you standing here? Go, this is your mark-sheet. Do the farming!" He cried and threw my mark-sheet.

"Sir, my admission . . . .?"

"Go, now there is no seat in this section, all are filled; see any other college!" He said rudely.

"Sir, please!"

"Just see, there is no seat, now. You must have been here earlier." He got angry. He showed me the list, the name of the students who took admission in eleventh-B, mentioned in it, "Is it any time of admission? All the admissions are closed now!"

"Sir, please . . . ! May be any corner! Please, sir!" I was a misty-eyed boy there; I requested many times. "Sir, I will work very hard. God promise, I'll be the topper in any case!" I said, my words and my behaviour very braggadocio.

"Sorry, there is no seat!"

"Sir, please . . . . .!" I said.

He was in hurry. He was going to leave the office. "No !" He shook his head and left the room—

While I kept standing there for four-five minutes, my eyes grew misty. I stood alone in the office with some hope still, ***God, please*** . . .

I had a wan face, on the chest of the auditorium of the college— the college pinching in my eyes. Principal's answer delivered the blow with all force, my mind unable to bear.

"Hey, any prob?" A healthy boy with a brawny body touched my back.

I spoke nothing and didn't have an eye-contact with him also— I was serious.

"I'm the president of this college and have some responsibility towards you all new students." He had an act of sheer bravado.

I looked at him, in his politician's dress.

"Admission?"

"Yea."

"You look serious," he said, ".... in maths ?"

"Yea."

"Madam, Dengua Machachhaar is very-very stubborn!"

"Who *Dangua Machachhar*?"

"The principal— we have coined a phrase!"

I smiled, my smile was the smile of any sad person.

"Bloody bastard, never listens to anyone" He said, "When his pops have their boots on his head, then he licks the bottom!" He said.

"*Yaar*, I'm dying to get admission!" I looked at him hopefully; caught him with my right hand on his shoulder.

"I can feel." He said with sympathy, "Madam, then don't be Wally here. Go to Anil Bashisht. I tell you, your admission will be done–he will do, his pop will do!"

I remained at his tongue but with no respect towards his idea. Whatever, I was into the doldrums. At 10:15, I left the College.

I was going back to pavilion, being compelled. I was in bus.

Wakey-wakey! My inward soul walloped me one hundred times.

Suddenly, I got the bus stopped and got down. Now, I'm to get admission, anyhow, I thought and anon had reached the MLA Anil Bashisht drum ling in the way.

My luck! He met me at the time. By mistake if I had eaten some 15 minutes more, he would have gone to Delhi and I couldn't have had a talk.

*Anil Bashisht*, an MLA of two tehsils named Badalia and Kankora was a RSS leader and had a powerful say with Bal Thackrey, the head of RSS, along the nice repo in B.J.P.— in Ayodhaya Mandir issue he played an important role. He was a great worshiper of God Rama, and always was robed in yellow clothes, that's why, he applied a chandan-tilak on his forehead.

"Jai ram ji ki pandit ji!" I wished him with my both hands, as I entered his office— he was alone there at the time I reached.

"*Jai ram ji ki!*" He gave me a politician's smiling face, "Come, sit."

I sat beside him on a green colour sofa. I noticed he was busy with some files as the principal became during the conversation.

The room was not much large but was enough to provide the place for 50 people at a time. It was well decorated.

"Sir, I have a work!" I spoke, having three-minutes wait.

"What?"

"Sir, I'm to get admission at *Jain Inter College*"

"Then go to college—why have you come here?"

"Sir, I have been there."

"So?"

"Sir, I have a nice percentage but the principle sir has denied even then."

"Why?" He entered upon my matter.

"Sir, he said there is no seat now."

"... Too observant of you!" He smiled, "Who sent you here?"

"None!"

"You're Name?"

*"Butterua; Butterua Giri Goswami!"* I said in deep husky voice and all eyes swung to him.

"You are *Brahmin?*"

"Yea"

"Very sharp-eyed!" He smiled again, "Would you take tea or anything?"

"No, only a glass of fresh water."

He called someone, and in two minutes, there was a glass, with cold Pepsi in it.

"Nowadays, students are not so innocent, they are the pop of big hitters, high voltage current!" The cheerful MLA said to that man who gave me the black colour Pepsi, just now.

"Hybrid seeds are there *pandit ji* . . . !" That person laughed and then they both smiled. I also had a gracious smile for the company sake.

"Just give this letter to the principal" He pushed a letter written on a *letter-pad* and said, "If even then, he doesn't listen, make me talk."

He gave me his cell number also.

I fetched that letter to the principal. It was 12:40– principal was going to leave the office. That peon also was there who arranged my talk with this principal earlier.

"You haven't gone so for?" The principal said, shocking as he found me again in the office.

"Sir, there is letter for you— just take a look." I put the letter, given by the MLA, on his table.

He lifted it and went through with his sharp eyes. Till then, I wondered in the room— there were many medals, shields, trophies and cups, wall–mounted and covered with a thick glass.

"*Anil Bashisht ji* is your relative?" He said shocking.

"That is written in it, you can read!" I had some rudeness in my words.

"You should've told it earlier." He said, "Ok, now come on 27th— your admission will be done!"

"Thank you, sir!" I was very pleased, now. I got leaving the office, while—

"Sir, villagers are very cunning! If they want something, they get and if they don't want, that's another thing!" The peon spoke to the principal— but I could hear properly; I was at the door.

I smiled, the principal as well— I stole a look-see.

As I was told, on July 27th, I moved and my admission was done, a special note of thanks to God!

# 2

"Hey, *madam*!" That president who met me at the admission time came near to me, crying– while he was sleeping under a tree, somewhat far from the college gate, inside it.

I was a bit late by the time. It was past 7:30, already. Moreover, it was my first day in the college. I had no uniform, no bag slung over my shoulder. As any student of a Degree College goes, I came like that. Some books in my right hand and a yellow T-shirt, navy blue jeans and a pair of relaxo company flip-flops, I was decorated with– my jeans, pretty long, touching the earth, and my coiffure, similar to that of *Ajay Devgan*.

"Hey, madam! Where are you going, no uniform, no bag? Are you coming from any farm?" He said.

"Yea, so?" I answered with strict words.

"Don't get angry, yaar! I just asked." He said remorsefully, "I didn't mean to pass any comment!"

"Then, why you stopped me?" I read the time in my wrist watch, "It's 7:50; my class missing . . .! Here, I'm already late and you. . . . !"

"A class potato!" He smiled cunningly, "Good. . . . ."

"A student must be! He must not play with his studies— as you are playing!" I noticed his red colour bag under the tree— of course, he must be bunking the class.

He laughed.

"Any mean?" I said and stepped ahead.

"Hey, madam! Don't go! Don't go!" He warned.

"Why?"

"*Madam,* you are novice. You don't know the history of this college. Here, tuition affair has a say. Students are beaten for it. I've been studying here since 9th."

"All guff! First, you guys don't study and then if you are smote, you give it a new name— *tuition teasing*!" I gave him a face of any grandfather.

"Okay, go missy go! I'm not preventing! But remember, I'm not fibbing!" He said.

I left him drinking water, near the gate, at government hand-pump.

Eleventh-B, the class of *eleventh-maths* was on 2nd floor. I went. I was on the last stair while I peeped from there– here, in the class all the fascinating stories flying around the college, looked becoming true. Means, that boy was not fibbing!

"*Aian-aian*, if you don't take tuition, be ready; you will be beaten daily." Dr. P.K. Jain, the lecturer of Mathematics, very hard and the bloody hungry dog for tuitions, was taking the class. His left hand injured; he pulled the hair of a girl, "*Bolo-bolo*, will you come or not?"

"Sir, it's not fair!" A boy said, his words hard.

"Just shut up or else!" The ghost left her and embarked on to him, *Aian-aian*, what's not fair? What's not fair? *Bolo-Bolo*, what's not fair?"

"Sir, beat us but don't beat girls!" he said in a low but confident voice, while tears misted his eyes.

"*Aian-aian*, do I feel good? *Bolo-bolo,* you are so weak! Why don't you take tuition?"

He spoke nothing.

"*Aian-aian*, when will you come? *Bolo-bolo*!" He left him shrugging. He stood in the middle of the class.

I stole a glance of the view going on in the class, me a poor little mite!

***Eina!*** This is a great college, that currently occurred incident effectuated me a lot of nervousness. Many hot blobs of sweat slipped over my face. I dreaded to think what would happen if I go— my mind snag geld! I took out my handkerchief and wiped the face. I ruminated for thirty seconds and went ahead fearlessly— an idea occurred to me.

*"Aian-aian,* so late!" He came up to me, giving a dangerous attack, "No uniform, no shoes, and no bag! *Bolo-bolo,* where from?"

I didn't care of his questions.

"Sir, are you *P.K. Jain Sir?"* I asked freely– that president who met me at the college gate, told me about this teacher, already.

"Yea, so?"

"Sir, I'm to take tuition, my brother would come to you, he has advised— you teach nice!" I lied; did the flattery, following my plan.

*"Aian- aian,* so come in. Why are you standing out?" He made that boy run, who argued with him just before, back– he was sitting on the monitor-seat– and made me sit there. He drilled all the class, *"Aian-aian,* this is a very good boy, tuition first, entry after!"

He left the class at 8:20; his period got over ten minutes before.

Next three periods bunked, no teacher peeped into the class. At 10:30, the bell rang. It was half-time, i.e., repast time. All the students ran towards the canteen, me also.

"Hey, yellow T-shirt!". An student called me up, "*P.K. Jain Sir* is calling you."

I went up to him. He was sitting in staff room; and having fun with a ma'am— the ma'am was unmarried and looked like an item girl, more than a school teacher. She had an attractive elongated face, smoky eyes and a long blue hair style- her age 24, fixed.

*"Aian-aian, Saxena!* This is a boy! He asked for tuition first, entered the class after." He made me introduced with a teacher— he was somewhat thin but handsome enough. That was *Gaurav Saxena*, the best teacher of physics.

I wished him.

"... Your name, *Bete*?" That newly introduced teacher asked.

*"Butterua; Butterua Giri Go Swami!"* I told him, while my mind intinerant on a porn magazine kept on the table before them what a shameful nuisance!

I noticed only three people in that room– he, that newly introduced Saxena sir and that nubile ma'am.

*"Bete-bete*, I'll give you full marks in practical. Come to me also, eh?"

"Er, I'll think." I said, "Now, may I go, sir!"

*"Aian-aian,* go! Play!"

I turned to leave the room.

"Come here, *Butterua*!" Suddenly, I heard a dazzling voice of hers, while I was at the gate.

I again went up to them. She gave me a slip; and was gonna say something, but saxena sir spoke in middle, "*Bete-bete,* this is *Sakshi* ma'am, teaches English, very good teacher, *bete!"*

I wished her with no word, only by head.

"*Bete-bete*, ninety three marks in English in Intermediate! Wish her, *Bete*!"

She laughed, "He has wished already!"

"When?"

"When you were in your *bete- bete*."

A laughing point!

"Butterua go to canteen and fetch three teas or coffees." She said, "Whatever else, I've mentioned in this slip".

I went to the cafeteria. It was 300 mtrs far from the staff room, of the college boundary. Many students gathered there. I put the slip on the desk of the coffee corners and received three cups of espressos in a plastic–tray— no kettle.

I was backing; in the way, that boy who warned me very first, met again.

"Hey, madam! How do you feel now? All is ok, or . . . . . ?"

He asked , coming with me, his words cunning.

"I'm ok. And, I'm feeling good!"

"Really!" He had a dazzled attack, "I'm shocked, how?"

"It's the mind, madam! And, it's not given to every one. Also it can't be valued; otherwise all the haves would have bought it."I smiled.

He laughed at my words-framing.

"Would you take coffee?"

He smiled.

I gave him a cup and also lifted one own self. I sipped. He sipped. We both sipped, stepping forward.

"Your élan!" He said.

# 3

Interval got over. *Gaurav Saxena* Sir, whom P.K. Jain sir made me introduce to, in the staff room just some minute before, came with a light blue colour register in his hand.

"Good morning, sir!" All the students stood up.

"Good morning!" He sat in the chair, made from *sheesham* wood and put the register on the table. "Sit down, guys!" He said after keeping us two minutes in our standup-position.

We all sat, paying thanks.

He turned over three big *Kalia Nag's* hoods like pages and put the point of his blue colour butter-flow pen at fourth one, so as to take attendance.

He closed the register as I registered my presence as the last student at the number hundred twentyth. He took a sharp look of the class with crow-eyes, with twenty seven students absent.

He left the register on the table and passed the half an hour wandering in the balcony. The class got stuffed with noise during the time.

"Stop, this infernal noise" He came into the class with a thundering voice, but became a sweet candy in few minutes, "*Bete-bete,* now, your classes are going on, *bete*! So, don't bunk the classes now— your syllabus will suffer, *bete*!" He said.

No one spoke anything.

"And also start coming to tuition, *bete*." He gave an in-depth lecture on indefinite pronouns but not subjective, centred on tuition. "*Bete-bete,* if you come for tuition, all will listen. I will too listen, principal will too listen— many benefits, *bete*!"

All the students peeped into the fucking mean of his— it was horror and infamy. I yawned. He noticed but said nothing.

"Sir, sorry to cut you shot— period is gonna get over. Have mercy on the subject also." A student who was at my place before me and who was sent back, stood up and said, having been bored by his all guff.

"Do shut up! You people no manners! Haven't your parents taught you?" He banged his fist on the table, with stiff anger . "*Bete-bete*, I'm very bastard, *bete*! I never do the students, bete! But, *bete-bete*, I never pass the students also, *bete*!" Indignantly, he wagged a finger three times.

It was not any docile prob. All the students were up a gum tree. He repeated his hackneyed subject tuition how many times, don't know.

"Sir, what if any poor student is there and unable to take tuition?" That girl whose hair, P.K. Jain sir pulled, said hazily.

She was *Mani7ha,* the most beautiful girl in my class and may be in the whole college also— I heard her name when S*axena* Sir took attendance.

*"Bete-bete,* that student should not study here *bete!* Its better to get your name struck off from the college, *bete*!" He said, "*Bete–bete*, I told you about myself, *bete*! I'll never allow to pass *bete!* I'll never pass!"

Now, of course, all the class was to face this gut-wrenching test, very hard task!

His period got over. He went down, without teaching anything; I noticed all the students had their faces down.

Next all periods empty.

At 12:40, we became free from that jail.

"Hey, yellow T-shirt!" I heard a voice in my back, a group of girls coming, hogging all the way there— it's a habit of girls that they walk on road in group and hog all the space.

I was not used to talking with girls. I looked back, but

ignoring, all came in my way again; I was a nebbish. I looked around. I was hogged by the girls from all three sides— only a student, that too from junior class, was ahead of me I felt suffocation.

"Hey, yellow T. shirt; listen *yaar*!" The voice entered my ears again.

I got more nervous.

"I'm not yellow T. shirt. I have my name!"

All the girls laughed.

"Sorry!" The girl who spoke in class gazed at me, ". . Your name?"

"What'll you do?" I said rudely and nervously, my voice different.

"I'm just asking, *yaar!*"

*"Butterua* . . . . ." I said, "You didn't listen in the class?"

"Sorry, I could not hear; that *Aian-aian* was there." She coined a new phrase for P.K. Jain Sir.

I glanced at her for a while— her egg-shaped face was decorated with florid complexion, sly eyes and stupid lips, enough to sex-up her image. She was a gentle student in a simple college uniform like other girls— white *salvar- kameez* and a same colour tippet on it. Her glossy hair were sleeked back over her back that were back-combed looking much more thicker, with a simple clip in her hair.

I was lost some where for some time.

"You are so active!" She gave her left hand having a sexy look, "Any way, I'm *Mani7ha* . . . .!"

I disappeared from there as ***Muni Narad***, a surprise!

# 4

*Amee* was my chum who would reside near my place. After leaving my books at my place, I directly went to him, without having lunch. At the time when I reached him, he was in his *khapral* or *chopal*. He lay in a loose cot, the cot almost frayed; his jolly company, a four-band radio was on. I went there to share the experience of my first day in any college.

"Hey, *Amee*! What's up?" I slapped on his left thigh— he didn't notice me while nearing him.

He got shocked. I noticed a lot of sadness and tears in his eyes. He sprang up on the cot wiping his tears, "*Butterua*. . . ., you have come?"

"No, my spirit is here!" I said

He gave a weak smile. He put the Radio off. I sat on the edge of the cot. I took the radio and started fiddling with it.

"Have you taken your lunch?" I asked.

"No!" He spoke thirty seconds later when I asked again.

"Why?"

He spoke nothing but stared weeping.

"Hey, *Amee*! You are weeping! What happened?" I turned down the volume of the radio and put that on the earth. I wiped his tears.

"I wish, my mother were alive!" He said sobbing.

"Hey, what happened? Tell me!" I said.

"*Yaar*, my *bhabhi* always criticizes me. Whenever, I go to eat, as a queen bee she always remarks *how much I eat*.

"Now what? Rest of I know, you have told many times. Tell what happened today?" I said.

"As I went to wash my hands to take lunch she started saying, *Dal* has been finished, chawal has been finished and rotties are no more, and then I came back."

I had a lot of sympathy towards him. He was not literate. He was a hard working boy. From dawn till dusk, he would remain as busy as a bee with tilling; watering the crop and rooting out the natural wastages from it. His life was so hard, moreover the behaviour of his brother and broyee towards him no extant! His broyee was somewhat literate but, very fatty and black complexioned as gorgon.

"Okay, just come with me. I also haven't taken anything—both will eat together."

"No, *yaar,* you must!" He said feeling embarrassment.

"Shut up! How long will you be hungry?" I pulled his hand, our friendship an indissoluble friendship.

My mother served the food. Only, we both were eating. The food was cold.

"*Yaar, Amee*! Why don't you speak to your brother?" I looked at him.

"He won't listen."

"Why?'

"He is cowed by her coy activities. He is completely in her hands. She leads him by her noise." He said.

His mother was no more and father very old. Two-three years before, after two-three months of his brother's marriage, she died due to T.B. His brother's marriage was a shotgun marriage– she was already one month gone with his brother before their marriage. They both eloped from the college; a passing infatuation must be the reason!

"I think, before your ***Bhaiya-Bhabhi's*** return, your mother had died!"

"Yea!" He felt something and started weeping.

"Hey, don't weep, *beta*! I'm here; I'm like your mother!" My mother wiped his tears by the edge of her parrot-coloured *sari*,

"*Beta,* never feel shy—— if you are hungry, ask me; you are also *Butterua-like for me!*"

We both took the lunch and he went out after taking his fill. I noticed a torn black colour chintzy pants and a green shirt on it.

My mother, an ocean of love— she came to me having a glass of milk in her hand while I was studying on the roof, around 10 pm.

"Retire to bed, *beta*! It's too night. Rest of study, continue tomorrow." She put the glass on my stool, made from wood. She sat much close to me on the cot, I sat on.

"*Mummy*, I'm to be the topper. For that, I will have to burn the mid night oil!" I said in reply.

"Do, but be aware towards your health also. It's falling down." she murmured, "The nights are already so short; dying before being born and you . . . . . . !"

"Mummy, I'm to be the topper!" I took the glass in my hand and started sipping it.

"Shut up! Take this milk and be in your bed. A lot of time is there, keep doing your study— I won't say anything." She said.

Actually, all the mothers are so. They can't see the drops of sweat or blood oozing out from the body of their children. They are very soft!

My mother was used to doing all this . She was always providing me with a glass of milk and a long lecture— it's her routine.

"*Mummy,* you were saying so, last time also." I said.

"*Beta*, as long as I am, I'm saying. When I die, I won't say." She said, with seriousness in her voice.

"Then, somebody else will be there!" I smiled.

At this, she suddenly started laughing.

"What happened?"

She didn't answer, but carried on laughing. She laughed and laughed.

"Mummy, what happened to you? Why are you laughing?"

"You know you would have been of six or seven, due to some reason, I got crossed with you and stopped talking with you. You tried a lot but I didn't speak. Else, annoyingly, I said I'm not your mother-vother, whoever is there, talk to her." She said, "You know then what you said?"

"What?"

She couldn't tell, her inward feelings beyond.

"Oh, *mummy*, now tell!"

"You said sobbing, if you are not, don't be; when my wife would come, I would call her mother."

"What–what?" I laughed; I broke the limit of laughter.

I finished the milk and she went down with the empty glass that she had carried with the milk in it.

I couldn't forget this incident.

At 11:05, I slept. Now, I was in any dream—I put my books on the desk. There, I found a half page of a rough note book, with some words written on it.

*Hey, gorgeous boy!*

*Who are you, I don't know but whoever you are, in fact you are a thing very sexy, bloody magician! I'm impressed. I'm in love with you. Please call me, please. . .*

*You can call at +91-09536402222, but please at mid night because that will be the chance when we can talk openly in right?*

*Must call, I'll wait!*

—YOUR MANI7HA

I went through the letter three times. I glimpsed her. She was gazing at me playing with her lustrous hair; her blonde hair tumbled in a cascade down her back—her beauty and vivacity superb!

I came to my place. I called her as it was planned.

Radhe-Radhe-Radhe, Barsane Wale Radhe, and the bell went on, a hypnotic song was there.

*"Hello!"* An engaging voice knocked me to speak, but I didn't.

I became dotty and larking around as I heard, a great cassis in her voice. I heard and heard and lost in an erotic world. I tell you something nourishing got into to me.

She disconnected the call.

I was on my bed. Her lovely face, the viridity on her foxy lips and glazing eyes were before my open eyes, shaking their booties. I was completely arrested; her voice as if has started tilling of my inward feelings.

Intuitively, because I wanted to appreciate her voice, I dialled her number again.

"Hello!" The same botylicious voice was there. But I spoke diddly as earlier.

She disconnected again.

I dialled again.

"Hello, who is there?" Slightly yelled was this voice. She said angrily, "What's your prob? Why are you teasing me at this time?" She cried, so thunderous!

One, who barks, is a dog!

I fell in a garden of love. There were buds, beautiful flowers and a lot of sweet smell, being mirrored. By buds–so many sittings together and nourishing the love. By beautiful flowers–a fantasy flowered love life and getting a lovely flower. And by sweet smell— spreading the sweetness of love all around as the smell of fresh rose.

I was of course a mad!

"Conjecture, who can be?" I laughed, as she repeated *hello-hello* more than three times.

She tried forty seconds but couldn't get. "Sorry, you are out of my range." she said innocently, "You tell please."

"Try- Try!" I said.

"Sorry, I'm not getting!" She left her voice loose.

"Don't over tax!" I said, "Didn't you put a letter in my desk and ask for calling you at mid night?"

"Me?" she laughed, as if blowing air of early dawn all of a melting glacier, so cool!

"Yea!" I said lazily.

"Mr. you are misled. It's a wrong number." She became a gentle girl.

I laughed.

"Why are you laughing?" She said, "Are you ok?"

"I know you girls by your blood. I know you. You do so! You lie!"

"I'm not lying"

"Good! Very good style my darling, very good style!"

"Hey, hello, mind your language first and tell your name, then talk." She said seriously, "Otherwise . . . . ."

"Otherwise, what?" I said, "Didn't you but the letter in my desk?"

"Which letter? What letter? And what desk you are talking about?"

"Darling, my tongue twisting *rasmalai*! Your voice is so sexy in anger?" I said.

"Shut up, be in manner!" She said, her voice hard, "To whom you are talking?"

"Aren't you *Mani7ha*?"

"Who *Mani7ha*? I'm not any *Mani7ha-Vani7ha*!" She said carelessly, the anger in her voice.

"Hey, don't be so. I'm scared of!" I said naughtily.

"Be sure, I'm not fibbing!"

"No, your voice is same!"

"Shut up!" She shouted, "If I said I'm not any *Mani7ha*, means I'm not. Why don't you understand? Why are you arguing?"

"Ok, tell me one thing!"

"What?"

"You like bud or flower or its smell. If you are not *Mani7ha*, I would judge in a ziffy." I said— actually, I did not mean these words of mine; I spoke just like that

"Why should I?"

"Tell, please!"

"Bud!"

"Me too!" I cried, "Hundred percent you are *Mani7ha*—you are fibbing, here!"

"Surprise!" she laughed, "You are next to the dogs!"

"Why?"

"You know, why the dogs are used for detective work?"

"No!"

"Darling, dogs have an excellent sense of smell. They can hear ultrasonic sounds."

"Thanks for this compliment!"I smiled.

"You are so sweet! Sorry, I was just kidding!" She said," I'm really sorry!"

"It's ok!" I said, "Any way, I want these naughty things from you, always."

She shied.

"I love you my green chill, I love you!" I became *majnoo*, "I love you too- too- too . . . ., too -much, you my sexy *Mani7ha*!"

"*Humm* . .!" She muttered shying, " I know !"

"Okay, leave it. Tell what are you doing?" I said.

"Nothing, I was just studying, but your call disturbed."

"Ooo . . . . . , my call disturbed you!"

"Sorry, I'm kidding!"

"I like it." I said, "Any way come to my place."

"Why?"

"I'm just saying, come!"

"At this time?"

"*Yea,* so what?" I said, "I'm alone at place; no one is here. I have many coverings, beer strong-one, and mood also. So come on, baby! All the night let's go!"

"*Shuttt...* up!" She cried.

"Shut up, for what?"

"Stupid, it's me; *Shakshi,* your English teacher! She said.

"What? I got surprised!" I fell down on my face, on my bed. Would she have really recognised me? What would I have been feeling then?

My dream got broken.

# 5

Next day, at the same time, I be took myself there in the class, with my dress same.

It was the period of *Skakshi ma'am*. She was on the podium and was writing something on the black board, a piece of pink colour chalk in her hand. I noticed her black-colour Black-Berry phone, on a green colour register, on the table.

Also, I noticed an orange-colour *sari* with golden border, many pin-pointed stars glinting in the same orange but some dark *palloo,* in the strong light of three *CFLs—s*he hung it in her V-shaped left hand.

There was the death in her quilted golden *saneeled* blouse, a *Rampuri-Chhuree!*

I had a call of nature, very hard to control.

"Ma'am, may I see the *loo*?" I stood up and asked—I was sitting at the same place, I sat last day.

"Why?" she spoke while writing, a question not worth asking.

I got nervous. All the students had cunning inward smiles across their faces. All were misunderstood, along with me.

". . . .*Brooker T. Washing Ton* kept wondering before the eyes of principal?" She completed the sentence. In fact she didn't listen to me so for. She turned her face. "Aren't you writing?" She said, as she noticed me standing.

"Ma'am, may I see the *loo*?" I showed my pinky.

"Why? Haven't you seen it so for?" She joked, with some smile lay on her lips.

*"Ma'am,* please! May I go; it's out of control!" I requested, ingloriously.

"No, only two questions are left; sit down!" She threw the chalk on my seat. She shanghaied me again in to writing down. She now, selected a green chalk from a box— the chalk-box kept on the table, with many different colour chalks in it.

"Sit down!" She said again, her voice rude. She came on podium and busied herself in her work, again. The podium, a curvedly made thing was somewhat above the floor.

I sat down. I, a poor child, and a helpless boy looked around, all the students had their hands fast.

Her writing was cursory!

I noted some words, but I felt uncomfortable. "*Ma'am*, please . . . . .!" I requested again, ergo.

"No, only after five minutes!" She said.

Piss, I felt very hard. I requested and requested but got all refuses.

Anyway, her answer, bête-noire for anyone in the situation— I asked three times more, the pressure of piss next to control.

Never! Suddenly, I shocked all the class, along with the English teacher. I went out of the class, my behaviour betokening no respect towards the say of teachers.

Sorry, matter was so!

For this problem, arrangement was on the ground floor I went downstairs.

Rats! All the *loos* were latched from inside, my bad luck!

I kept waiting. Every second was like an hour for me at that time. As much as could be controlled, I did. But it was a hard puzzle.

"Come out! Come out!" Thunderously, I started crying. I kicked all the doors, very hard, but no response.

After a great toing and froing, I decided to see any of the girls' *loo* — a dangerous chance!

Having seen here and there, very quickly I gave it a go—

actually the *loo*s of the girls were not far from ours. The door was shut but not latched or bolted from inside.

Eeee. . . . . ! A female voice cried. Was there any girl in the *loo*?

*Yes,* there was . . . . ., an incident asinine and shameful! My eyes took a photo of all her hidden zone, her *salwar* opened.

I vaguely remembered, she was *Mani7ha* who communicated with me while backing, this day before. My piss went where, don't know!

I broke out in a cold sweat. I, an over wrought boy didn't see the face of the college for next seven days, all the class bunked. I was much more embarrassed and frightened, besides. What if she would have gone to the principal, my mind filled with many more whys, whats and hows. My nerve-racking thoughts had thrown me in a difficult situation.

$8^{th}$ day, I remembered my college, that too at 11:05. Interval got over just now five minutes before, *bête-bête* in the class; and the class jam-packed— it was the test, first one, today.

"Just drag your benches ahead, all the guys!" He, a bloody *jacka-bapes* ordered all the students throwing his hands.

"May I come in, sir?" I knocked him, as I caught the class-door. I had some books in my right hand as I carried earlier, but with one difference, me in uniform, a gentle student now.

"Butterua, at this time, *bête*!" He looked at me.

"Actually sir, I have carried my luggage today— I have rented a room." I fibbed, "Sir, after adjusting all the articles in the room, I rented, I saw there was some time, so I thought why should I miss my rest time and have come."

"Good boy!" He smiled, "Just see, *you ne'er-do-well*-what passion he has towards study, while you haven't left your beds so far." He commented looking at all students.

"Sir, he is coming after seven days, you don't know?" A voice thrilled me; *Mani7ha* raised her voice.

"Why?" He looked at me.

"Some work, sir!" I fibbed once more.

"Okay, come in and sit there, near that girl." He nudged me to sit by *Mani7ha,* on her bench.

It was test, so all the girls and guys were mixed, otherwise all the girls put their jacksies on their reserved benches, partially in left of the guys. No boy was allowed to sit there.

I had to sit there with her, *bête-bête*'s order. She was sitting on second one from ahead; I was wall-wards, only two students on a bench.

My condition I knew— no one could fathom. My eyes couldn't face any one in the class.

"*Bete–bête,* take out a pair of pages *bete*! Everyone, *bête*!"

We all obeyed his words.

"*Bete-bête,* it is your very first test, *bête!* Do fair! And remember, bête! Numbers will be added in the result, bête!" He instructed.

He gave five questions on the board and spoke to do, "Each question has two-two marksvalue."

All the students were in field, along my bench partner. But I was fiddling with my pen, doing the post-mortem of its— all parts on the bench, the cap separate, the rifill separate and its point separate.

Twenty minutes passed, but my note book was longing to be touched by the point of my penquit fair it was. I wrote nothing, the *loo* episode in my head.

Mani7ha did her head up and looked around, *bête-bête* in back, in last. She gave her eyes to my test paper. "*Butterua,* do! Don't be nervous! And don't be worried about the matter— a lot of the time is there to waste after the test." She entered into the spirit of my feelings, all the words in her eyes.

Wonder! She guessed, I was thinking that? How I felt at the time, I can't explain— it was quite different. I had this sort of feeling very first time, a different energy in myself.

"Stupid, do the test! Only ten minutes are left!" She said her voice slow.

"- - - Enough!" I whispered, looking at her and set the pen. In rest ten minutes, I did four questions, with one left. Reason,the time got over.

*Bete-bête* collected all the test papers and left the class.

I paid thanks to her after the class.

# 6

Next day, at 5:50, in morning I parked my wildfire city bike at the place of *aian–aian*, my purpose was tuition. I reached there from my place, riding 24 kms. I was in my uniform.

An aunty, may be the wife of *aian-aian,* pointed towards me her finger to go upstairs. I noticed she was in a jade green night gown.

There were 24 stairs that I climbed. For fifteen minutes, I alone kept sitting there in the room he would tutor in— it was my first day. No other student was there. Three benches were placed alongside a chair. Five students could sit on each.

*Aian-Aian* entered the room in sixteenth minute. He was wearing a slaty and white mixed polo-shirt and black pants, on his thick set physique, clothes code matched.

"Good morning sir!" I stood up.

". . . . . . Morning!" He smiled. I sat down without his any permission. *"Aian-aian,* alone?" He gave a kicker.

*"Sir. . . . !"*

"You have carried your books?" He asked.

"*Yea!*" I took out the book of logarithm, written by *Kumar Mittal* and a rough note book. I paused it.

*"Aian-aian,* you know what is logarithm, you are going to study?" He asked.

"Yea, a little bit, learnt in $9^{th}$." I said excitingly.

"Good!" He smiled and started teaching; digged the history of logarithm.

"Sir, at college an incident took place with me." I interrupted him, while he could write only log $(mn) = logm + logn$ and log $\frac{m}{n} = logm - logn$

"What?" He raised his eyes up.

I told him all that happened in the *loo*.

He laughed, "*Aian-aian*, don't worry; I'm with you!"

"Sir, I'm very embarrassed!" I said.

"*Aian-aian*, forget all, it goes! And anyway, it was her mistake, not yours— she must have latched the door. Why she didn't?" He said and made me feel easy; patted on my cheeks, "Don't feel fear, I'm here!"

"Thank you, sir!" I said.

He put the point of his cello pen just now, I interrupted again, "One more thing sir...."

"What?"

"Sir, how about this, all room jams up with the students?" I talked about the room, I sat in, at the time.

"Never!"

"Sir, make me monitor of my class. I would see all; I promise the whole class will be here!" I said.

"What?" He said, "I can't believe it."

"Believe me, I can do so!" I said.

"Okay, let's see in the class; make me remember there!" He said.

At 7:03, he left me.

At 7:20, I reached the college. It was the first period at 7:30 *aian-aian*'s one. He came with his register at 7:40, ten minutes late by his time.

He marked the attendance and started walking in towards the students after closing the big file that he carried.

"Sir, any monitor must be in the class!" l whispered as he passed across me.

He winked. He went up to the table and sat on it having his legs in the air, "*Aian-aian*, is there any monitor in your class?"

He looked at all. No one spoke.

"No, sir!" After forty seconds, *Mani7ha* dared to speak.

"So, far?" fabricatedly, he got shocked.

Once again there was the same silence what was sometime before.

*"Aian-aian,* your class teacher *Saxena* is so lazy; hasn't made any monitor so far!" He sat properly, his both hands on his both thighs and legs swaying in the air, "Okay, lemme do; I make!"

His examinee-eyes got searching the candidates, able to monitor, "Hey, stand up!" His sharp eyes plumped for Mani7ha, "Would you like to be a monitor?" He asked her.

She did her tipped and hair, as she stood up. She felt her *salvar-kurta* somewhat rumpled; so she made them also.

"Aian–aian, would you like to be a monitor?" He asked again.

She looked at me. I stole my sight and had my head down. She stood silent, her eyes agreeing.

*"Aian-aian,* put-up your hands together— she is your second monitor!" He announced.

The room filled with noise, the noise warm.

Two minutes later he moved his eyes towards me, "*Aian-aian*, will you be monitor?"

"Yes, sir! He must be!" *Mani7ha* spoke before me.

I looked at her with her superb excitement. All the students okayed and started clapping before signature of *aian-aian*.

He smiled and said, "*Aian-aian*, you both come. This bench is oft– reserved for both of you. Sit here, always." He nudged towards the first bench in the middle row.

"Sir, we both, together?" I said, my voice looked outrageous.

"So?" He said, his voice loud.

Bulb got fused!

She smiled while I stole a glance. Now, we both were the

incoming CRs of our class. Out of compulsion, I was there with her on the same bench; she just came on, me a badly nervous oke!

Two minutes later after sitting, I stealthily larged the corner of my eyes her-wards, her eyes looked waiting for it, I did. I squeezed myself. Her silent lips became naughty. She laughed, keeping her face hidden by her both hands.

I felt shy. Here, hardly, I could dare to have my eyes up and she......

# 7

Next day at 7:35, *bete-bête,* in place of *aian–aian,* appeared in the class, *aian-aian* being absent. He had the test papers, taken two days before, in his left hand.

*Mani7ha* and I sat on our reserved seat.

"Good, seat has been beautified with monitors; nice!" He smiled. He kept the all test papers on the table and called both of us. He said to her to separate the testpapers of girls from all and to me to go down and be there with his register.

Within in a ziiffy, I was there— *Mani7ha* was still doing her work. He was in balcony. He took the register from my hand and came inside the class. "Help her!" He nudged me, while I tried to see the seat.

She smiled.

I had to stand with her. In the period, we did our work and he did his— he marked the attendance.

"Sir, these are!" She said, as he closed his register.

"Okay, now take your seat, *bête*!" He said.

We both took our seats.

"Do your tippet." I winked her, a little portion of her boobs visible.

She made it. She looked at me and smiled, a stupid girl!

*"Bete–bête,* you haven't done fair *bête;* very bad marks, *bête*!" He said, "*Bete-bête,* I wept while checking, only six students in blue moon, bête!"

All the students flinched at his last dialogue.

"*Bete–bête,* the passed students are— *Mani7ha*, bête, scored seven, *Aiece*, bête, scored seven, *Pharat*, bête, scored, six, Udit, bête, scored four, *Sindhi*, bête, scored four and *bête–bête, Butterua*, scored three." He announced the names.

He flung a dangerous sight on rest, "Just go in the balcony and be cock."

"Sir, girls too?" *Pharat*, a raillery spoke.

"No, girls will be standing, having their both hands up." He roared, "just move . . . . !"

In few seconds, all the girls looked in their position having both hands up; stood at their places. And the boys were out.

*"Bete-bete,* take these papers and put before them, bête, name-wise, bête!" He nudged both of us once more. He was on his chair and doing something with his register.

We followed his words.

Now, there in the balcony the cocks were reading, a rad scene!

"Excuse me! You guys listen, please!" I came on podium as bête-bête left the class, with next period empty—he freed all the students two minutes before he left the class. "Now, this class is under the flag of my monitory." I said.

"So?" *Mani7ha* interrupted.

"You don't speak, please!" I said, having my eyes at my flip-flops. It's shocking, how I dared to speak and also how I climbed on the stage.

"Okay, carry on." She had her both elbows on the bench with 'Ë', an upside down V-shaped figure and fixed her chin along the face in an 'U', formed by her palms.

"Dear friends, I always will try to do my best for you, but you all are to be with me." I said, "Before continuing anything, I would like to know one thing."

All the class had the eyes at me, expression looked asking word **WHAT**.

"First of all, tell please, are you all satisfied with me, as your monitor?"

Neither anybody said 'yes', nor any body 'no'— all were silent.

"I'm not!" Suddenly, a boy, the president who met me very first, raised his voice.

"Your name?"

"*Pharat*"

"Any reason?"

"No reason, but that is my position— you have snatched."

"Okay, come here."

He came on the podium. "Who would like to vote him— raise your hands, please?" I said.

Only two hands, in back were straight, the rest of class ignored. Both who raised their hands, were his friends— *Udit* and *Sindhi*, intelligent, but naughty boys.

"Just see, they have chosen me. I didn't snatch anything." I said.

"Whatever, but very soon you will have to leave this seat— I have a strong say in politics." He said rabidly, going to his seat, his irritating eyes seasoning proud.

I kept looking at him, all the class as well.

I had cunning smile across my lips.

"You were saying something." *Mani7ha* knocked me, breaking her sitting style. Now, she sat straight cross-handed.

"Sorry!" I broke my silence, "Dear friends, it's not any intelligency to see this day like days every day. It better to listen our teachers; take tuition!" I lit upon the main subject.

"Just get in his back, you bloody flatterer dog!" He murmured angrily.

"Shut up!" I cried, my voice got twittering in the whole class, "shut up your offensive language— this is a class, you know? It seems, your parents haven't inculcated you any manners of talking." I humiliated him.

"So you teach, please!" His both friends spoke. They came ahead and sat with that rude boy on the same bench.

"Let the time come, obviously I will. I will have to— your behaviour is telling." I said.

"Good dialogue!" *Pharat* said and they both started clapping "Mindblowing, yaar!" He also made noise with his clapping. It looked that they tried to pull my leg.

"I'm not talking to you, be silent!" I cried.

"How will you, you have no mouth!" He shrugged.

"Shut uppp....., this is your monitor and your monitor is warning you to be silent or to leave the class, otherwise.....!"

"Otherwise, what?"

"Butterua, don't argue with them; they are bloody wolf-whistler." Mani7ha said to me, "You carry on . . . . . !"

"What? you are speaking so!" His tongue stopped, all noise stopped. "Mani7ha, you are giving a name of wolf-whistler . . . . . to me?" He had a lot of emotions of any love lorn lover in his voice.

Mani7ha ignored him. She was doing her hair during all the time he remained on. She held her clip in her mouth, I noticed.

"Yes, so; aren't you?" She said after fixing her hair in the hair clip, at the time he ended.

"Nothing!" He became serious. In next forty seconds, he left the class and his both friends followed— it looked he loved her and now obviously will weep, his heart broken.

"Sorry!" I said, "Pardon them, please; I'm apologizing, on their behalf. Actually, they are hurt by the cruelty of the teachers; anyone can be so. But they are good at heart. Now, it is our responsibility to ingratiate ourselves with them." I said, or better say, won the heart of the girls, my ingenuity superb!

"Dear friends, tuition issue is not any tiny problem, and also is not the only one before us. It's a dangerous disease and is all around. We are to eradicate it." I said.

"How?" A girl spoke, named *Aiece* or something—I'm not sure.

"Start going to tuition. And then see, they will teach in the class also." I said.

"And fees?" Mani7ha asked with eagerness.

"Any way, if we go somewhere else, then we pay or not? So, what's wrong in going to our own teachers?" I said.

All class had to think what I said about.

"Don't worry, I'm here. Your friend is here. I won't let anything wrong to be done with you, I promise." I said with my all heart, "Believe me!"

"Okay!" Mani7ha lifted her cello pen and pulled its cap out from it; she looked at girls, they nodded. I looked at their anties, they also nodded.

A puzzle looked near to be solved.

# 8

*Aian-aian* off his nut! *bete-bete* off his nut! They both off their nuts! Their minds stopped working— matter was so, any one could have been. All the class was there at their places.

A laughing subject, no one of the either of the two had enough place to make sit, even. It was the first time; they saw the all class in their tuition.

I was all in all, now.

Seventeen days passed. All the class was going but *Pharat* and his group not, still. I was worried.

"You have any commission?" Mani7ha did her eyes at me. At that time, we both were in canteen. In seventy days, she did enough; now, I was somewhat familiar with her and could talk to any girl.

"What?"

"Nothing, I'm just kidding." She laughed, "Anyway, why are you so rigorously trying, tell no! Nowdays, *aian-aian* and bête–bete are also roaming around you always—what's the reason?"

I had a popcorn in my hand. I sat on the edge of a low wall, under the tin shade , eight lying bricks up and joining two pillars, a grotty little canteen.

"No reason, only tuition." I looked at her, "Mani7ha, this is the college my father studied at. It would have been a very good college by this time but now . . . . . .! Any how, I'm to improve it."

"Is it? Then, I'm also with you!!!" She also sat on the same wall that I sat on.

"Thanks!" I said.

"What thanks? You villagers really have no manners."

"Eh?" I got wired, "What I did now?"

"I'm here for a long time and you are eating the corns alone. You didn't ask me even." She snatched the popcorn.

I laughed.

"You saw *Pharat*?"

"Yea, why?"

"He is a good boy. I must talk to him."

"Should I look for?" She said in the twinkling of an eye.

"Your greatness!" I took the popcorn in my hands.

"A raconteur!" She felt her fingers on my head softly, as a sign of friendliness.

In a single minute, she did her work; *Pharat* was there with both of his friends, before my eyes. She also stood there, very close to me.

"What?" He said as he came, with tone as serious.

"Nothing; have a seat!" I said and moved my eyes in triplicate, nudging him to sit on the wall.

"Don't sit, yaar— I'm sitting!" Mani7ha sat on the place, where she sat just before.

"Any way you have a strong say in politics, you said, a day after I became the monitor." I had my eyes in my corns.

"Yea, so?" He said, "Any work?"

"No"

"Then?"

"Take corn." I stretched my hand, "To whom-whom do you know?"

"What will you do?" He smiled, also lifted some corns.

"Tell!"

"To *Rahul Gandhi,* to *Azam Khan*, to *Shashi Tharoor,* to *Rikka Vey Ahalubalia* and many others."

"Do they know to you?"

"Are you no mind?" He laughed, "There is a plenty of people around them always. They don't know any one but we all know them".

"Wrong!" I stretched my body again and gave the popcorn to him, "You don't know any of them, you told just now. But now listen, I don't know any of them but they all know me!"

"What?" He pulled my leg, "Off your trolley!"

"Have you?" After seventy seconds, I spoke, "I give you proof."

"Okay, give."

"To whom you *wanna* talk?" I said, my voice confident.

"To *Rikka Vey Ahalubalia,* you are a little child that's why." He smiled almost cunning.

"Okay, follow me!" I jumped from the wall and moved towards the class.

"*Rikka Vey Ahalubalia* lives there?" Sindhi laughed, they all, as well.

I stopped, looked back and gave a witty smile, "Come!"

In six minutes, I carried them all in the class. I sat on the table. "Any one has a white paper?" I asked.

"Yea, I have." A boy said.

"Get me." I said.

I took the paper, lifted a long note book to put the paper on it and a pen of *Mahi7ha*. I wrote a letter and folded it. I took out a rupee and put it on his palm . "Just buy an envelop to keep it in and press this letter to him." I said and gave him the letter also.

"Mhm. . . . !" He looked at me doubtedly.

"Don't look at me like this. Just go and see— not only he will listen to you, on the contrary will provide you with snacks." I smiled.

"Let's go, guys!' He had his eyes all around. He got positive answers.

"Yea-yea, hotfoot it! What are you thinking about?" I showed even more confidence.

"Okay, let's see!" With the purpose to pull my leg, he along *Udit*, *Sindhi* and four other students became ready to go.

"*Mani7ha,* you also must take a look!" I whispered, looking in her eyes.

"I think so." She said and also followed them.

You know what I wrote in the letter? Don't know, well, let me tell! It was—

*We are;*
*Can change the all—*
*The rule and the rulers;*
*The air and the weather*
*We can compel the God—*
*To come down*
*No God. No any other thing*
*We are the only power on earth*
*God needs us, we don't;*
*We are—*
*The key to your lock*
*We can give you chair*
*We can drag it*

*Dear Rikka Vey Ahalubalia Ji*

*This is Butterua, a social worker. Here, I'm sending some guys to you; attend them with all your heart, please...*

*You understand the meaning of please, no!*

*Jai Bharat!*

*Butterua*

*Pharat* had a lot of pride, but now has got it out of his system, his face down.

"Hey, now are you ok?" Mani7ha looked at him with naughty eyes as we met next day at college.

"What happened?" I said almost facing the sort of egregious trouble— I tell you I didn't have any term with *Ahalubalia* but because of being egoist took that risk; though, may be, my *letter* idea cast any spell.

"He got fainted there!" She laughed.

"What?" I pulled the question mark, some shock lay in my words, "I mean, why?"

"*Yaar*, I'm befuddled! He really knows you!" A surprised officious boy said, his words bedraggled.

"I never fib!" I said with an ego-trip.

"Sorry, yaar!" He spoke slowly, "I didn't know, you villagers are so cunning."

"You wanna talk to his mother?" I smiled.

"No, let it be— it's enough!" He also had a synonymous smile like mine. He gave his hand, after one and half minute of silence, "Friend?"

I went into his eyes with my smiling sight. "Okay!" I also stretched my hand, the right one.

All the guys clapped with noise.

We palled up. Here, it is a great fact, at college if you have tussle with some one or some one fights with you in early days, you both become friends.

At the time, we all naughty guys were in our chemistry lab, the last period of the week.

"Hey, what sort of noise is this?" *Dr. Vedpal Singh*, The lecturer of chemistry and our practical teacher cried. "Just issue your necessary things and be in your laborious task, soon."

Mani7ha unzipped her back pack. It had been kept on the cement- made rack whose edge she rested her back with. She took out *a* note book and tore half page to make a slip of names, in order to issue the apparatus.

"*Mani7ha*, our names also, please!" *Pharat* said to her.

She looked at me.

I nodded.

She mentioned their names and moved towards the lab incharge.

The lab was filled with apparatus, many chemical bottles in the racks, test tubes, stoppers, and funnels in the test tube racks, and also two-there microscopes in the cupboard near the door of incharge room.

I noticed seven wash bowls in the middle of two racks, each.

Our whole class was grouped, forty students with me.

In three minutes, *Mani7ha* neared us with a Bunsen burner, a dropper and a flask in her hands. "Go and carry yours one." she said.

We all also collected our apparatus.

We were to recognise the basic and acidic radicals from the given chemical liquids.

The practical was interesting and no boring. *Mani7ha* stood much closed to me, near the wash basin, and Sindhi, *Udit* and *Pharat*, facing both of us, in another side of the sink. All the arrangements of the practicals were on a long rack, with the enough space on both sides of the room; marbled nicely.

I lit the burner and began heating liquid in the test tube. I had used paper with many folds of it, to hold it.

Eee.....! I suddenly cried wincing. Actually, my finger came in touch with the glass and got burnt.

The test tube fell down from my hand.

"*Butterua....!*" *Mani7ha* caught my that finger and took it into her mouth, "Idiot, can't you see – why don't you work under the watchful eye?" She scolded, exhaling cool-cool breath on my burnt finger.

I could do nothing, except gazing at her. She behaved as if I was any beloved of hers or a baby deeply related to her. Now, she was doing her work and I mine; taking every reading of her heart.

"Now, leave it; I'm ok!" I smiled.

She got shied. She left the finger and turned away.

*Pharat* plundered the whole scene. He felt this, for he left the lab before the practicals got completed.

We did ours, this first practical nicely and submitted the objects five minutes before the period got over. All the guys got their attendance marked and left the lab as the bell rang— we along with.

# 9

After the day, when the incident took place in the lab, *Pharat* started sitting at back, in the class— three days passed.

Now, he was quite silent, away from his group and not talking wild card–alone, serious.

It is with every one that if your loved one is with someone else, you feel tight, but by mistake with your naked eyes, if you see any sign from your heart's side towards another one, you can't stand anymore— you go mad!

It knots you!

He had love for her; I smelt so, his behaviour different.

Any teacher, around forty, I don't know his name, was there in the class— the period of Hindi. He came third time during my 25 days' presence.

He was fatty and black skinned. He had worn a white *kurta-pajamas*. I noticed a fashionable eyeglass on his big eyes, its lenses black and frame thick, little dark colored.

The '*padas*' of *Soordas* on, so boring! Students in back were flying the air planes, made of papers.

His period got over.

I stretched my body and neared to *Pharat*, "Hey, dear! What happened? Why are you wilting face— any prob?" I sat on another bench, a hand much distance far.

He didn't speak.

"No coming, no talking—— anyway, what's the reason?" I lifted his notebook and started opening its pages.

"Butterua please don't talk to me at this time; I don't wanna speak to any one." He said.

"Why?" I shut the notebook.

"I don't know." He said and took his notebook from my hands.

"Okay, madam, as you wish!" I smiled, expected he would feel fine— you know he would use this phrase for me, but now had given up.

He didn't response.

I read the situation. I left him. I dragged the table somewhat ahead, upto my bench. I sat on it and kept my both legs on my bench, on my side. I took out my butter flow pen from the chest-pocket of my shirt. I started playing with it.

I was silent.

Also, there was a pin drop silence in the room.

*Mani7ha*, in an awkward way wiggled with her bottom on the bench— she looked naughty in her feelings. I noticed, she was still shying although the lab incident got over two-three days before. She was with me on the same bench but quite apart inwardly. Although, time to time, we exchanged glances but she, a wimpy girl kept stealing her sights, all the time, with a decent smile.

She tried hard not to speak to me but—

"Hey, don't be stodgy, speak something. I'm getting bored!" She snatched the pen from my hands, with a childish cry.

*Pharat* did his ears.

I looked around. All had their eyes at me.

"*Bharat mata ki jai*!" As *a* ding bat, I jumped from the table.

"What?" She laughed, almost looking surprised.

"You spoke to speak so......" I said innocently.

"What was that?" She looked at Sindhi and *Udit* and they both peeped into my eyes— they both were sitting on the same seat they would sit on, usually.

"Nothing!" I trivialized the topic, "Let's play *antakshree*. . . .?" I suddenly said and took my pen from her.

"Yea-yea-yea, your idea mind blowing!" *Aiece, a florid complexioned and ebriated big-big eyes girl* cried excitingly, standing up from her seat-she was sitting on the left of *Mani7ha* on wall-side seat.

I looked at *Mani7ha*.

"By the way, idea is not bad!" She nuzzled with her erotic lips.

I stopped my sensitive eyes and ears at the speaking style of that nymphet and willowy body girl, her style sexing up. If someone else had been in my shoes, he would have been nutty as a fruit cake and would have raped her.

I was quite still.

"Okay, lazy bones, get up! Be in groups; C'mon, soon!" *Aiece* handled and made the groups.

And antaksharee was on!

There were two groups of the class-first one of gals and second one of guys. *Pharat* didn't play but for the sake of formality, sat with us. *Aiece* requested so and I also said.

Only film songs were allowed.

The antaksharee took many wriggling twists, all the time our side under pressure. Two-three times, guys wimped out but *Udit* and *Sindhi* pulled the whole team out from the hot water.

So far, I spoke not a dickybird. *Pharat* also was no word. He sat much close to Mani7ha, only a hand length far while I was at the back of all guys.

Chance went to girls. Mani7ha sang a very troublesome, old song and threw ***'La'***, the forty first alphabet in Hindi. Everyone of my group felt themselves as if before *Bali*, the brother of *Sugreev* in *Ramayana*— all were without words.

*Mani7ha* had a dekoo at my face; she started counting the seconds, tik-tik, one! tik-tik, two! tik-tik, three! tik-tik fou......!

"Hey, stop-stop! I'm here!" I stood up; all guys looked at me hopefully.

***"Languria Naikoo Pump Chala De***
***Haba Likar Gyee Pyeea Ki***
***Pyeea Ki***
***Ardash Karoon Kela Maiya Ki."***

I sang and all the guys started beating the benches. They cried. They whistled. A lot of noise in the class!

The noise went up to ground.

"What is this?" *Mani7ha* stood up.

"A song, or what?" I laughed.

"From which movie?" She questioned.

"Am I hanging the name?" I said— secret, this song was not from any movie; some where I heard a no sense song!

"No-no, this is not any song-*wong*! It won't go! It won't go!" She disagreed and gave me a lot of hassle, all her group similarly.

"Why? Why not?" All guys forced arguing.

"No! No! No!"

Now, all were haste ring out, a rigorous argument in the class and cacophony no answer— I tried to dictate it.

"Why is this all noise ?" Suddenly, *Bijendra Singh Dhaka*, the president of disciplinary issues appeared. He was so tall and strong bodied that all would fear even by his appearance. All class became tongue tied – so shocked!

He arrived there with his all his unit, the *Dengua Machchhar* along with unit, rich enough with thirteen people in it.

"Sir, the period was empty, so we thought........" Mani7ha dinged.

"So, you will make a noise?" He lifted his hand to slap her.

"Sir.....!" At the moment, *Pharat* caught his hand with an involuntary cry, his eyes redlike a roaring tiger.

Tik-tik, one! Tik-tik, two! Tik-tik, three! Tik-tik fou......

The issue became large. Now, there was a monitors' meeting, the main issue was how a student dared to catch the hand of a teacher and now what with him – should be pardoned or should be shown the way?

A peon started the generator. We all thirty four CRs took a move towards the meeting hall.

The meeting hall was upstairs, on 3rd floor. It was a big and nicely decorated room; made especially for the purpose of meetings only. There were forty arm chairs, in two rows, with an enough space between both—twin arm chairs in each side. On the face, there was a long podium and a long furnitured table, with a thick glass on it, with twelve swivel chairs on back, of it. This hall had two doors and a long glassy window of 3 meters x 8 meters, covered with a maroon coloured curtain, on the balcony side, somewhat up from the floor.

The whole room was airconditioned.

We all took our seats. *Mani7ha* sat on my left, on the wall side. We both sat at second number, from front, in the left row.

At 11:40, *Parag Jain*, the president of all *Jainas*, in the district and also the president of our college, came into the hall we sat in, *Dangua Machchhar, Dhaka* and nine other responsible people, along with.

We all stood up.

"Be seated!" Dangua Machchhar waved his hands.

We sat down. They also graced their seats. Parag sat in the line of *Mani7ha* and *Dangua Machchhar* giving the space for two people with him, with *Dhaka* on his right.

*Parag Jain* was spiffed up with a blue shirt, matching black pants, brown Lee Trophy oxfords and a green tie— his looks undoubtedly formal. He was healthy enough, height somewhat six feet and imbued with fair complexioned skin.

He was of forty.

For a moment, the room was without any noise.

*I noticed Dangua Macchchar saw Parag Jain* having a serious face. "Dear, monitors! There is a shameful subject, due to which this meeting has been held." He broke the serene atmosphere and the meeting was on.

All the monitors looked at the faces of each other; seemed, as if they were put in a place where they had been never before.

"A boy from 11$^{th}$-B, has raised his hand on *Dhaka* Sir-not a tolerable subject. May be, tomorrow it is with us. So, what must be with it" Tit, to get the solution, we all are here." *Dangua Machchhar* said.

All the monitors were silent.

"No, Sir! He didn't raise his hand, on the contrary, he only caught the hand of Dhaka Sir, while he went ahead to slap me." *Mani7ha* said.

"Oh, so he is from your class! Okay, describe that happened there before your eyes.

She told all that had taken place in the class.

"Both are the same thing-you catch the hand of your teacher or raise it on him." He said and waved his head. "Don't know what sort of students are coming nowadays."

As you are needed, I wanted to say, but I ignored all. All the monitors did not answer.

"Anyway, now what should be done with him?" He asked.

"Whatever you want!" *Mani7ha* said.

"He must be expelled from the college." One monitor said. "Or he must be given a chance to improve himself, with a strict warning."

"Sir, expel him, so that no other incident would occur next time in future." Another monitor who was from 12$^{th}$-C, said.

"Sir, do, as you wish." A girl, a monitor from backside said.

"Sir, say to him bye-bye sans thinking, otherwise these case will keep coming before us forever more and more". A girl sitting in front of me, said.

"Yea, the college is also thinking so." *Dhaka* said, "Now, he is expelled from the college."

"Dear monitors! You know this meeting is held to see the problems of yours and to solve them anyhow. Now, if you have any prob speak out without hesitation. That will be listened and will be solved." The principal said.

"Sir, so many benches are broken in our class." one monitor said. "And sir, the ceiling fans are also out of order."

"Sir, there are many cobwebs in our class. At least, they must be removed." A monitor of a junior class spoke, his attitude holier-than-thou.

All laughed.

"Sir, *samosas*!" Two peons entered into the room. They had two big boxes— each with the *samosas* in them. They brought them from *Durga's* shop, as could be seen wrapper on boxes.

"Okay, distribute! But. . . . let sometime pass, till then, put them there." The principal said and nudged them to put the boxes near the gate.

The mouth watering aroma of pies made every one mad.

"So, guys! This student, named *Pharat*, a bad character boy, has been expelled from the college. His name will be struck-off from the register and he will not be coming from tomorrow; college has decided— that's it!" *Dangua Machchhar* said.

He nudged the peons to distribute the *samosas*-meeting was near to over.

I couldn't control myself.

"Excuse me, sir!" I stood up with a ferocious voice, now a sirocco in the full hall.

"Eh?" *Dangua Machchhar* looked at me.

"Sir, that student you told about, named *Pharat*, a bad character boy, belongs to my class and he is not gonna leave the college; he will come, no siree!" I said.

"What?"

"Yea, He will come and will come. I am saying, if he doesn't come, all class also won't come. There, he was not alone. All the class was there."

"Who the hell are you, a saying boy?"

"The monitor of his class."

"So what?" he cried, fervidly.

"Don't holler at me; I may fall down!" I spoke confidently, some smile in my voice.

All room laughed.

"Shut up!" He glowered at all the monitors.

I had an inward cunning smile on my lips.

An 70 year old, fair complexioned and healthy, with height that of Big B, a good looking boymust be an responsible personstared at me with sharp sight.

"Sir, no one was there in the class. So, what should we have done in that leisure time?" I said, "We started playing *Antaksharee.*"

"Good, you could have studied!" He said.

"Sir, what were the teachers doing in that period?" I questioned.

"They must be having any work." He said.

"That work could have been done in any leisure." I said.

"There is a lot of burden nowadays." The *Dangua Machchhar* spoke.

"So what?" I scowled to him. "Thirty thousand rupees are not less. Ask any labourer, then you will come to know. He sweats out all the day, then he gets only a hundred rupee leaf. And you, you get one thousand doing no work."

No one among all of them had any word to speak.

"Sir, this is our money, don't take undue advantage of it." I carried on.

No one spoke.

"But matter is not this; the matter is why a student caught the hand of a teacher?"

"Why did he raise?"

"What? You will create noise and a teacher can't beat you, even?" *Dhaka Sir* spoke. "Those were the days, a teacher would have all the rights. He could have scratched the skin of a student."

"That was the time. All the teachers were so. They loved their students. But now......, all are selfish; bloody air looking fox!" I said.

"What?" The principal said.

"What what?" I changed the topic, "I came here to get admission. I got fastered. I wept. But no mercy! Many excuses there— you are late, seats are over and blah-blah-blah!"

"Of course, you were late!"

"Then, why my admission got done?" I cried. The conversation between both of us had many sinuous steps. The feud over the matter went on for a long time.

His brain scrambled.

"*Beta*, at this time you are a child. You don't know anything!" He sizzled.

"No, I'm not any child-*bild*! I understand all! Any phone comes; any letter comes, and all the way is opened! No, care for our sweat! No value!" I threw my hands, looking up at him with a scowl.

"Tell one thing. You have denied to do any work of some one and if your father forces you to do that you have denied, then what will you do?" he fattish zed, "Won't you do?"

"It means, all the politicians are the pops of yours! You are nothing in spite of being a principal!" I went ahead with my words scouting the answer out in his question- the scowl and a sort of smile mixed.

All the students laughed.

Shame-Shame! Fie-Fie!

He had his face down, fessing up.

"Sir, when a hombre sires, he has some responsibilities; and he must think!" I taught him a nice lesson.

*Parag Jain* who didn't speak any word so far, looked at me, sizing the scraggy boy up. So far, he had scratched the surface of the matter, going on between both of us. He sojourned every one with his eyes, his eyes some calm, some serious.

No noise, so any peace not yet.

"What is this all?" *Parag Jain* spoke with a serious voice.

"Your homage, Sir!" I awefully looked at him, "Sir, no one was in the class and and all class wanted to play *Antaksharee*. So, that was on. Suddenly, *Dhaka Sir* reached there and raised his hand to slap this girl, sitting near me and that boy we are talking about, caught his hand— that's it!!!"

"Not this one, politician one— I heard, just now." He said.

I became elated and started eating the story, occurred at the time of my admission.

"You look excited! Be in a fine fettle with your words!" He spoke gently. He nudged a peon who stood near the gate, in side, to get me water.

He provided me with. I sipped a half of glass. I put it in the tray, he held.

"You are at home?" he said.

I nodded.

"What happened? Now on!"

I told him all happened with me at the time of admission.

He looked at the principal. Still, his face was down with a lot of repentance on the matter.

"Sir, all would be there as it is, *Pharat* will come. He will not be expelled!"

"Okay! But it is the first and last chance." He was strict with his words.

"Thank you, sir!" I said

All class clapped

The amiable president smiled, as though solaced by some memory.

# 10

"*Butterua*, you all people are going to *Aian-aian* and *bete-bete*. So I think, me too must be with you." *Pharat* said, while we all were on stairs, coming down-all classes having got over.

"You're welcome!" *Mani7ha* spoke at once, almost using my words.

"It's better, you make us talk." He said, hesitatingly.

"Okay, let's go now!" I said.

"Yes, it's fine!" *Udit* kowtowed to my idea.

In two minutes, my idea was respected. *Pharat* took out his *Yamaha* bike from the stand and we moved towards their places here we were four on one bike, how thrilling.

I tell you, *Pharat* was a perfect rider. He showed many daring-dos; held the bike too superbly. More over, the weather was so nice. For me, it was very first time that I sat on the pillion of *Pharat's* bike.

Any way, time was so nice!

"Hey, what happened?" I asked when he suddenly applied brakes.

"Nothing, just see ahead; patrolling is going on." He became tense........... *Chitrole* is there; so dangerous!"

I enlarged my eyes and noticed around hundred meters away some cops were on their duty; checking the bikes. Because of fear many more bike-riders had parked their bikes on side of the road.

"So, why do you fear so much?" *Udit* spoke out with a tingle of energy.

"My idiot dude, *Chitrole* is there, you know?" He said, "He never uses stick, but always makes sweatout; coercing into cock."

"He won't do anything. We are students, by the way."

"So?"

"*Pharat*, I have heard, you have a nice say in politics– so, you can do something, at least!" I said to *Pharat*.

"Yea, I have, but......" *Pharat* looked in confusion.

"But what *Pharat*?" *Sindhi* said.

"Sindhi, you don't understand. One can save another one, but how can if he own it." *Pharat* explained his compulsion.

"So, what do you say, we stay here or...?" *Udit* said.

"Let me think!" *Pharat* said.

"Hey, I've an idea...." Sindhi suddenly cried.

"What?" *Udit* turned his neck.

"Just turn back the bike!" he said.

"Why?"

"Just turn first of all; don't question." He insisted and on his saying so, the bike was reversed.

"Hey. stop-stop-stop." he cried all of a sudden and got down the bike as the bike was stopped.

Now, he was stepping ahead and our eyes were fixed on his each further act.

He went up to a mango-shake shop. We were able to notice a healthy man on bike with his wife on pillion and a little girl in her lap— they were enjoying the taste of mango-shake.

*Sindhi* reached them. And, we sharpened our ears and eyes, both.

"Sir, could I have your wife, please!" He said a little later as he completely figured her out.

"What?" the man got surprised; almost shouting.

"Nothing!" As our work gets completed, I would bring back her to you, I swear..." He said, and—

"You bloody.....!" The balloon of his anger burst and we all disappeared from there.

Suddenly, our bike stopped. And we were before *Chitrole*. Now what, God knows!

"Park it aside." A cop said.

Now, we were truly worried. I noticed many more people there, by the roadside in cock-position. For some time, I felt we also were in their shoes— sweat started dropping down from our faces.

"Licence?" Mr. *Chitrole* stared at *Pharat*.

He didn't speak, and we as well.

"Good!" he smiled almost criticizing, "No helmet, no licence and moreover four people on one bike."

"Sir, actually we......." *Pharat* tried to explain but—

"Shut up! Just go and take your position; be the cock, like them!" he cried.

"You know to whom you are preventing?" I suddenly came out with illiterate tongue.

"What? What you said?"

"Nothing!" I said and took the hand-set of *Pharat* from his pocket. "Just take this phone; dial any number and say to him that you have prevented *Buttarua* – result you will come to yourself." I was confident as *Amitabh Bachchan* in *Buddha Hoga Tera Baap*. And this time, *Chitrole* also had to think– I tell you, I'm a true fan of *Big B*, so his dialogues are mine, logic!

"*Butterua*, what are you doing this?" *Pharat* tried to stop me, while he was himself confused in this new incident.

"No, *Pharat* let me do!" I said almost crying at *Pharat*.

"Okay, get the cell— I would talk!" *Mr. Chitrole* took the phone and started dialling a number— now, how I was feeling, only I know or God knows.

"You were fooling me, hey?" He talked to me with egregious gestures as he finished the call with S.P. and got no words in our favour.

"Sir....!" I tried to say.

"Shut up!" He slapped me, his palm as hard as stone. "...And be the cock there!" He cried ever more.

Now, we had no option else. Soon, we were going to be cock.

As I ducked, suddenly, I lit on *Mani7ha's* presence there – a no purpose, cooky girl. So far, I didn't feel that she was coming with us.

I at once went back to that *Chitrole* and said, "Sir, beat me, however much you want. But don't make me cock!"

"Why?"

"Sir, one of my class-girl is standing there. If she watches me in cock form, she would tell the whole class. And then, a lot of insult, a lot of humiliation— sir, I've my position in my class." I said.

"So?"

"Sir, please...." I requested him.

"Shut up, don't tamper with my patience. Go and be a gentle cock!"

I listened to him but didn't follow his words, moreover I started weeping.

"Okay, don't weep, go! But never break the rules of travelling in future." He said after five minutes when I carried on weeping.

"Okay, sir! Thank you........!" I thanked him wiping my tears.

However, we escaped from that ghost. We were discussing all the way about the just-occurred-incident.

"Now, what happened?" I said, when a little later, *Pharat* stopped the bike again.

"Both sirs are there!" he said and parked the bike.

*Mani7ha* stopped her scooty after us.

"*Mani7ha*, it's not good thing to roam around with guys!" I said getting down the bike, as I saw her before my eyes.

"All goes in this age!" She smiled and made her hair, parking her scooty. The weather was nice and pleasant. The air was blowing freelyone wanted to feel it always.

"No, it's wrong." I said.

"You idiot, I have some work here." She cunningly tried to bury the conversation into end but I could judge that she was lying.

"Then ok." I smiled.

Roadways station was the place, from where a person could take the rickshaw to any other place. Their places were more than three km stone, still.

"Good afternoon, Sir!" I touched the feet of both of them.

"Bless you!" They both had their hands on my head by turn.

*Mani7ha* wished, *Udit* and *Sindhi* also touched their feet. They similarly blessed both of them.

But *Pharat* didn't touch their feet, He only wished.

They both minded it, And *Aian-aian* took it to heart. "*Aian-aian*...!" He enlarged his hand, the bowl with a water ball in it, he had.

"No, sir! No!" I had towed three steps back— I actually thought he was providing me with it, *Mani7ha* and all others felt similarly.

But..........!

.......... He threw all the spicy water of water ball and that water ball on *Pharat's* feet! I couldn't understand anything.

*Pharat* was shocked.

"Sir, what is this?" I asked with surprise. *Mani7ha, Sindhi* and *Udit* had their ears and eyes on my words.

"*Aian-aian*, this boy has no manners. Can't he touch our feet like you?" He said loudly, having his eye on me, "Bolo-bolo. . . . . . !"

"Sir, he is a Muslim and Muslims never touch the feet of any one." I said.

"This religion is bad; very bad!" He abused the Muslim religion and humiliated him badly, but indirectly.

He had to touch their feet, after all. During this time, many people gathered around us.

"Sir, he and all three standing nearby, wanna come to tuition." I said, as the matter got some settled.

*Bete-bete* looked at *Aian-aian* and *Aian-aian* looked at me, "Okay, as you wish – if you think, carry them tomorrow."

"Thank you, Sir" I said.

From the next day, *Pharat* and his all group started going to tuition, my heart; garden-garden.

# 11

Our coaching time going on; *Aian-aian* was on as an FM Radio. As many of students would reach the tuition late, the prob of all guys occurred to me suddenly. Actually, they were villagers. And their places were far away; I felt about them. I took *Aian-aian* in a side, out of the couching room.

"Sir, many of students gonna leave the coaching!" I said when he asked me the reason why I had interrupted him in middle.

"Why?" He looked at me startling.

"Sir, they are villagers and they have to cover a lot of distance daily."

"Yea, it is." He agreed.

"Sir, now you will have to face a lot of loss."

"A great prob! It will make me bald!" He said comically.

"Sir, I have an idea."

"What?"

"Sir, is there any inn near about?"

"Yea, *Rastogi Dharmshala*, a stately building is there; not much far, hardly half km from here."

"How many rooms are there?"

"Five *barats* can stay there at a time."

"So big?"

"Yea...."

"It's nice." I said, "At least, triple story building it must be—I think."

"Yea….."

"Sir, do a work; get an agreement done of the last full floor for two years and put all the students there."

"There may be loss."

"Why? Who said?" I made him understand, "Indirectly they will have to pay the rent— increase their fees. All are under the pen of yours. At last, get all."

"Yea, idea is not bad." He smiled.

We both came into the room. I sat on my seat and he stood behind his chair, having his both hands on the edge of the head of his chair. He looked every one seriously. "How many students are from village?" He asked the students to raise their hands.

Almost all hands were up, except *Aiece's*, Mani7ha's and other seven's.

"You have to face many probs while coming?"

"Yea, sir!" All those who raised hands, said in unison— all were parroted.

"Well, soon, your this prob will be solved. I'm thinking to take an inn on rent for you all."

"…Really?" A student said while rest of all showed a fake surprise which looked more real than the real one.

"Yea…." He shook his head with stateliness.

"Thank you, sir."

"What thank you? The rent you will have to pay."

"So what? At last, we will clear all the accounts."

He smiled and came on shine-board with a black marker, after a minute.

"Wow, what a pleasant surprise!" *Aiece* cried, flushed with success—*Pharat* was there near the room, we were sitting in.

*Aian-aian*, with his complete attention, was on the shine board "What happened?" He turned his face, with surprise. He stopped his hands.

We also had our eyes opened, no guess about his coming, then.

He entered the room sans any permission.

"Pharat......!" Many guys fluttered their hands around him, wildly, their purpose to communicate. But he didn't listen to any one and sat backside on a broken stool, a flummoxed boy.

"*Aian-aian*, so late! Where were you so long?" *Aian-aian* said. "After four days you are showing your face!"

"Sir my mother-in-law got died." he sought excuse, night off the bat.

All students laughed.

"What?" He smiled, "You are married?"

"No, Sir not my own ; my brother's one." He said with the heebie-jeebies.

"So, what you did?"

"Sir, I was at home."

"House keeping, sir!" *Aiece* spoke and fluttered her eyelashes at *Pharat*.

He looked at her but didn't speak.

Before *Aian-aian* might have put any other question before him, I held all the matter and took it away from the head of *Pharat,* "Sir, will it be holiday on *Janmashtami*?"

"No, everyone is to come; no holiday is there!" He said loudly.

*"Right-ho!"* I said. Anyway, we had to satisfy ourselves, only with a rebellious streak.

*Aian-aian,* left us at 7:10, ten minutes late by his time.

The students, for whom I talked with *Aian-aian* for an inn, so as to shift them in, were worried. *Now what? How about the rent ?* They discussed each other, stepping down.

I streaked down the stairs; unlocked the chain and pulled out my *ampala khatara, parting the cycles*— we would use a chain for binding all the cycles in order to prevent from being stolen.

Now, I was on foot, having both handles of the cycle in my hands.

"*Butterua.....*!" *Pharat* cried as I stepped ahead. I turned back my head. Surprise, he was by cycle not by bike! I noticed, even now, no other was there except him.

I stopped.

He came up to me.

"Hi, how are you?" I spoke, giving my hand. We both had an informal hand shake.

"You didn't talk to me." He said, ". . . .Annoyed?"

"No…!" I sighed. We crawled being on foot.

"So?"

"Your mind was off!" I smiled, "That's why. . . ."

"Sorry!" He gave a serious fall.

Any reason?"

"Yea. . . ." He sighed, "That I would tell you any other time!"

"Is all ok?" I knocked him as he went cool with some emotions.

"You know Mani7ha and me, I mean we both have been studying together since 9$^{th}$!" He said, "How should I tell you that she is in my all heart, in my eyes and in my all bits, all the time. I don't know why I can't stand any one in her company?"

"You love her?" I peeped into his eyes.

"I don't know."

"Tell!"

"May be."

"What may be? There is difference between may be and is."

"So, there is an is."

I smiled.

We both got on our cycles and paddled our speed slow and

lazing. "You know, in lab when she stood near you, at that time I also felt but when your finger got burnt and she took it into her mouth and blew the breaths on it, then I couldn't stand. And. . ." He stopped speaking, his voice of a disappointed lover.

". . . And then, you left the lab, right?" I said, "Yaar, I also was thinking somewhat so!"

During this separate conversation of ours, *Sindhi, Udit, Aiece, Mani7ha* and some other guys also neared us. Therefore, our conversation was got disturbed.

Now, we all were riding hogging all the way— I was to left.

"Any way, what happened in meeting?" *Pharat* started the conversation from a fresh point, once more.

"Nothing. . . ."

"Why do you fib?" *Mani7ha* spoke, "Tell clearly."

"What happened, tell no!" *Pharat* said again.

"Nothing happened. She is just speaking." I said.

She smiled.

*Pharat* wondered at our conversation.

"You were going to be expelled. It is *Butterua*— touch his feet— he righted a wrong. He faced all the teachers and saved you." *Aiece* spoke.

"Who told you?" I looked at her.

"Any one." She smiled.

I looked at *Mani7ha*, my eyes skeptical.

"No-no, I didn't tell anyone." She spoke childishly. I was forced to smile at her innocent face with her eyes crinkling with laughter.

And I practically smiled.

"*Butterua*, don't play with me! Tell me, what happened?"

"What should I tell you if nothing is there?"

"Uff, *Butterua*! Don't be now?" *Aiece* said.

"A donkey never understands a request, but does *dhenchoo-dhenchoo* if he is in mood." *Mani7ha* passed a comment.

"What?" I smiled.

All laughed, except *Pharat*. "Okay, don't tell-I know already".

"How?"

*Hunnnn*.....! Suddenly, a truck pulled out from a distance and looked streaking off down the road, while I was going to answer to that HOW.

Now all the guys came in line. I was the engine of this train. I got scared of, as it passed through us. I used brakes and got down the cycle with no alarm; all got down.

"What is this?" *Mani7ha* got annoyed. She murmured holding herself while she was just after me. It startled her, along with everyone to find me stopped suddenly.

"Sorry!" I shrugged smiling, "I'm not much familiar to riding. And that's why, not perfect at; I fear traffic."

She smiled, anger mixed in it— her smile inward one.

# 12

It was Sunday; 11:00 am. I stood on flyover near the railway junction, many lines passing through it. I was only lounging, without any particular purpose.

The bridge was very large and had two footpaths, two low walls along, at each side.

There was a divider in middle.

I stood on east of one footpath, facing the sun-rising side.

The deity looked in the favour of weather, the pleasant wind, all around, puttering in my ears. Many clouds and clouds like black smoke of moving trains, were floating in the sky, blanking it out. It seemed, possibly soon, it would rain, like blazes.

My all heart was in the delight due to that beautiful weather.

"Butterua.....!" A male voice pierced into my ears; it was Pharat, his voice quitely familiar to me. He must have glimpsed me.

I turned my face.

He was by cycle and looked coming from Aian-aian's side. He was in the other side of the divider. He had to take a long turn to come up to me. "What's up; cut up?" He, a dab hand cycle rider said, as he reached me— he had his one leg on footpath and another one on pedal.

"Eve teasing?" I patronized him, no respect for his question.

"No!"

I had a perfunctory smile across my face. "Then how are you wondering here?" I said.

"I'm coming from Aian-aian."

"Any work?"

"No."

"So?"

"Yaar, I'm thinking to be shifted to city— I also have probs while everyday commuting." He said.

"So, you looked for any room or not?"

"Not so far."

"Try, you obviously will find."

"Yaar, can't you shift me with yourself?" He put an astute question.

"Me?" I bleated feebly, "Yaar, don't mind! You eat meat like many rubbish things. And I do not eat even onion or garlic. You understand how can I?"

"I understand, yaar!" He said slowly, "Okay, if I don't then.....?"

"Then no prob; let's go right now." I said preemptorily.

"And luggage?"

"That will come; carry any other day."

"Thank you!" He spoke as he reached the room. "How old it is!" He discussed about the location of the old building.

"Yea, but it is!"

"No prob." He smiled.

By evening, he fetched his all luggage. And alongwith, Sindhi and Udit also were there just as the free drops of rain from sky, or as a compliment. Now we were four in a room.

We all perfumed the whole house with our presence. Now, our landlord had to miss us if we were not there only for a day—they had become used to us.

There, Aian-aian, took the last floor of inn as he had told, on rent for two years; he got an agreement done and promised that all the rent he him self would pay, whether any student paid or not.

All the needy boys got shifted there. And for the girls, there was a facility of richshaws to pick up and drop up, from and to their places.

Slowly–slowly, three months passed, and our half yearly exams were on. It was 2:00 pm. We all were studying.

"Pharat, you have fifty bucks?" I asked, having my both eyes on my lesson.

"No."

"Sindhi, you....?"

"Sorry........."

"And Udit you?"

"Only twelve rupees are there."

"Oh, shit!"

"Why? What'll you do?" Pharat asked.

"Gas cylinder may get finished any time! May be tomorrow or day after tomorrow; only one-two days it may pull." I said seriously.

"And exams are one after another, continuously, no gap." Pharat also got serious.

"Hey, what is there to be serious?" Sindhi spoke, "We may borrow from any one."

"Why?" I stared at him, "You would show them, you don't have even fifty bucks, while you're at room."

"..It's also a matter!" He said.

"So."

"Sorry, yaar!"

"Butterua, I have an idea." Udit spoke.

"What?" I said.

"You know, there was a tiny birthday party here, some days before?" He said.

"Yea....."

"There is a big cylinder, kept downstairs, in a room, close to the stairs. Hundred percent there will be some gas in it-think so."

"Good idea!" I smiled.

"But what about valve?" Pharat said, "Without valve how would it be done."

"That I have!" He showed the valve.

"Genius......! It means you have this idea in your mind, for a long time." I said.

He smiled, "I was thinking to save money for the next time."

"You look some ahead of me!" I gave a lovely slap on his head and closed my book, "Okay, let's lift the cylinder upstairs." I said.

Pharat and Udit, like thieves, went down and carried the most wanted thing in the room. I had my sharp eyes on any incident, likely to occur.

Our cylinder was 5 kg one, not big one. Pharat held it on and carried one big cylinder; connecting both with their mouths with the valve-he made the most of that tiny valve.

The gas must have been going into our cylinder.

After 10 minutes, we dismantled all the arrangements and like a hot potato, threw that big cylinder where it was.

"It is somewhat weighty, now." Pharat said, as he lifted the 5kg cylinder to examine it.

"It seems so." I also noted the reading.

Whatever be, a great problem got solved. After that, we all slept. Next day we got up near about six.

I went into the kitchen to prepare tea. I tried hard to burn the oven, but shocking!

"Pharat!" I cried.

"What happened?" He along with Udit came into the kitchen while Sindhi went to bathe, with bathing arrangement downstairs.

"I think, yesterday the cylinder got over-filled!" I smiled.

All worried, but everyone had an inward smile.

# 13

We had to go for the exams empty stomach.

I sat in room no. 27, and by luck got first seat. No one of my group, was in that room— I was alone with juniors in left, right and back.

*Shakshi ma'am* was in my room, on her duty; she was with an old sir, a teacher of junior class. The old sir was black complexioned, not much fatty but looking not villinous— his fashion high, no beard, no mustache. He had a purple turtle neck on black jeans along black sneakers with white sole and no sign of age.

And she was wearing a yellow V-neck cardigan on a green *sari*, with a pair of wheat-colour pumps.

The bell rang. Both teachers started distributing the question-papers. Damn it, three papers of my class fell short!

The exam was that of English.

"*Butterua!*" She gave me a key, "Take it and go downstairs, in the staff room. There in cupboard no. 5, search locker no. 7, unlock that and take out all the papers— they will be in a black colour cobra file. I forgot them there!"

"Within a jiffy, I'm here back!" I took the key. I went down. There I searched the cupboard and then locker. I unlocked it. I took out the papers. As I was *gonna* close it, suddenly by chance, I had my eyes on that porn magazine what I saw on the table in very first meeting with *bete-bete* and with her.

Since before it, I never saw this sort of any magazine all my life, my heart vilified! I looked hither and thither— no one was there. And then, I opened it. The pictures were really smooth and erotic— very soon I felt it.

I kept turning the pages over. Hardly seven-eight pages must have been gone, I closed it— I felt someone coming there in the room. A peon came inside the room and went out without speaking any word.

At the time, I was very light with my feelings, with my body as well very excited inwardly. I opened the magazine again and got feeling them. Suddenly, **a letter fell down from it.**

I picked the letter up. I again looked hither and thither and unfolded the letter after taking it out from the pink envelope—

*Dear darling,*

*It's long time since, we did it. Now, soon we are gonna get a chance to do it. On Saturday no one would be at place—all are going to attend a marriage in Delhi and would be back till Mon, but I'm here as I need to be in bed with you, with an excuse of exams of students; how sweet!*

*My spicy sauce, I'm really very excited. So, be ready, on Saturday.*

*With many sweet- sweet kisses!*

*Gaurav Saxena*

"Oh, God, It's going on here!" I got surprised as I went through the letter. I thought to show it to all college, but when I peeped into their ages and their means, I dropped the idea.

I put the all things in the locker and locked it. I came to my class with a bundle of papers.

"It took a long time you to come back—was there any river in the way?" she said, as I gave her the papers.

"Ma'am, the room was locked, that's why..." I said.

"Okay, sit down." She said and gave a paper to me. At 11:30, the exam got over.

"Hey, you didn't fare well?" I asked my roommates when I reached my room—all three of them already were there.

I couldn't receive any answer, no one rolled the tongue.

I stood with my both hands on hips.

"What happened? Why are you sitting so quite still with a pale face?" I asked changing the clothes. "You haven't changed so far?" I said— they still were in their uniforms, sitting on the bed with the faces as if some one had died in our room or as if they all fell ill.

"How you did?" *Pharat* spoke, his voice like a patient of T.B., some coughy.

"Nice!" I said, "And you.. . .?"

"But, we didn't."

"Why?" I asked. I had my blue sweater in my hand. I hung it on the hanger— the hanger we menagingly made using some nails on a board of wood and that wood stuck on the wall with two nails on each side.

"The hunger. . . ." He blew with nascent words.

"Not hunger, the pangs of hunger!" *Sindhi* cried.

"Oh, so that's why, you are sitting so; this is the matter!" I slapped on his hippo campus, sitting on a chair. I had dropped all the uniforms and wore another set of clothes.

He hindered, I looked at *Udit*, smiling.

"What I did? I gave only my idea. Why you accepted?" He cried, "If it had been good, you wouldn't have praised even; your mouths would have been closed then. But now.............."

"Don't open your mouth, mood is very off!" *Pharat* warned him.

"Oh, shut up, you guys." *Sindhi* said, "It's only first day, think how next five days would be whiled away?"

"Let's see." I said.

"You must see. But I can't stand the hunger any more. I'm going!"

"Where?"

"To the railway station."

"So, there you would ask people for the loaves of breads?"

"So what? I would scratch my skin and would tear my clothes. Or, I would wear dirty old and torn clothes." He said, "And anyway, no compromise with stomach!"

"Right!" I said, "But, where would you get clothes from?"

"From any roadside."

We all laughed. "Good! Very good!" I shook my head left-right.

"*Bat* happened, *Buttalua why all* of you are lapping?" Our landlord, a lisper, papery and snub-nosed, unpleasant faced man of 35 spoke, his entry was a sudden surprise—he stood near the door, out of the room.

"Nothing, uncle ji, a matter of college." I said.

"How *wad yol papel*?" He said.

"Nice!" I said.

"It mutt be!" He said.

"Just come, come inside. Take a seat." I said for only formality sake.

"No-no, *flol had* been end. So, I *thot bheet* must be got *glinded*." He said.

"You didn't go to office?" I said.

". . . .*Jat* now? I go *aftel* 12." He said in proud.

"Your job is good!" I looked at him and then passed a smile towards my group.

He was an F.O. in SAHARA, a finance company of *Subhrat Rao*, which provides the Indian cricket team with uniforms.

He scattered a bag of wheat-grains on the floor which he carried to show the sun.

He went downstairs, as his work was done.

"Yaar, I'm hungry; please, do something!" Pharat cried childishly.

"So?" I said, "So..... I became silent; and started smiling little later after the last word I spoke—suddenly, an idea occurred to me".

"What happened?" *Pharat* knocked me. "What happened? Why are you smiling?" He said surprisingly, *Sindhi* and *Udit* also wondered at this.

"You are hungry?"
"Yea. . . ."
"There is an idea!"
"What?"
"Be silent up to evening"
"What?"

The evening dawned. The landlord came upstairs. He filled all the grains in the bag and kept it under the tin-shade, ahead of our room.

He went down.

"Bring the electric rod which we use for warming the water and carry the *stainless-bucket.*" I said, when time passed the ten— the landlord got slept by then.

"Why?"
"You are hungry?"
"Yea."
"Then . . . ."

"I wonder what you will do with them, a mad boy." *Pharat* murmured as he came to me with the rod and bucket.

"Bring water in it!" I said, giving him the bucket.

He brought the bucket with enough water in it. "Now what?" He said in a tired voice.

It was the government of *S.P.; Azam Khan* was the minister from the city at that time— so, electricity was there all the time.

I plugged in and put the rod into the bucket. I went out of the room and came inside with about 2 kg wheat in a bowl— I carried the bowl from the kitchen. I used the bowl three times, meaning thereby 6 kg wheat.

"Wow!" *Pharat* cried going mad with surprise. "What an idea, sir ji!"

I smiled. "Fetch salt". I looked at *Sindhi,* a quest!

I put the salt in the wheat corn. The water boiled, the grains of wheat also boiled.

Our hunger got satiated when we ate them.

Five days we managed with them, thus, a nice experience.

# 14

Slowly-slowly the Saturday came. The incident of letter was in my mind always. I was not properly ok with my feelings and also couldn't do well in exam.

It was the exam of physics on Monday, so there was tuition at six and the next day there was Sunday. By the way, no tuition classes were there in the all exams. But we insisted bête-bête and.....

*Pharat* had an ***hTC*** handset, a very expensive one. His father, a respected business man, dealt in menthol. I gazed his mobile for fifty five seconds in his hand.

"*Pharat*, can you get me your cell for one day, only?" I said with an idea in my mind.

"Why? Why for only for one day? Take it for forever, as a gift from my side." He smiled.

"Thanks!" I sighed and lay my back on the back of the chair I sat on.

"Any way, what's the matter that you are asking for it?" *Sindhi* winked.

"I'm to shoot a ***b. f.***" I smiled.

"What?" They all got shocked, "Speak once more!"

"Yea!" I stole my eyes.

"Where? We mean, with whom?" *Sindhi* asked, his style cunning.

"Any *setting* is there!" I said.

"Oooo....!" *Udit* and *Sindhi* cried in unison, "Why so late, then? There is a good work?" *Sindhi* snatched the cell from the hands of *Pharat* and got me.

"Is that *Mani7ha*?" *Pharat* doubted.

"No!"

"Then ok!" He said, "*Yaar*, please don't do anything with her; she is your someone else like."

". . . . . Not that!" I smiled.

"Best of luck!" He said.

"But *Yaar*, I don't know how to use it— you will have to teach me." I said.

"Why are you worrying for that; three-three experts are here!" *Udit* laughed. They all laughed. And all the night they taught me using the cell.

A heuristics!

At six, we all moved towards the couching of bête-bête with the pricey set in my pocket. I was in somewhat black jeans and dried hay coloured jacket— it was so cold and the room we took coaching in, with no door, so tough!

Tuition got over at 7. It was dark all around. All students started going out one by one through the door, *Mani7ha* as well— bête–bête was already gone.

I went in a corner and tried myself so as not to be seen by hiding. But the one who is so famous has little places to hide, *Mani7ha* looked at me— she had her eyes always on me. "Hey, *Butterua*! Ain't you coming?" She cried.

**"Shsss…!"** I had my right hand's index finger on my lips. I nudged her to go and not to leak it.

She could understand nothing, but thank God she went and I think, not surely she wouldn't have opened her mouth before any one, her both hands into the hip-pockets of her my jeans-coloured bolero.

I hid myself in the benches but I could manage to see all that was going on outside.

Ten minutes later, when all the students went, *bête-bete* came and switched off the CFL of the couching room.

At mid night, around one, bête–bete got strolling in the open fresh moon light, the moon in the age of seventeen, so sexy! He was only in underwear and a white colour sando-banyan.

Suddenly, an scooty stopped down, at his gate—I heard a voice. I last saw her share fly beetling off down the road.

My doubt was correct, *Sakshi ma'am* was there.

"Any day you will kill me." He said and lifted her in his arms and teased her lips.

"You too!" She went up to his nose with her right hand's naughty fingers.

He took her into his room.

I came out and made a beeline for them. I went up to the window of his room from where I could see everything clear—his bed chamber was expensive and lit with bright light of four *CFLs*. I put on the video shooter and fixed it at the right point.

He was springing her. He was taking rounds on his legs keeping her in his hands. She was laughing and he as well.

"Hey, shut the door first!" She said— actually the door was slightly opened.

"Don't worry, no one is here!" He said.

"Even then......"

"*Okhay- okhay*!" He shut the door using his right leg like a horse; neither latched, nor bolted— it was opened in all respect.

"Hey, now, would you put me on the bed or keep swaying in your arms all the time?" She smiled. He threw her on the white bed sheet-covered bed.

"Now, what should be done?" As an innocent boy, he itched his hair.

"Whatever, you want!" She lay on her back, on the bed, her both hands stretched and pins also.

He sat on the edge having his left hand in her V- shaped legs. He was gazing at her.

"C'mon, baby!" She said.

"So sexy!" He climbed onto the bed properly. He caught the pompom of her bobble hat and pulled it out and threw it. He tried to undo the first button of her *denim jacket*, at the moment she took a bit of his hand into her mouth.

"You are already so warm, you don't need any cloth." He capped her. He put off her jacket and threw it also. He put off her both moccasins and insulted them by his habit. He turned towards her jeans. He did her cloth-made belt undone and pulled her jeans out. He threw it also. He put her inners also off.

Now, she had only a chocolaty colour decent bra and a black colour thin lyre underwear on her 24-aged hot and red body, and socks too.

"You look not less than *Pryanka Chopra* now!" He moved his fingers on her boobs

"Have you ever seen her in this position?" She did her eyes large.

He smiled.

"You, sexy boy! I understand your feelings!" She sat and pulled her socks out. She threw them.

"So, let's play!"

"Ooo - - - - - hunkk!" She smiled.

"Hey, my *Ram Swaroop* is worried some more for two-three days."He patted her thighs as he came on bed again.

"So what? My *Ram Pyaree* so does." She parked her wild, glassy and erotic eyes on his words.

"You are no answer thing!" He flattered.

"What's there to say, that I am; many boys are dying always on me." She overtaxed.

"You are so squat!"

"That also I am." She had not thank in her voice.

"You are very seductive and overloaded with natural pulchritude!" He said.

She was sitting in front of him in his V- shaped pins, her head pillowed on his chest. He had taken a support of the wall for his back. He had pinned her down, his both arms around her neck and his chin on her left shoulder. I was unable to see his face or eyes even, her step-cutting hair on his head covering it almost.

He slightly, squeezed her balls.

"Aaaa... aa.. a! You bloody monkey!" She did her head up.

"What?"

She laughed and bit in his hands and ambled as he tried to catch her. He followed her and again took her in his strong arms and once again threw her on the bed, a slushy laughing in the boudoir all the time.

He tore her bra and pulled her underwear out with the help of his capped teeth.

She also did same with him.

Now, they both were naked, on the bed facing each other— they were on their knees and on their hands. Like a bitch she stared at him and he also climbed on her as a dog. They quarrelled each other for some seconds.

At last she lay as a sultry fish and he came on her. "Beer?" He ogled her eyes.

"Am I less than any beer?" She had a carnal voice, her eyes I can't explain—so sexy!

"Now, their pillow talks were on.

"No, darling! Beer is in your every bit! "He jammed his lips and nose and all mouth into her lips and also licked her breasts.

He was playing with her *bhonpoos*.

"Play, play and play! I'm enjoying; carry on!" She pressed his head in the upper warm pitch to be nuzzled, forcedly using her both hands. And hebit, her nipples and lips and cheeks with no teeth, but with lips— I was a peeping tom there, all the time.

**"Ahha- - - aha a a - - -!"** She took sexual breaths, her eyes closed and lips slightly opened. "Gaurav!" She gave a soft cry, and held him close— the climax great!

Well, this is it! Their all act secretly saved in chip to finally arrive on screen, all neat and crisp. Ah, that sounds sweet.

# 15

The exams got over. It was December 23rd. We watched Robot in *Pharat's* cell and played cards for sometime after that—time was difficult to spend.

At one, I prepared tea and we all took it. Even then, everything looked a boring box.

I lifted my books which I didn't feel like. And they made a mind to tease the people.

Pharat dialled many numbers; all were guessed and not surely correct, his many tryings failed.

The call rate being free, after 11:00, in Vodafone.

"Hey, be silent now!" He cried as the bell looked going— he had the call hand free.

"Hello!"

"Yea, who is on line?"

"Your sister. Will you talk?"

He disconnected the call at once. We all laughed and kept laughing until he tried again for the next.

The bell went again.

"Hello!" A female voice said.

"Kashish speaking?"

"No."

"Then?"

"What will you do?"

"At least you must tell."

"Why?"

"Oaf, I'm asking that's why."

"It's not Kashish – that's it."

"You are speaking from *Lucknow,* no?"

"No."

"It seems so by your voice. Any way, it is so sweet!" He buffered, "And I think you will be very decent too. There is a beautiful couplet for you. Would appreciate it?"

"You bloody bastard! So many slittos I will beat on your head; you will forget to make any one appreciate anything." she abused him very much.

*Pharat* became silent, his face worth watching, so comic.

He disconnected the call again.

"Will you try again?" I laughed; other dudes also gave me a support. Here, I tell you *Pharat* was the sort of wolf-whistler, bloody loafer usually flirts. He had many affairs. Here, I remember, once he teased a girl and in answer she threw her sandals on him just to hit but—you know what he did— he took a catch and ran away with her sandals; and poor girl kept on beating her feet with annoyance.

"What are you looking like this? Hone your talking skill." I said. I shut up my books. "Okay, dial any number and get me the cell; I show you how to talk." I said.

He followed my words. "Here it is." He got me the cell—the bell was going.

"Hello- - -!" By luck, a female voice was there. It was sweet but some sleepy, my ears peaked.

"*Aye Mona*, my darling! What happened to your cell? I have been trying for a long time but it was out of coverage all the time." I used my talking skill.

"Sorry!"

"Sorry what?"

"Where have you called?"

"Wherever, but it is at the place I wanted."

"A wrong number?" She said.

"Yea."

"I know you guys; must be studying."

"Yea, but how you guessed?"

"I'm also a student." I heard she smiled, "Just now, few minutes before I closed my books!"

"A hard working student!"

She smiled and I could hear her silken voice, "No, it's my 12th there, that's why!"

"A cunning boy!"

"Sorry, I disturbed you at this time!"

"It's ok."

"Anyway, where are you speaking from?"

"From *Sarvodya Nagar, Kanpur*."

"Where there is the head office of *Dainik Jagran*?"

"Yea-yea, by the *big Bazaar*" She said, "You have been to *Kanpur*?"

"No."

"Then, how you know this much?"

"Actually, I'm a poet as cum-as student. From there, usually my poems are published, that's why." I said.

"Good! My luck; I'm talking to poet." She said, "Would you write anything for me?"

"Why not?"

"So please!"

"It will take time."

"Okay, sms after composing anything."

"Your words on my head!"

She laughed.

"Sweet girl! How far is it IIT from there?"

"Not much far, hardly two-three kms." She used her mind, "Why?"

"Nothing, I asked just like that."

"An IIT maniac?"

"Yea."

"You didn't tell your name."

"You told?"

"Sorry," she smiled, "It's *Anjali.*"

"And here, *Butterua; Butterua Giri Goswami.*"

"Sweet name!"

"Friend?"

"...... *Hunnn,* lemme think; you guys are always cunning!" she smiled.

"Have you thought?" I knocked her after forty seconds.

She laughed, "Okay, done! But never cheat me....."

"I promise!"

"Sweet boy!" She said. We both talked for twenty minutes, our talkings formal, but romantic also.

"So, you a sweet baby, it's my exam there; let's talk tomorrow!" I fibbed.

"Tomorrow?"

"Yea."

"Of what class?"

"It is eleventh."

"Okay, do study." She said, "Sweet- sweet good bye!"

"Good bye." I disconnected.

"I can't believe it!" *Pharat* was surprised and *Sindhi* and *Udit* also.

"It's the skill of talking!" I smiled giving him his phone. I held my books again. Still, he was without any word.

*"I am sheila, sheila ki javani......."* His cell phone cried just after one minute.

"Hello." *Pharat* received, his voice heavy.

*"Butterua?"*

"No, his friend!"

"Where is he?"

"Here he is; talk." He spoke in phone and gave the cell to me.

"Hello," I said, my voice sweet.

*"Butterua*, where are you speaking from?"

"From your heart?"

"Oh, shut up, *Butterua.......*" She laughed, "I'm asking the name of the place, you are calling from."

"From *Rampur."*

"I didn't ask, that's why— sorry."

"Sorry, for what?"

"I disturbed you."

"How cool!" I smiled.

"The girls are always so."

"May, I don't know."

She laughed, "*Butterua*, whenever you come to *Kanpur* call me. I'll receive you, right!"

"Okay."

"Surely."

*"Okay, baba*! Now put the phone."

"Good night." She said.

"Guruuuu............. *!" Pharat* started catching my legs and my chin also," *Guru*, you are really *Guru;* only you can save my life. Please take out some solution. I'm dying every moment without *Mani7ha*. Please- please—!" He cried and cried.

The room filled with laughter, the cacophony touching the high point.

"Leave my legs, please!" I pulled my pins and squeezed myself.

"Please!" He said," I won't leave until you listen to me."

"Oh, shut up!" I cried.

All became silent. They started studying, a deep study now. I did my eyes up; he was weeping many tears, pearls-like, on his book, "Okay, I'll do your work." I whispered.

"Thank you; thank you very much!" He started again-a boy with crocodile tears just before.

# 16

*Modi Motel* is the best restaurant in all *Rampur*, but a restaurant not any cabaret. Once, I thought to collect my all friends there—just to get together, and to make a friendship between *Pharat* and *Mani7ha*.

"Let's go." I said to Pharat with no clue of my mind.

"Where?" He looked at me in a strange way.

"To Modi Motel." I said.

"Why?"

"*Mani7ha* has invited" I fibbed.

"Any function?"

"No, only to get together." I said cagily.

"Then, you must go—you are invited."

" . . . . . You are too."

They looked each other, a compadre.

"*Aye*, stop this all and be ready; I'm downstairs, looking for a rickhshaw."

I buttonholed a rickshaw puller as I reached down.

They were there in half an hour; failing the females in doing make-up.

We hired the rickshaw and sat on it. I asked the rickshaw puller to park *Modi Motel*, a place about five kms from our place.

"Butterua, how am I looking?" *Pharat* ruffled his hair. He was in nice and expensive cloths— a black wellingtons, caddis-coloured jeans and a shirt beet-coloured, casual and stylish.

Our clothes were also not bad.

"Really, killing, a boy in cahoots!" I said, "Believe me, If I had been a girl, I would have married you, all cases mine."

All started giggling and kept on.

"What happened?" I asked the *rickshaw*-puller when he stopped the three-wheeled vehicle suddenly.

He stood on the road, catching his stomach "Let me laugh first, otherwise, I will die." The 35, strong bodied and black complexioned man felt pain laughing.

He started pedaling after three minutes and dropped us the designated place in about 10 minutes.

I cadged the fare of *rickshaw* off *Pharat*.

He paid one hundred.

We entered the expensive restaurant. *Mani7ha* and *Aiece* were there already before us— I managed to call them, my purpose being to make a friendship between *Pharat* and *Mani7ha*. They both were wondering in the corridor and seemed to have just arrived.

We waved our hands for 'hi' and went into the main hall. It was big enough to provide the place for 90 people, many tables and chairs arranged into it.

I booked two tables, a table with four chairs. *Udit* dragged another table and lifted three chairs to the place— he conflated both the tables a dovetail.

All sat— *Mani7ha* and *Aiece* in right, *Udit* and Sindhi in left and *Pharat* on my face. *Mani7ha* was beside me and *Aiece* very close with her.

I noted all the walls of hall were decorated with pictures of different varieties of food-vegetarian and non-vegetarian, both.

A waiter came close to us with a long menu.

*Pharat* chose *dal-makhni, Udit, Sindhi* and *Aiece palak-paneer*, but *Mani7ha* and I made no choice. "*Butterua*?" *Mani7ha* asked me to choose something.

"You must." I looked at her.

Mani7ha ticked off the *kari*.

I gave the menu to the waiter.

"You didn't choose anything?" *Mani7ha* sulked her face.

I smiled. "You all have chosen, it's enough. I'm in you all." I said.

"Just see his talking. . ." "She said with her brow, smiling and looking at *Sindhi*".

"Sir, all the things are ready but for *kari* you will have to wait— it's in the wok."

"How long will it take?"

"About fifteen minutes?"

"Okay." I shrugged as all of my mates gave their expression positively.

"But get us some newspaper or magazine, if there they are." *Mani7tha* spoke as he was going to leave our table.

"Ma'am, what should I carry; news paper or magazine? Both are.. . ."

"Then, news paper."

"Ma'am which one— English or Hindi?"

". . . . English one"

"Ma'am, Times of India or Hindustan Times?"

"Any one, you want." *Aiece* said smiling.

The waiter brought up the TOI.

**"Wow!"** Mani7ha cried as she took the paper in her hand.

"What happened?"

"Just see, *Anna Hazare* has shook *U.P.A* Government, very strong man!" She said excitedly, "Now, of course there won't be any corruption."

"Why?"

"Now, there will be ***Jan Lok Pal Bill***— youth against corruption!"

". . . . Bribe dances, even then." I remarked with a cryptic smile.

"How come?"

". . . . People are very shameless, There is a note— put a note of ₹100 on one's one palm and a piece of bread on another one and keep on using your boots on his head, even then the next day, he will vote for you." I said.

"May be."

"What may be? *Mani7ha,* our Constitution is very fucking. It is cadaverous. Here, although there are many rules, but many lacunae in every rule." I assuaged with a candenza in my voice, "Miss *Mani7ha*, you know what is the reality? Here, howsoever much you can carry on with rules, carry on, nothing bad with you! No doubt, unless, two-three babies would be born, there is not any response." I used my right hand to pump the balloon, peskily.

They all broke into laugh.

"Stop, *Batterua*!" *Mani7ha* caught my hand. She laughed and laughed and laughed, "You use slangs?" She met my eyes, her laughing turned into surprise.

The waiter knocked at the time. Very first, he served a mug of water and then steeled plates, finally meal.

"No, but whenever I come in touch with these sort of things, I have no control on myself."

"A pesky boy! Learn controlling. It is a dangerous thing." She touched my right hand— it lay on the table.

It perturbed *Pharat*. I also had a strong shock. I pulled my hand. She glimpsed him noting all.

"Oh, hush up it, *yaar*; the party is getting cold!" *Aiece* said.

"Oh, sorry!" I grated and the party raring to go.

"Oh, yes I'm going to forget an important thing!" I blew a Bronx cheer.

"What?"

"Why you don't speak to him?"

"His eyes are not good." She had a raspberry at me.

"What?" I looked at *Pharat*, "Just see the doctor, first of all."

All started laughing. "Not in this manner." She said smiling.

"Then, in what way?"

"He always looked at me with a different sight— I don't like that." She cleared in conspicuous words. "He must remove the things he had in his mind always related to me. If he can, I have no prob." She shrugged with a smiley, a pretty vivacious girl.

"Okay, he will— I hope so!" I said, "Now, you will....?"

"I have no prob." She repeated her words, putting the spoon in her mouth, *kari* along rice in it.

"Good, now you both shake hands." I said and all started clapping along myself as they shook.

We left the restaurant as our lunch was finished—*Pharat* paid the bill.

# 17

It was 6 p.m. of the same day. We managed to meet again in *Ambedkar Park*— an open, lush-green and good looking ground, on the highway, in the middle of CRPF Camp and flyover, the same flyover which leads to *aian-aian's* place. There is a railway track behind it.

It was evening time, the weather pleasant!

The park was getting stuffed with people, mostly with the ones who thought it to be a nice place to pass off the night.

"What a nuisance!" *Pharat* sulked his face, we all are in the meadow, near the effigy of *Dr. Bheem Rao Ambedkar*, "Just see this is the condition of our Indian parks! A park like thing is for us, but here . . . . .!"

I looked at him.

"And see here, to the parks, what sort of names are given?— *Ambedkar park*, Gandhi park, *Kanchan park. . . . . ,* bloody fucking! Are these any names?"

". . . . What sort of they must have been?" I smiled, a verbal gymnastic in my voice.

*"Laila-Majnoo Park, Heer-Ranjha Park, Banti–Babli Park;* many names are there, they could have been." He gushed, "Some *Eros* must be in the names as we find abroad."

In fact, if there is some one and that is new to something, has much passion in itself—*new suit, new boot, new rangoot ask for polish!*

Here, *Pharat* looked following it.

"Let's go there!" I cruised my eyes around all the park looking for a sitting place, a shade, there in the mountain side-the mountain artificially made.

"Oh, yes, why not? Why not?" He threw his hand.

We turned towards the shade, the shade not good enough—why we chose that park? Was there no else place?

We all sat on the cement-made benches, under the shade, near the bank of brook, the brook arising from the mountain.

For some time, there was a conglomeration of thoughts which we had.

Finally, we climbed on the mountain.

I took an emerald stone to sit on, *Mani7ha* and all others also. The colour of her short skirt and of the stone she sat on, was same, the stone all black.

"Butterua, you really don't know riding?" *Aiece* started as she found no topic to talk.

*Pahrat* laughed as he remembered the incident of the returning from tuition of *aian-aian*.

"Don't cackle this much; I can defeat you on your own pitch, however hard nut you are!"

Ho! Ho! Ho! No one could control the laughing like thing, leaving me. "Laugh. . . . ; must feign laugh!" I looked at Pharat.

"Okay, have a bet!" He said, smiling.

"You will be defeated." I said, confidently.

"Let it be, you tell!"

"It's a Byzantine matter— you will have to repent."

"It's up to me. You tell are you having a bet?" He congealed with his words.

"Okay done!" My tongue slipped as I looked at *mani7ha*. Here, one thing is notable that I was a mediator, or ownself a part?

"You know he is. . . . . . ?" *Sindhi* looked at me.

"Whatever, now he needs a treat, keep waiting?" I smiled with ebullience in me, "He is a child before me!"

*Mani7ha's* mind was conking out. "Let's go? It's too late." She crumpled up or jumped down from the stone. Her short-black skirts flee. She put her both hands on her thighs, preventing it— a sexy figure, yellow top with white short sleeves smiley face on one side and opened hair; her little bit out. Oh, god! Stop it, otherwise. . . . . ; all the guys are *gonna* commit suicide— sure!

"Of course, it's getting dark." I looked hither and thither, and we left the park— for 45 minutes, we stayed there.

Next day, as the prayer ceremony got over, I went to *aian-aian* and asked him to get the the event done.

He laughed, "What have you ; you know he is the pop of riding?"

"I know."

"So?"

"Sir, please, however, get this cometetion done!" I requested.

The principle sir gave the permission.

Now, all the teachers and students gathered in the ground. Pharat was with his wild fire city bike, an *Atlas company* cycle, showing his gymnastics riding in the open ground.

It was like lion and a jackal face-to-face. A heavy defeat this time—sure! The people's gesture there elucidated it.

Pharat! Pharat! Pharat! The ground support with him, some buddies, hidden in the class-rooms were compelled to be there in the competition arena by the chants, the atmosphere electrifying.

"Wish you best of luck!" Mani7ha showed her thumb as I passed through the stairs—she stood very depressed, standing near the entry gate, worried and doubtful.

I thanked. I smiled as if the ball was in my hand. I noted her perplexed and a girl like a confused bee in her mind as I stepped ahead.

*Aiece* came close to her.

I, a biped, went forward, towards the game committee— now, the competition was under the auspices of the college. All noise disappeared. *Pharat* was also called.

I propped my cycle against a tree.

He neared us-happy, smiling and whistling. He front-braked and the cycle lifted up, from the back. Pharat! Pharat! Pharat! Once again, a big noise got dancing.

Waving his hand, he paid thanks. "What's up, buddy?" He conked me, a sign of love. He parked his cycle on its stand and shook hand, a lot of proud in his words and style, eliciting his poor attitude.

"Fine!" I smiled, feeling the pain in my head.

". . . . . .Now see, who needs a nipple?" He smiled. He had thrown all wicked means; he had in his mind, elliptically.

"Go back. You have some repo, now. And, I don't *wanna* spoil that, otherwise. . . . . .!" I said.

"Otherwise what?"

"I never insult any one." I explained him.

He laughed "You won't be changed!"

"Again, I will have to say— don't laugh this much, so... !"

"Well, will you get me *Mani7ha* if you are defeated here?" He smiled, his style dishonest, his voice low but high enough for me.

I smiled and only smiled—doff, I already, myself worked for the same purpose, but here he. . . . . . !And any way, was *Mani7ha* any property of mine?— Idiot! Dodo!

". . . . . Mani7ha!" I elided smiling and tried with my eyes to search the heart-touching, soft and milky, elfin-faced, bountiful dove— she was there on the same place, quite silent, quite still and deeply thinking, a serious girl. "Forget her!" I said suddenly, as I touched her with my eyes— don't know how?

He took it to heart.

*Dhaka sir* had a mike in his hand. He was speaking loudly and loudly on it, to announce the competition.

He went up to him and asked for the mike. He got it. "Didi tera kya hoga, didi tera kya hoga; anke. . . . . ." He sang dourly a song dancing and walking around me. Whatever, it was a great insult of mine.

All the college supported him.

I had myself still and serious and in deep thought.

I was feeling all but—

Suddenly, I also started dancing. At this, all the crowd was astonished; Mani7ha broke into tears— she couldn't tolerate my insult.

Here, I was a very different boy, inwardly so palsied and so courageous out-wardly. So far, I was not prepared for the race and neither aware, even. I didn't feel anything about the coming result. And a notable thing, what will I do now, I didn't know.

I was dancing and dancing and dancing. Although, he stopped, but I even then. . . . .

I was being mocked.

"Butterua!!!" *Mani7ha* shook all my body— she came up to us, an annoying girl. It looked as if all that was happening to me, was not happening to me, but on the contrary, to her. Why did she felt so?

I stopped. My heart palpitated. It was beating rapidly. Now, in fact, the state of everybody's eyes gave made my palpitation tougher.

I watched every corner. All the crowd was at me, their sight so different. All were silent.

*Aiece* also followed her.

"Ask him not to be mocked and to come back." *Aiecc* elbowed her and smiled cunningly, "Otherwise. . . . . .!"

"*Butterua*, please. . . . . ; everyone is laughing at you!" She was worried, a cachet in her voice. She knocked some sense into me.

". . . .A child he is, still!" I smiled, as if any great idea was in my bonnet, or any *Rustam* I was.

I took the mike.

She closed her eyes, communed with nature and surprise. . . . ! Now, of course it was— an elegant solution to that prob in my mind. "Never, no one can defeat me. I challenge you all; I challenge the whole world! No one can defeat me! No one! Here, no one has drunk this much!" In a loud voice, I spoke in the mike, eloquently.

My words and my passion emasculated all the supporters of his. Now, all wondered. All were in a doubt there. Was there any alien with me?

"Sir, the rules will follow my words." I gave the mike to *Dhaka sir.*

He looked at *Pharat.*

"Okay, done!" He nodded.

"Now, if you can defeat me, I of course will drink your piss— must try . . . !" I said to *Pharat*, my words hard.

His face pale as he found me so strong. "Let's see!" He lisped.

"Tell, what do you say?" *Dhaka sir* said.

"Sir, if he follows me in all respect, I will be defeated then." I said.

Pharat silent, his tongue forgot commenting.

The principal sir gave the permission and competition was on.

I held my cycle, no spoke, no brake and also no mudguards, the cycle was a *khatara*. I asked a peon for the black-burnt mobil-oil. He got me it in three minutes. I doused back one tyre of my cycle with it and threw the can.

All people were surprised!

". . . . . Now, follow this line!" I said as I pedaled with elegance in my words.

Uuuuaaa- - - - ! All people started crying. They were shocked at this. And never ever they must have thought that I did.

*Pharat,* a poor boy tried. He cycled following the prints,

but fell down very badly. He got eluded and clobbered— my idea nicely dovetailed nicely the situation.

*Mani7ha* ran towards me. In the way, there was *Pharat*, his cycle was on him. *"Pahle kaha tha mat khel. Le ab jhel!"* She commented taking revenge of the insult of mine that he did, lifting the cycle up, palling around.

Till then, I also was there. "What happened, *Mr. Rider*?" I smiled. His face down, he spoke nothing.

# 18

Hoouoo!!

I was thrilled. I left the cycle. I was at parking, parking my well known *khatara*.

"…. scared of?" *Mani7ha* laughed as I looked at her.

"Intoto not……." I held my cycle.

She parked her purple colour *magna*, a ladies *Atlas company* bicycle.

"…. Ergo, your cycle was dropped from your hands?" She smiled.

"Actually, suddenly it occurred." I excused.

"Don't fib. I know you got shocked." She started climbing the stairs, me along.

I gave a gummy smile.

"Hey, I wonder how you defeated *Pharat*?" She came before me as we reached landing.

"A magical surprise . . . . . ., whenever I'm in trouble and you are before me, I myself don't know how I get the ideas?"

"You love me?" She blew her genteel tongue, salivating; her eyes scaling.

"Eh?" I smiled.

"Any way, I love you…." She said, her eyes melting, voice mellifluous, but both not formal.

"… Hey, stop!!!" A male voice stopped us as we neared the class room of ours — *Pharat* was there. It might be possible that he could have touched the conversation, we had.

"… How come!" I left my mouth opened as I turned neck.

He hasn't been talking to me since the time of the competition!" I said.

"Why?" She stared at him and took a nice class.

"Sorry!" He said, "Actually, a setback to my mind, I'm a master of riding, but he put me to rout... how come? He can't cross even a road if it is nodded, even then!"

"..... Gratuitously mad, a boy stupid!" She laughed, "So what? It's a mind — every one doesn't have every thing in it."

"Right!" *Aiece* also had dropped herself there.

We all entered the class.

*"Butterua,* you know anything about ***Masani***?" He rumbled, not a sincere boy.

"What *Masani*?"

"It's some Devi"

"It's not any Devi, a bloody bitch she is!" I said, "... For what you are grubbing about?"

He didn't speak

"May be to get any magic power he would persuade her—don't ask!" *Aiece* said and we all guffawed.

In the evening, he was at the room with a *barfi - sweet* box in his hand.

". .. . Sweet?" *Sindhi* asked.

He spoke nothing — something was fishy! I ran with my mind and remembered the topic of ***'Masani'*** raised at the college. I guessed all.

It was the night of black ***amavasya***. An a*mavasya* night is thought to be good to persuade black powers.

My guess was right, he was there in a crematorium, alone, at midnight, around one o'clock. The whole caboodle he had with him— a sweet box, incense sticks, hair of a girl, a piece of somebody's clothes and some black u*rad*— I could see this all when he burnt the fire.

I had been there before he reached.

He threw all his clothes and became totally naked. He sat cross-legged and started throwing the grains of ***urad*** into the fire and time-to-time burnt the hair and the pieces of clothes he had.

He sat on his knees and hands and touched the earth with his head. Then he murmured something remaining only on knees and cupping both hands. And like a funny left-field, he got dancing around the fire reciting— ***Jai Masani, Jai Masani,*** . . . . . . . .

And once again, he sat on his knees and hands.

Now, I had a naughty prank in my mind. I took a solid piece of clay and threw upon his bottom.

Now, he became active and looked hither and thither. He was surprised and scared, both.

Hoo ha-ha haaaaa. . . .. ! I appeared there before him, a complete ***symbolic man;*** all clothes dusty and covered with the leaves of *paker* tree.

He ran very fast, leaving all his clothes.

*I lifted the sweet box. There, by chance, I found a paper which was carried here by Pharat; Hey, Masani! Be appeared, I pray to you, I am at your feet. Be happy. And listen to my request. I want a girl. That is Mani7ha. Get me that sexy, beautiful and 16 old girl. I want to get my leg over her only — nothing else! Fill my wish, my desire to the full extent.*

I was surprised at this.

I saw hither and thither and opened the box. I put a piece of *Barfi* into my mouth—so sweet!

I found myself there alone. I also got scared of.

I quit that place immediately.

# 19

All girls were surprised. All boys were surprised too. The whole class surprised. I was not exception, at—

No period, interval over. Slowly-slowly, the class gathered. Mani7ha was a thoughtful girl since morning. I noticed a lot of worry in her eyes and she looked anxious. She, suddenly, left her seat and went on the podium, a myopic oaf! She took a chalk and decorated the board, the writing curlicue—

*I think, now you won't let me remain alive!*

The quotation not muzzy!

She was an enigmatic girl in the whole class. She came back to her seat. She looked at me baffling and left the room, leaving a message on a paper, on the desk— ***Butterua, If you wanna see me alive, meet me outside the college as soon as possible; I'm waiting for you at the station, your favourite place. Remember, I have salfash, a very dangerous poison with me.....!***

Booby, the matter not mystique!

After all, I had to reach the venue before the time. She was there at the beauty spot, awaiting  banging the walls.

"Hey, *Mani7ha*! What is this all for?" I boomed, as I came before her.

"You blockhead! Bloody dog—duffer!" She cried, with myriad abuses for me. What a welcome!

Her anger lovely!

"..... Anything wrong with you?" I smiled.

"You stupid bloke, a very boor! Why you ignore me always? Why you.... ?" She, my very close friend caught my collar and broke into tears.

I was silent.

She shook all my body. "Why don't you understand my feelings? Am I mad? Do I have horns?"

"Don't know, I can't say." I burbled.

*"Shut up! Shut up!"* She pushed me.

I got shocked.

"Butterua, I'm always thinking about you! I love you! I love you, my partiality....!" She wept with more tears.

I pored over her eyes and boned up on all the steps of hers since I had been in the college and— hey presto, I got melted!

"Sorry!" I smiled, "I think, now you are out of your tube top with your bosom!"

"What?"

I seized her. I pressed her hair. I kissed her; on her lips and on her neck in the right side, and wherever I could.

She became a buoyant ***Nagin*** with her arms around me. Now, we both were necking.

For fifteen days we both pootled on the ground of time, only kiss went on, nothing else!

Soon, there was a birthday party at *Aiece*'s place for her younger sister. And we all were invited, *Man7ha* as well— the party bourgeois.

A lot of noise, bloody poppy cock! The D.J. was on. The invitees on it.

"Hey, c'mon baby! Let's dance!" *Mani7ha* pulled me, pootling on floor.

"I can't!" I said in the bedlam of that place.

"Hey, don't be party-pooper. C'mon shake your poppet!" She showed her energy and I was there on the floor, dancing bovinely.

All were there with their all party spirit.

The song, **I am *sheila; sheila, ki jawani***....was on.

The dancing is a poser for me I came down from the floor before going— but kept on lip— syncing all the time.

Mani7ha danced like a lady possessed. And I got gob smacked.

As the song was over, she put her left hand on her head and right one on the red-lined collar of the top, very near to her breasts, her eyes up, long-long hair opened out and free. She wore two big-big, thin hoop earrings, a golden orange rinkled long skirt and a top on it, beautified with sequins, her style erotic!

"Oh, boy! Your dance!" I complimented her when we both were in the dining hall—all the friends were on the floor; we secretly left them.

"Bowled you over?" She smiled.

"Very much! I felt like. . . . . . !" I stopped my tongue.

". . . . . Felt like, what?" She looked at me cunningly, her heart seraphic.

"I got getting randy and felt like to jump up on you!" I said.

"So, let's go!"

"Where?"

"To my place."

"You are alone?"

"A bloody hound!" She bowed her head with smile, "Yea, parents are out of station and will be back in two-three days."

"Good!"

"Let's go now— my dear boyf!" She enticed; lured sedatively.

"How are you by?"

"By scooty."

"Okay, as you wish! Let's see— one day in *sasural*!" I shrugged.

She smiled, "Your bounden duty!"

We both skipped off the party at 11 O'clock, for the place of Mani7ha—we came without telling anyone and not eating properly.

She rode fast and very soon we were at her place. She fetched me to her boudoir and left me alone for the time she changed her clothes.

Surprise! All room bedecked with the photos of mine, the photos were very seraphic ally bordered, with many bougainvilleas around them. I wondered how she would have collected them. I was really bedazzled.

I kept standing till the time she came.

"You are standing since then?" She switched on the T.V. making the bed linen and pulled me on the bed to sit on.

"...... You look sexy!"

"Just tune in— *Raaz* movie is there!" She smiled.

"I haven't come here to watch any boring movie." I said.

"So?"

"Let me watch this one movie!" I said, my eyes on her cleavage.

"What one?"

"This one!" I nudged towards the ample zone of hers, a boob tube is worn where.

"Naughty boy!" She smiled, "Okay, park your eyes anywhere, you want." She gravitated towards me. She put the remote in a side on her bed.

"Really!" I looked into her eyes.

"Hoon. . . . !" She played with the nails of her left hand's thumb and index finger, her expression a beery mixture of drive, shyness and naughtiness along smile, some raisins in it, and an Essex girl!

I had myself closed to her. Slowly-slowly, with my eyes and fingers along I went up to her bazoom and stopped there.

Affww.... ! She sighed as if one had thrown the drops of cold water on any hot oven. "No!" She caught my hands.

"What?"

"It's not fair!" She said, a girl in a semi-trance state.

"The go-ahead granted!"

"Not for your fingers."

"Please; it's me!" I flaunted.

"So?" She stoked.

I stared at and—

"One second!" She paused to remove her clothes and took out a thin rubber covering, a prevention for pregnancy and any sexually transmitted disease. It was kept in her innerwear.

"You knew it?" I smiled.

"No, but ever since you came in my life, I have been keeping it always in this safe place, looking for the chance; and that I got today." She bit the wrapper of sheath and put it on my palm.

"What is done by it?" I asked intentionally.

"Idiot, it is used to stop a warm girl or any woman to become mummy."

"I would use it as a balloon in the childhood", I said, becoming her partner without any clothes.

She smiled. She lifted that prophylactic and used where it is. She lay to be sedated.

"Any way, how long have you been in love with me."

"When you met me very first time, near the gate while backing off our place; I gave you my hand and you got disappeared, since then." She sat and had her both hands on her knees, "Any way, why you country people feel shy so much?"

"Don't know. But all the villagers are so!" I said

"How stupid they are!"

"Yea!" I looked into her eyes dishonestly.

"Hey, stop your eyes. Otherwise, I would lose my control!" She said, lying again— her Eros strong.

"After all, you have had your control on me, a wily fox!" I smiled and jumped in the battle field. "How do you feel now?" I asked after some seconds.

"Some different!" She smiled.

She pressed me to her bosom.

Each of us spurred each other. We both got panting in that particular game. "What is this?" In the nick of time, I held her tightly.

"I also don't understand!" She also winced.

....Huffing and puffing! Only, huffing and puffing— no voice! The whole nine yards got over. I kept lying on her for some time after the passion repressed for years came forth unleashed and then crept in a side of hers.

We had lost our virginity.

"How cool it was!" I looked at her, a gobshite.

"Now, I understand why a girl gets ready to elope with a guy—really, it's so sweet!" She stretched her right leg on me and raised herself on an elbow, covering my face with her stupid hair." "Any way, they do nothing wrong." She said with a strong kiss on my lips.

I smiled. I threw her and came on her. I bit her and kissed her all the time; rubbed her breasts passionately.

"Once more?" She smiled with strong sedative effect in her eyes.

"No!" I left her. I put on my clothes.

"*Mani7ha*, what do you think about *Pharat*?" I said to her. Still, she was on bed, a naked and thirsty bitch.

"Nothing!" She said "C'mon, no!"

"No, it's enough!"

"A dirty boy!" She left the bed.

"No, he is very after you!"

"A girl understands every thing; another thing doesn't enter into any further step whatsoever about them, otherwise she understands. . . ."

I smiled.

"Yea, I know. But, I have a sexy boy— you!" She took her underwears to put on.

"No! He loves you, before than me."

"So?" She popped on her checked *payjamas*.

I looked at her excited knockers—those were larger than usual, and stiff.

"I didn't need any *tom-dick-harry!* I always wanted a off-screen hero, and that you are!" she put on the same colourful sleeved checked shirt, of what her payjama was. She started buttoning, no blouse, only a thin bra.

"But, *Pharat* is not any *Tom dick harry*—he can make you mummy every month of new-borns." I smiled.

"Shut up!" She pushed me on the bed— I was on the edge of it. She pinned me down by having my pins in hers— she stood and I lay on my elbows, my bottom on the edge. Slowly-slowly, she bent her waist and gravitated to my face with her sexy eyes. "Never say so, again! I am on this earth only for you— that's it!" She said, her voice some serious and some funny; I couldn't judge.

"Let's go!" I ogled her, changing the topic.

"Where?" She couldn't understand.

"In bed!"

"Again?"

"Yea!"

"Why not?" She started undoing the buttons of her shirt.

"No-no-no! Please, no!" I laughed and laughed—how crazy the girls are!

# 20

My darling lived not much far from my room. And it was dead of night; 1:30 a.m. The electricity supply was still there.

I made my mood to reach my residence.

She lay pliant in my arms, on the bed. I played with her secretive zone.

"So, now you are skipping me, in this burning night?" She did her head up.

"I'll have to."

"Why? Can't you spend your night here, with me?"

"My luck green! But my mates will worry if I don't reach the room."

"Fucking . . . .!"

". . . . Otherwise, many questions will be there!"

"So, let them be!"

"Mani7ha, it is you who kindled my faith in love! I can't tolerate any wrong comment towords you from any mouth— I worship your love!" I spoke slowly, in a state of preoccupation, "So, please. . . . !"

"Okay," She sighed. She got down the bed and stood before the mirror, gazing at herself. "Should I drop you?" She spoke turning her face towards me.

"No, never! It will expose the affair!" I smiled. I too left the bed.

"Okay, as you wish— good bye!" She said.

"Same here!" I said.

"Go carefully. It's too night." She said as I left her at the gate.

"Nothing can harm me, if you love me!" I stopped my feet and got gazing at her, "There is poetry in all your gestures!"

"Now go, otherwise . . . . . . !"

"Otherwise what?"

".....Don't complain then for not letting to be gone."

I laughed. "Bye!" I stepped ahead.

She was nearly going to close the main gate, when I entered again.

"Now, what happened?" She said as she found me there once more.

"....You look beautiful!"

"Go..., otherwise I'll off you!" She cried, pushing me.

Here, at O' level, I took only a subject— love! I was obsessed by the pleasure; I got with her in the knees-up and in her boudoir. The olfactory heart of mine, a free ladybird was smiling and dancing in an amusing spot. I was very cool. I was whistling and singing the song, ***I am sheila; sheela ki jawani***.

All the dogs were out, barking!

I chose a bypass to reach my place. There was a *banty dharam kanta* in that Podunk way and also a crematorium, most morasses, same one where *Pharat* came some days before. This feary zone was occupied with many bigeucalyptus trees, along with one very thick banyan tree in the crematorium.

I was plumb in my mood, the poignancy of the bed romance in my mind all the time.

"Hey, where are you going there?" A black unpleasant obese bloke came forward to prevent me. At the moment, the lights went off—it was dark everywhere, now.

Sensing danger, an onslaught of fear struck me— I was very afraid at that time. I looked at him, but didn't stop there nor anywhere else, main reason being the crematorium actually.

My speed was fast. I skittered, a boy not remarkably poised.

My tongue morphed the track. Now there was ***Hanumaan Chalisa*** on it, not *sheila ki jawani.*

The area passed off. I looked hither and thither, no menace now. I continued again the same song— *I am sheila; sheila ki jawani. . . . .*

I was a boy, plumb up the pole!

At 2:40, I reached my room. *Pharat, Sindhi and Udit* were there already. "How long is it since you came?" I asked.

They all were po-faced, "Where were you?" *Pharat* asked. He was skolly here.

". . . . . . . In the party!" I said.

"Oh, skipped it! We scoured you everywhere!" He cried.

"I was there!" I smiled.

"Shutt up!" Sindhi skirmished, "We tried to get you everywhere."

He plied me with many questions.

"My pop, I was there! I was watching movie!" I said.

". . . . .Okay, tell! Which movie was on?"

"I don't know the name. But it was very fantabulous; you boof head bleb, can't understand it!" I said.

Many questions, many answers—very hardly, nattily, I could escape from their *chakravyuh* and could save the pregnant reason.

At 4 a.m. we took to our beds.

There was no sleep in my eyes. The pole dancing girl was there in the tulips, in the roses all the time. Too cool, pleased as punch I was, a boy no tuppence for anything. Her luminescent lovely face made me wacko. My all mind got turfed out of my sense.

I was mad in the high noon of love, ludicrously killing the night, turbidity strong!

Next three days, I didn't appear at the tuition and coincidently, *Mani7ha* as well. There at the room, I was an animal, hibernating all the days, all the nights.

"Hey, get up! It's too night. Let's take dinner." *Pharat* awoke me, on third day.

I checked the watch hung on the wall; 11 pm, "You have prepared?" blinked sleepily.

"*Yea*, you must wash your face."

"What's there?"

"Your favourite— *khichri*!" He smiled.

"*Oh, shit*!" I sulked my face.

I, after washing my face sat on a mat on the floor of the room; *Udit and Sindhi* too.

*Pharat* carried the cooker and four plates along, four spoons and four bowls with curd in them. He also fetched fresh water in a jug, four glasses as well.

He served the *savermati riced-khichari* in all four plates— the *khichri* yellow, seasoned nicely with mustard *oil*, cumin-seed, turmeric and green chilly in pieces, salt was reasonable; many pieces of potatoes and tomatoes alongwith the corns of pea were there in it.

The aroma was mouth watering!

". . . . Good cook!" I smiled as I put a spoonful *khichri* into mouth— it was so delicious.

I applauded.

"Thanks!" He said.

We were in the meal. During it, *Udit* spoke, "*Yaar*, now adays *aian-aian* is very much angry."

"What happened?" I spoke.

"Nothing, today *aian-aian* beat a boy very badly, many slaps, many punch." *Sindhi* said.

"Why?" I asked.

"He asked him something and he couldn't tell, hey."

"You ken?" *Udit* stared at *Sindhi,* "Fees matter must be there!"

"What?" I looked at him, with surprise.

"*Yea*, for three days he is keel hauling the guys everytime, having any base." He said.

I kept silent for twenty seconds. "Who was that boy?" I asked with my eyes up.

"*Harshit*"

"*Harshit*, who?"

"A boy, once who gave excuse that his harvest got destroyed due to the flies—a lame excuser." *Pharat* said.

"I think, now I shouldn't be Luddite!" I spoke in a strange way.

"What?" *Pharat* looked at me doubtfully, a hilarity on mat.

"Don't laugh." I said to them, suppressing my own smile, "What the hell! Nowadays, even a new-born child is using a mobile but I am not. I think I must."

"How are you talking here, I don't understand; I'm confused!" *Pharat* said, putting some more *Khichri* in his plate.

"It's beyond your ken."

"So tell, no!"

"You have a mobile?"

"*Yea,* but it is kaput."

"Get me."

"What will you do?" He asked as he collected all the utensils.

"The treatment of the teachers"

"What?" He said, his eyes dilated with surprise.

# 21

I dialled ten digits, perceiving something as intellectuality; the number of *Anil Bashishth* an M.L.A.

The bell went.

"Hello!"

"Jai ram ji ki, pandit ji!"

"Jai ram ji ki!"

". . . . *Butterua* speaking, pandit ji!"

"Oh, *Butterua*! Hi there, how are you?"

"God's favour and your blessings!"

"Nice, it must be actually." He said, his voice richly ornamented with goodwill for me, "What about your study?

"It's nice!"

"And . . . ?"

"Every thing is fine."

"How you remembered today?"

"Actually, a work !"

"Speak out!"

"*Pandit ji*, you know many penurious students from little dorms usually come to my college. They are too poor to deposit their college fees even. Hardly, they do it. And now there is a precarious problem of tuitions, else. For the teachers, it's a nice business here." I said with polyvalent talking skill, "They say—however hard you work, if you don't take tuition—you won't be passed."

"It's predominately going on everywhere, not a new thing!" He said.

"*Yea*, but . . . . !" I stopped his tongue.

He ruminated over. "Okay, you speak!" He said boisterously.

"*Pandit ji* at the time when you got my admission done, the students in my class were being beaten, badly, only for the tuition! I carried them all to the teachers, so that they mustn't be beaten and could pass. But there is the fee-deposit conundrum now." I said; a mealy-mouthed boy.

My words roped him into doing something, at least, for us.

"You are brahmin, right?"

"Yea"

"*Pandit ji*, you are also too much!" He chuckled rumbustiously, "Of course you would be a very good leader any day, undoubtedly!"

"May be," I smiled, "But, I'm dying to be an engineer!"

". . . . .Thirty six situation, then!"

"Yea."

"Okay, make me talk to the teachers, whoever it to be is." He said.

"That I'll do! But *pandit ji*, It's me with them, so... !"

"Cool, make me talk first!" He laughed. "Anything else?"

"No, nothing else!"

"Then ok!"

"So, I'm calling you in morning!"

"*Yea*, of course! Of course!"

"Well, good night!"

"Good night!" He disconnected.

"Wow, what a contrivance!" *Pharat* squealed as the conversation between him and me ended. He kissed me on my cheek, his excitement supper.

The game was gonna be pepped up!

"Let's see, what happens tomorrow?" I wrapped the blanket again. And, at 12, we all were fast asleep.

On the morrow, at the fixed time, we reached the *aian-aian*'s tuition. Many students were absent, even then the room fully packed. Actually, half-yearly exams were already over and annual ones were on the verge, approaching soon, so both kindred spirits, *aian-aian* and *bete-bete* were very worried to seize their fees.

*Aian-aian* entered the room. We all stood up wishing him.

"Sit down!" He waved his hand.

We all sat.

*Mani7ha* was there much close to me, a girl wrapped in a nice dress. Every touch of her body with me, uncontrolling one— I was having the continence, hardly.

"*Mani7ha*, your fees . . . . .?" He asked my pole axing beloved.

She stood up. My eyes also stood up with her. She hid into the gestures of my face. "Sir, it didn't occur to me!" She paled at.

"You are always a forgetting girl." He gave a menacing tone, "Just, sit down!"

She sat down, with an inward smile.

"Hey, blue shirt! Yours . . . . . ?" He stormed.

"Sir, my father is not at place." He stood up squeaking.

"And next?" He said annoying, "Your mother won't be . . . . , hey?

"No, sir! I have carried! I'm not like them." He said, his voice riotously funny.

"Good boy!" He said smiling, "So, get!"

He frisked his pockets, but—

"Sorry sir! I forgot my billfold in another jeans." He said. I tell you they all were following a plan; and making him fool.

"Of course, Sir! Tomorrow I won't forget it!" He said and sat down without any his permission.

He didn't notice it. "And about you.....?" He nudged towards another one student.

"Here you are, sir!" He said as he stood up, putting his hand into the right back pocket of his jeans. "Hoa!" He got shocked, his pocket torn—no real palpitation!

"What happened?" *Aian-aian* became active. "Sir, the money has fallen down some where; the pocket is torn!" He palmed him off.

". . . . Why you kept in that one?" He cried.

"Sir, that time it was not torn"

"Then, why it is now?"

"I don't know?"

"I don't know! I don't know anything!" He started-weeping, "My money has fallen down. How will I collect this much money again?"

"Just sit down. Don't weep." He sympathised with him, "Why didn't you see earlier, a lazy boy?"

The atmosphere was tense in the room, no one speaking.

"And what about you?" He said to the next student, a few seconds later.

"Sir, actually my cow went down like nine pins!"

"So?"

"Sir, all money was spent in her treatment." He said, a melodramatic character. Everyone had an inward but irresistible giggling. And *Mani7ha.....*, she had her hanky on her mouth.

He stared at her, but spoke nothing, "*Aian-aian*, at least some one must give!"

No one spoke.

"I don't know anything. Whether your cow gets sick or died. I don't bother. I need my fees. Get it till tomorrow. How you manage it, you must know!" He goaded perilously.

"Sir, this 4th sum is some more tough, please tell it!" A student stood up.

"Don't deposit fees and suck up my blood!" He was there, a squalling filthy soul.

He got prostrated.

"Go, today I won't teach you!" He said, "Carry your fees first, then. . . ."

I blinked towards *Pharat*.

He dialled the same 10 digits of ***Anil Bashishth*** and gave the cell to me.

"Hello!" I said, "*Jai ram ji ki pandit ji*!"

"Jai ram ji ki!"

"*Pandit ji*, I talked to you yesterday regarding...... I reminded the previous night conversation.

"Oh, that! I remember." He pulled his voice.

"Yea, he is sitting close to us. Just talk to him." I said.

"*Yea-yea*, make me..." He said, and I handed the cell to *aian-aian*, "Just talk; *Anil Bashishth Ji* is there!" I said.

All the students stood nimbostratus around him, as he took the phone in his hands.

"Hello, *jai ram ji ki, master sahib*!"

"Jai ram ji ki"

"Here, *Anil Bashishth* speaking!"

". . . An M.L.A.?"

"Yea!" He said, "*Yaar, master sahib*! What is the matter of these students?" He probed.

"Nothing!"

"No, they are saying you are forcing over much for the tuition fees!"

"Oh, that!" He exclaimed, "*Pandit ji*, actually, ever since they have been coming, none of them has paid even a single penny! So, you must tell what should I do?"

"Yea, of course that's a wrong thing. But master sahib, nigh on all of them belong to very poor families! How can they, you must think." He said, "*Yaar,* they are studying, It's more than enough. At least, you must feel them!" He proselytised him.

"You tell *Pandit ji*! What must I do?"

"Give the fees-concession to them!"

"And what about my family? My better half always asks me for two hundred rupees daily, and my little one every day spoils a hundred rupee note. How would I manage it? Where should I throw them? Where would I carry my stomach?"

". . . . . . Your monthly income is there!"

"*Aian-aian,* why should I? I have taught them all the year. I have worked hard!" He murmured.

Now, an interesting parley in the room!

"You forced them, so they had to come to you, otherwise....!" He said, his voice rough.

"No-no-no, who said I forced. I didn't said to any one. They came by themselves." He said.

"It means I'm lying!" He got riled.

"No, tell who said?"

"Whatever, hush up this matter. Give them their fees concession— I'm saying!" he propelled him.

"So?"

"Means, there is no matter of my saying?" He got niggled, "*Yaar,* you are in government job and earning so much. Don't earn from these children!"

"*Pandit ji,* why are you teasing this poor? You are a nob and also in government. If really a prop you are, pay their fees. Why are you nipping at my bread?" He grizzled him.

"Master sahib, I am cool. So, it doesn't I mean.... !"

"Okay, tell! What you mean?"

"*Yaar,* I'm having a request!" He laughed.

"No, it can't be done. I have sweated out all the year...!" He protested at.

". . . . . You don't love your job?" He said, pronto.

"I love. I love it the most."

"So?"

"*Pandit ji*, it's not fair! I am saying, it's not fair!"

"Don't teach your granny how to suck eggs. I'm not any newbie!" He said getting all riled up. "Give them concession. That's it!"

"Okay, as you wish!" He spoke, not an agile male body. It propitiated him, "I'm giving you all your fess concession." He propagated.

"Thank you, sir!" I took the phone from his hand, being in a *never-never* land, a profuse thanks for him.

"If any thing else occurs, call me. Don't be hesitated". He looked cosseting us.

"*Yea-yea*!" I said happily

"Good bye!"

"Good bye!" He disconnected the line.

Here, *aian-aian* pared his cheep character off. He sat propping himself upon one elbow on the table, "It's a nightmare! *Butterua*, I tell you!" He said as I paid thanks to him, "It's only $11^{th}$. There is $12^{th}$ also. I would see how would you run your mind there—practical marks are in my hands!"

He was noisome, a night jar.

"Sir, we are compelled!" I said, "And about practicals...., its long time. Let's see!"

"See. And see. But, I warn you, nothing will work then!" He spoke irritatingly.

"Let's see!" I said, "Well good bye, now!" All the students waved bye-bye.

He didn't respond.

# 22

My next stop was *bete-bete,* I mustered some of the students, packed into the staff room. On the same day— the interval on!

At the time, he was talking to his, you-know to whom. She was sitting in front him. As he looked a swarm of locust coming towards him, he was on the edge of a precipice. About her, an amusing thing— she shifted herself into a corner.

*"Bete-bete,* what happened? What happened, *bete*? Why are you all people here like this?" He was left his eyes wide-open, shocked. A lot of fear and nervousness reflected in his voice.

"Nothing..., actually!" I looked at *Pharat,* "You tell, no!"

"No-no, you must; you are nicely swatted up on the subject!" he took a swipe at me.

*"Bete-bete,* what are you talking about *bete*? I don't understand *bete!"*

"Sir, there is a phone for you!" I gave a sword play.

"Phone; whose?"

"Of M.L.A.; *Anil Bashishth ji* is there!"

"What a swizz!" He ostracized, "*Bete-bete* I don't talk to any politician, bete. They are very rude, bete! *Bete-bete,* they don't respect any one, *bete*! Very-very-very fucking they are, *bete*!"

"Sir, say only hello, please!" I insisted.

"No-no-no!" He was stunned, "*Bete-bete*, tell me the matter, *bete! Bete*, I would solve your problem here, without talking, *bete*!"

"Sir, tuition fees.....!" A boy from the crowd spoke.

"That . . . ?" He talked sweetly, "*Bete-bete*, If you don't wanna pay the tuition fees, don't pay; go! I won't ask you for that. But, for that don't make me talk to any leader, *bete*— they are bloody dogs, bark much *bete*!"

"So, you are giving the concession?"

I uttered.

"*Yea-yea;* of course, *bete*! Of course!" He said, his mind sweltering.

Every one of us paid heed to his every word. "Thank you, sir!" All the guys bowed.

We hightailed the staff room as our purpose got solved, all were happy to the hilt.

"A high-spirited boy!" *Mani7ha* ruffled my hair, a primordial signal of love— at the time we both were on hiking, two km. stone from the village, alone, in an village side.

She had a black ruffled piece of clothing along with a fine bra on her breast portion and bell bottom blue jeans down. There were many coloured balls of wool in that ruffled clothe of her. All I want to say is she primped herself.

We both came at the high point by her Alto. The way was very narrow and covered with sugarcanes from both sides.

"Just see! This is my sugarcane field; how sweet! "She braked the car. She opened its door and came out.

She was gazing at her field.

Suddenly, she glimpsed a butterfly. She started trying to catch it tills he was successful in her endeavour, "How lovely it is!" She showed me that colourful creature as she came upto me.

".... Like you!" I said, lying my back on the car.

She smiled.

"*Mani7ha*, I have predilection for this smile!" I took the butterfly in my hands. I flee it. Now I was romantic, actually.

"And . . . ?"

"I love your eyes!"

"And . . . . ?"

"Your nose is very colossal."

"And . . . ?"

"I find your fleshy lips very enormous."

"And . . . ?"

"And, come down; your neck is milky and really surprising!"

"And . . . .?"

"Sorry, now I can't tell it here!"

"Why?" she laughed.

"Let's come inside the car. . . . ." I opened the door.

She lifted her head up and squeaked, "You loafer; you . . . .!" She started hitting me with every thing that she was getting at the time; she was throwing the blade of grass, the solid clay and then her sandals.

"Hey, stop; that hurts" I said moving towards her.

"Don't come near me, you loafer." She laughed and laughed and started running from there. Now, she was running and I was following her; following her by the bank of river ***Koshi***. She was bare footed and suddenly—

*"Ouch!"* She cried and knelt down crying; actually, a throne pierced through the arch of her left foot.

*"Mani7ha* . . . .!" I cried; was worried a lot for her. I neared her. I pulled out the throne from her skin. "It's paining . . . . . ?" I said as I noticed the gestures of pain across her face.

"*Yea* . . . !" She smiled while feeling pain.

I took her in my arms and came to a spot. I tell you a girl is a feather in her ***boyf***'s arms.

*"Butterua*. . .!" She swilled her eyes to me; held my face with her hands clasped passionately and started seizing me by—actually, there was some anxiety in my eyes for her.

"You are ok?" I asked her when I put her on the barky trunk of a tree under one other *tad* tree. The trunk on which I kept her, was hanging over the same river, along it's all branches— the seen was so wonderful!

"*Yea;* I am!" She came with a pleasant voice, "You care about me so much, why?"

I didn't answer but kept admiring her.

"Ah, why?" At this time, she was cunning with her words.

"Actually, I've only one girl friend; and that is you; that's why!" I shrugged.

"What?" She said with a nonchalant look and then broke into laughter, suddenly.

"Mani7ha, I've something for you!" I said and went into the pocket of my jeans with my right hand; I took out a folded paper from it.

"What is this?"

"....Read; and let me do my work." I said; took a long deep sparkling sign with my Eros patently obvious.

"Hey, don't do anything wrong with me, right?" My wigeon said when I pulled her down; pushed her wiggly on the trunk; and came ownself on her.

"No baby, I'm sort of gentle boy. Don't worry!" I satisfied her but as well took a nosedive and to the nth degree I was in desire. My nose became the *Hitler's dog* and it started wondering into her hair. I was long past my honesty, not in my control.

"*Hey*, what are you doing this?" She pushed me. And, I tell you she tried to push me off.

"Trust me; I'm not sort of bad boy!" I hissed peevishly.

"It's not fair; I'm a baby of my parents!" She moaned in delight when I untied the knot of a ball of the wool to open the ruffled piece.

She overtaxed but not for long; soon she was mine. I pulled her hair and put my thirsty and languorous lips on her murderous one, wriggling my erogenous zone on hers— I was the pop of *Imran Hashmi.*

I was in. She was in. We both were out of our tree.

*Thuppp. . . .pp .!* Suddenly, something hit on my bonnet while I was going to undo the paterfamilias button of her piece.

"Ouch!" I groaned and held my head with my chin up. I could see, a monkey, hidden almost in the fruits of *tad tree, there.* He was smashing them to smithereens. "Heisting? Bloody thief! Just come down!" I cried.

*"Kheeh . . . . !"* He threw one more fruit on me. And, I escaped from it narrowly.

At this *Mani7ha* gave a *ho-ho.*

*"Kheeh- Kheeh!"* I mimicked the monkey modulating. I teased him crying, making faces, putting both thumbs on each corners of my lips and making all fingers dance.

He threw one more fruit.

*"Hey,* bastard! The bloody piffle of your pop! Just come down, come down!" I shouted rowdily, "How dare you roust us? You hell, just climb down!"

*"Kheeh . . .!"* He showed his teeth once more.

*"Obey,* to me?" I started throwing the dry solid piece of earth, crying and crying, "To me; to your pop! Bloody bastard, just come down—only once!"

"You are a monkey! Oh, yes, I knew it today!" She commented and laughed but I didn't support her, a joke mundane.

Here, I was silly, fighting with that monkey.

"Butterua, don't be mad. You know how large families these monkeys have—plus relatives!" She laughed and caught hold my hands while I was in high jinks and was carried on.

I stopped for a while but started again.

*"Abey, nincompoop!* The Chinese set are very cheap and the call rates as well. He will inform his all knowns and then, the life will be hardly safe!"

Now, I had to laugh at this talking manner of hers. Here, I was noting her childish innocence—she was really very cute!

"Leg it-ttt. . . .tt . . . t!" Suddenly, she cried pulling my soft white colour shirt while I was going to take my girl again—*actually, the Indian Army in Kargil, there!*

We ran towards the car.

Our breaths were fast, not in control when we reached the venue. Now, we both were laughing and trying to catch the breaths as well.

"Oh, God, how dangerous they were!" She said as we sat in the car, so as to come back.

"Where is that paper?" I asked her as I remembered the rule of flattery.

"Yea, here it is!" She said and came close to me see what I had written.

I unfolded the paper and recited it, explaining her everything. It was—

Oh girl! You're beautiful;
The most wonderful creation on earth
And bear the stamp of god.
I say you kill me
No one can stand before you
How ever, they always preen
And you, the fairy of present
Might be primping any time.
Your eyes powder 'blue
And nose the sort of
Rosy buds full of beer
And hair so smooth
I tell you you're sexy
One can judge if he feels
Your all zone so special.
I love you and your bits
Ever and ever and forever.
Here, oh, my doll!
I have the desire; both in bed
Thoroughly nude. . .
With a blanket soft.

"You're poet?" She lifted her face with *I-can't-believe-it* surprise, "I wonder I'm a girl friend of a boy who is not only a topper, but is a great poet as well; how lucky I am!"

"Don't be so happy. I'm not going to be a poet!" I said

"What's wrong in it?"

"I'm to be an *IIT*ian. I'm to fulfill the dream of *Kalpna Chawla*." I said, "You see, one day I will be the heart of India... ." I certainly lost mine and forgot all the world.

"Bless you, my boy! May your dreams come true!" She kidded as if she was any Goddess and was giving me a boon, showing her flat palm. She giggled on her own ,a childish attitude.

"You look so beautiful!" I said doing nothing but noting her all gestures and her face.

And, at this she got blushed.

I folded my arms around her once again. You know it comforts a girl to feel her boy friend's arms around her. "*Mani7ha*, I can do everything if your love is with me." I said nuzzling her opened hair.

"That is, you mad!" She hit me on somewhat up the nape of the neck and then turned away to start the car, "Any way, you can be a good poet also!" She suggested me as she turned the car back.

"I will be if I couldn't be an *IITian*. And be sure, very first I would come to your college as a chief guest; you will be dancing before my eyes and I will smile at my destiny!"

"..... So God must do it; I'm ready to be a *Nachaniya* for you! Oh, God, I pray, he must be a poet or an author !" She spoke out as if God was before her.

Here, she was mad all the time. Again and again, she was reciting the poem I had composed for her.

Whatever, at six we backed.

I was alone at my room— all were at their places just for the sake of enjoying themselves, no any other reason.

I was on my bed and my mind was engulfed with the pleasure of all three incidents of the day. I was recollecting everything event by event. As my mind was reminiscent of the *bête-bête*'s speaking style, I broke into laughter, an engrossing moment.

It became hard for me to control; soon it turned into coughing— actually, I was a patient of tuberculosis. I tried hard to supress it but no use, the enormity of the problem severe and enigmatic. It was being aggravated.

I had no control.

I had to leave my bed and had to come down up to the *loo*.

My all pleasure engendered. A bowl of cough came out from my mouth. At that time, my body was enfeebled and eyes strained.

I was huffing and puffing.

In fifteen minutes, I could come out of the *loo*. I directly went into my room.

I stood before the mirror. Now, a powwow occurred between my soul and me, my emotions ruffled.

I got filled with the stuffy feelings. This pernicious disease of mine permeated all the corners of my self respect. "*Mani7ha*, how selfish I am! I very well know there is no life of mine, even then....!" I cried and tears rolled down my eyes, "You idiot, why are you so innocent? Why do you love me so madly? I'm ditching you, you know, I'm ditching you!"

I kept on weeping and doing nothing. "*Mani7ha*, my heart! I too love you! But I'm not worth you; you understand I'm not worth you!" I cried, "Forget me, I say forget me!"

Suddenly, I wiped my tears and came to my books. I took out a note book and a pen from inside the closet. "My darling, however much you are enmeshed in my love but you will have to hold yourself. You will have to sever relations with me; you have to— I will compel you. . . .!" I entered into reverie.

I composed one more poem and put it in to an envelop. I gave that envelop to *Sindhi* and asked to hand it over to *Mani7ha*. And he did what he was parroted. Oh, yes the poem was—

You're girl
May be the daughter of beauty
So foxy, ball–breaking
May be your bazoom, your booty
Your long-long clouds
And may be smoothy hips
Of course an erotic pride
Must be lying on your lips.
May be Miss Mani7ha
Your every step killing
But it is me——

*You can't touch the ceiling*

I wept at my doing cheap and profane, *Hallelujah!* I cried as I hallucinated the voice of hers around me. I became mad. *I'm sorry! I'm really very sorry! Mani7ha, I'm not gonna be yours! I'm not able to behold you, you understand, no! Please, pardon me!* I couldn't hold myself; was on the rebound, actually.

I too, of course, was very sad after doing that unwilling work.

# 23

*Mani7ha* became red with anger as she got the letter. She directly came to my room. Her bad luck, I didn't meet her. Notice, she had never ever been to here before.

As she came to know that I was out of station— I was at my place—she left the room at once and didn't stay even for a single second, while Pharat kept offering water for her. Her anger at its height—she was enraged all the time!

Soon, our annual exams started.

She tried to find me there at the college desperately, but all her efforts failed. I would enter the designated place ten minute later than the beginning of the papers and would leave it half an hour before the bell rang.

I was not at the room during the exams. To the college, for the exams where I would come from and where I would disappear after giving the paper, no one knew, even my mates also!

The exams got over.

The results were distributed. I came first in my class as well as in the all sections of 11$^{th}$—*Mani7ha* was there waiting for me. But, I didn't reach. I asked *Pharat* to take my result along his own.

As she figured it out and also found my result in his hands, she snatched it; and cried when he asked it back. No avail! Now, speak to him to take it from me. Prize idiot the half-assed; over-taxes much *Sekhchilli*; don't know from where....! Now, go and say to him I won't give....!"

The news came up to me.

It gave me a sweet smile when *Pharat* told me everything mimicking her acting.

In fact, my attitude was bad—It looked eating her. She was profoundly mad, like a biting bitch, of course!

Here the condition of my heart also was not fine. I too was avoiding her as much as I could.

At night, in the moon light, I was on the roof, alone; I missed her!

I was at the lush green field; I missed her!

I was by the side of river; I missed her!

I was in the bed; I missed her!

Means, where ever I was, I was missing her; was weeping as to why I was a patient!

The summer vacation got over and the college opened. I reached the college—*Mani7ha* was there already!

"*Butterua....!*" She cried as she might have glimpsed me.

I wanted to disappear at once but couldn't do so; why, don't know.

She came up to me. "You half-assed; what do you understand you are? Bloody monkey; bag of bones!" She caught my collar, "Have you ever seen your face, you skeleton?"

". . . . . Today, I would see!" I said smiling.

"*Shut-ttt. . . . up*!" She puerile threw her hands, "What you wrote in the letter?"

"Whatever you read, that . . . . !" I said, trying to make myself bold and serious.

"Means?"

"Means, I'm a sort of lion and want a *she-lion* in life, not any deer like you!" I said, "The level is slightly askew!"

She didn't speak for a moment. "Means, you don't love me!" She looked askingly at me, freeing my collar.

"Ask yourself; you know better!"

"You did with me that all; so, that was what?" She cried and wept at her own words.

I didn't speak.

"Mr. It is me, a mad girl who roams around you always, or you are not handsome enough to attract even *Ramkali*, the ugliest girl in our class you understand. She had a tiff with me; commented a true thing." She commented a true thing.

I realized. I didn't speak but noted her words.

Once, *Aiece* carried all of us along *Mani7ha* to the *Sanjay Palace*, the biggest cinema house of the *district*. At the gate when we were entering the *balcony* corridor, we noticed a Punjabi-girl, slapping a boy—she was unmarried, beautiful like Mani7ha, a slim-girl.

"Look at there, a dangerous girl! Just see, how I knock her dead! And, how she becomes mad; wanders around me!" I king-hitted for their attention, particularly of hers.

Every one stared in astonishment at me. "Go, but be sure to be beaten!" Mani7ha laughed. "And make your head hard!"

I smiled; went ahead.

A cliffhanging moment, now! It was a luxurious hall and big enough to provide the seats for four hundred people around; I however shifted myself near that new girl.

In three minutes, the movie started. It was **READY**, a fantabulous movie. Casting was going on. "What happened there?" I gave an inviting smile to that dangerous girl—she sat in my left seat.

"Where?" She bent her head towards me.

Mani7ha did her ears. She was not much far from us; could see everything.

I nudged towards her with a smile, cunning.

She was invidiously a burning girl

"At the gate; you slapped that boy, no!" I said," Why....?"

"What will you do?" She inveighed, throwing her hands.

I stole a glance— *Mani7ha* was laughing.

"I only just asked; tell no!" I said shrugging and smiling.

"Here, I have come to watch movie. Don't disturb me!" She cried as the casting got over.

I bit my tongue, at once. Now, I had no topic to talk.

I ran my mind. But yet, no idea occurred to me; I teased my hair.

By god's favour, there on the screen *Salman Khan* ran after a man, spewing the clouds of fire from his mouth; the man was running fearfully, just to escape himself from him. Everyone was aching with laughter, that girl as well.

She had a *kurkure* pouch in her hands— its mouth was torn. "A nice acting . . . . !" She commented.

"Of course!" I agreed while I almost stole a piece from her *kurkure pouch,* "That's why he is a nice actor!" I spoke, biting the piece—actually, I wanted to knock Mani7ha.

That girl stared at me.

"Sorry!" I caught my ears, a nice pacification.

She smiled.

"Don't worry, I would get you the piece back!" I said reclining my seat, innocently.

"The same one?" She smiled again.

I didn't speak. But I was unable to stop my smile also.

"You live in this city?"

"No!" I said hurriedly, "I've come here just to impress a girl like you!"

"What?" She laughed.

"Would you love me?" My tongue, a Kalashnikov rifle, fired a kamikaze bullet of words. I was peeping into her eyes after the main thing having spoken.

"Are you mad?" She lamed into me, the juxtaposition of scale and excitement in her voice.

*"Yea!"* I smiled, "Anyone may be if any hot girl like you is there before the sight ."

Once more, the laughing got scampering from her mouth. She couldn't stop it, "A boy very interesting!"

"It must be if you like girl is saying!" I said "Any way, your laughter is inviting—I like it!"

"Thanks!"

"Your cell No.—could you get me, please?" I said at once, taking the advantage of the moment.

"You know, I am to strict towards the boys but here, don't know why I'm melting and talking to you—any magician you are!" She said smiling and unzipping her purse. She took out a visiting card and gave it to me.

The interval occurred.

All people came out from the hall; we both and all the group of *Mani7ha* as well. She had a strong jealous at each moment—everything was clear on her face. In canteen, we both remained for ten minutes, talking friendly and romantically, eating the *Chaumeen* and *Tikki* and *water-balls* together.

The movie started; and we entered the hall before it. I had popcorn in my hand.

"You know what happened in the movie till now?" I extended my hand to provide her with the corn, "Take your one....!"

She smiled at my talking manner. "Just watch, a romantic scene is there!" She forced me to watch when I was admiring her smiling face. I saw, there, on the screen the heroine was having romance with her boyfriend with an excuse of checking the records of his accounts.

"...... Interesting!" I slipped with my tongue, "Would you like to check mine?" Articulately, I said; my tongue hung loose and panted like a dog.

"Of course, come to my place!" She smiled.

I have inveigled myself into her affection. Now, she was

in my arms with all respect. *Mani7ha* was at this— she averted her face from our side.

The movie ended and all the people had come out from the hall, *Mani7ha* and her group as well; we were still there.

"So sexy!" I took a long sigh while we both were juicing each other's lips.

Suddenly, *Mani7ha* came; now, her story ended!

"You bitch, bloody scarlet woman! I'll eat you! I'll chew you! I'll cut you in to pieces!" Without any pause she assailed. She pulled her hair and cried pugnaciously, "How dare you to see my boyf; I'll pull out your eyes, you bloody. . . . !" She slapped her and then slapped her more.

I was smiling and looking at my girl. It looked she was not my girl friend but was my wife; her love and an arvo of the summer same. Anyway, have you ever seen this sort of an incident? God, I had missed that anger. I wanted to shoot it and play it on a loop.

"Hey, will you kill her?" Pharat held her hands, her burning anger at the hilt.

That girl couldn't understand anything, all gobbledygook to her. She went scarlet with embarrassment. She crawled from there; and me, before her!

# 24

*Mani7ha* appeared to get fully brushed aside by me. Now, her face was gloomyand melancholy, all the time—her heart looked broken!

Soon, she left the college. "Now, I won't study further. It is biting me." she publicized, before leaving the college.

I came to know.

I felt her. I wanted to associate with her. But the reason which prevented me from doing so asphyxiated me— how arrant!

My heart hung aslant, an overtone.

I oversaw the situation which she was burning in. As an effect of that, my puny mind pulsating and the salient function pulverized. What must I have done?

It was *Diwali* on Monday, two days later—so there were holidays.

I reached home.

The D-day came. All were busy with themselves. But I was perturbed, along in the jungle, emotions running high.

It embittered my mother a lot. "Where were you?" she cried as she found me before her.

I highfalutinly spoke nothing. I was in a sombre mood.

"Hiya, where were you? Why don't you speak?" My mother held my chin, "Any thing wrong . . . . . ?"

For a moment, I felt to reveal the matter. It shocked me. "No, there is no wrong!" I smiled. However, I managed all and didn't let anyone feel anything.

The *Diwali* passed off.

I reached the college after five leaves. Along with *Pharat*, *Sindhi*, *Udit* and me, very few other students were there, *Mani7ha* and *Aiece* as well—*Aiece* insisted her.

*Mani7ha* has become very poor in health, What phooey is it, *Mani7ha?* I wanted to ask but I didn't. I ignored her all.

*Ho-hum!* There was no period, all the day. "Hey, let's go to the shrine of *Munda Shan*—it's Saturday today!" *Pharat* said.

"So?" *Udit* looked at him.

"So what? Just take a going!" He said, "You know there whatever we ask, we get!"

"Really!" *Mani7ha* interrupted him.

"Yea!" He said.

"So, don't be late—let's go!" *Mani7ha* was ready. Thus, Pharat carried all of us to the shrine.

It's really very beautiful place near the Kemri Dam in Distt. Rampur in U.P. The scene was very heart-rendering! The shrine is hundreds of year old. It is known for animals' related problems. It is said, *having been here if one asks any thing, that is given and if any apparition or such sort of problem one suffers from, that also gets solved.*

We all went by a local bus. The bus dropped us at the Dam, only two hundreds metres away from the shrine. "Wow, amazing!" Aiece got stupefied as she glimpsed the sight of that marvellous point.

"You know it was sketchily built in 1964 and could become useable only ten years later—my grand father worked here!" He guided us, "At the time the work started, it was very sanky, but now how stupendous and scenically beautiful it is, just see!"

"Of course, it's a surprise!" I said as we moved towards the shrine. A lot of people were gathered in the large compound of the shrine. There were many young girls and similar aged boys crying—they were the sufferes. There were many exorcizers who were busy with their jobs.

Except me, all of us washed their hands, faces and feet in order to get into the dome.

"You're not coming?" *Pharat* asked me as he was gonna enter the main dome.

".... *Yaar*, I quail at these things!" I smiled.

"Shut up, *Butterua*!" He gave me a piece of his mind.

"Why?" I looked at him, "You fear our graven images, so we as well.... "I remarked waggishly.

His mouth closed!

They all went into and I kept standing outside. There, I saw a drama unfolding; a yay good drama!

"The water is falling down drop by drop, drop by drop; means, anything is there on her!" A *Mianya* was persuading his customer.

This blackclothed, around thirty, a long bearded healthy young man had some water in his right hand-palm and was dropping it slowly–slowly. Two old women, in black *burka* and a twenty year old girl were near him, watching every step of his.

They all were under an aspen; many asters behind him and clematis on the wall, along.

"*Mianya ji*, how it happened?" An old lady spoke.

"Some one of yours has done it. Something has been given to her in the yellow rice!" The *Mianya* had a serious face, "She went somewhere during this week?"

"Not to any particular place, but. . . . .!"

The same old lady tried to remember.

"*Yea,* two days before she had been to her *Phup-pho*!" The another one lady agreed.

"*Yea*, of course, it occurred there!" The *Mianya* cried.

At this, I could not stop laughing— I was not much far from that supposedly ***Dhongi Mianya.***

"Call that boy!" He spoke to a lady; and I could hear it.

I myself went up to him.

"What happened? Why have you so cunning smile across your face?" He looked at me and spoke calmly, "*Hiya, Butterua...*!

"You know my name?" I stopped my smile, sitting before him on my knees.

"I know everything!"

"Can you tell me my future?" I said and stretched my right hand.

"Fold it; I don't need it to tell you your tomorrow!" He said, "I know everything, listen, I tell you!"

I fixed my ears there, properly.

"Any girl is a votary of yours. She loves you very much!"

"And . . . . ?"

"You are a good student. And you want to cross any big competition!" He stopped his tongue, "But. . . ."

"But, what?"

"You won't do it!"

"What?"

"*Yea*, you won't study further. Your study will be spoiled now. And you will have to leave your house even!" He said clairvoyantly.

"And what about that girl?"

"You will be great haves, but not that you want to be—you will marry her!"

I was completely in his words; was listening to him heartfully.

"*Beta*, you are a T.B. patient. So, the oncoming hurdles are some more dangerous for you!" He put his hand on my left shoulder, "Keep this stone ring with you always. It will help you whenever you need." He took out a black stonemade redemptive ring from his pocket and put it on my palm.

"*Mianya ji.* . . . !" I couldn't speak ahead, the emotions hard. I touched his feet. I took out a tenor from the pocket of my jeans—

"No, *beta*! I don't need money! It is my work!" He said smiling when I tried to give him honorarium. "*Beta*, have patience now, a bad time ahead!"

I became quite serious.

I left him when he permitted me.

I carefully looked at that ring and put it into my pocket as I saw my friends coming out of the Dome.

"It took you a lot of time there!" I spoke when *Pharat* and others were giving me the *prasad*.

"A lot of crowd is there!" *Udit* spoke.

"You won't give?" I happened to ask *Mani7ha*, don't know how, as I noticed her standing aside, silent.

She sobbed and then broke into tears. "Butterua, why are you doing so? What shortcoming do you find in me?"

I was going to be emotional but I controlled hard over the arousing feelings in me and could make with difficulty myself calm, still and silent.

She put the all poly of *prasad* on my palms. "*Butterua*, why don't you feel me? I'm dying for you!" She held my head to make an eye contact.

I didn't speak; and my body quaked as she shook it.

She kept making emotional talk and weeping, but I didn't speak.

Suddenly, she stopped weeping, "Look at there, that crying girl; an evil puissance on her!" She helloed, giving me her puffy eyes.

I saw, there was a voluptuously beautiful, about twenty old girl, in red clothes with a lot of make–up on her face, with too much lipstick. One other *Mianya* in green clothes, an old exorcizer was standing near her; she was yowling.

By some *Kalmaas*, he had tied her hands with two poles in each side.

"I was simply on my way. Why she broke her smile looking at me?" The evil spirit cried from inside her body, "I found her nice; so I came to her!"

"So, what should be done, now? Are you gonna leave her or not?" The *Mianya* questioned.

"*Mianya ji*, I won't! I won't!" The spirit cried, "You don't poke your nose, other wise . . . . . . !"

"Otherwise what?" the exorcizer threw some water having given it any *kalma*.

"Eeeya. . . . . .eya. .!" The evil spirit cried, yanking her hands. The both pole she was tied with, started quaking. "No, *Mianya ji*, no . . . !"

The view was really overweening. It astounded me. "Now, see; you will find your *she-lion* in me!" *Mani7ha* puckered her lips.

I overstayed at her as she stepped ahead. What was she going to do, exactly?

She went up to the dangerous place; turned her neck and stared at me again. As if a lot of energy came in her, she held her breath and slapped her many times, tightly enough.

Yikes! I couldn't understand any thing. "*Mani7ha*. .. .!" I cried and she ran away from there. We all also followed her.

She is blind in love, my ticker philosophized and asked me, when I was in dilemma about the matter at my room, not to be negative all the time; all it was to sanction the file of her love.

All the night, I was stravaigging, there on the roof of our room, silently.

# 25

Slowly–slowly the practical exams approached. All the students from all groups were in the lab—it was the practical of physics.

The lab was more nicely decorated than it remained all the year.

All the students were given two-two practicals. I continued with first one, the practical really very tough. "What happened, *bête*?" *Bete-bête* neared me as he found me itching the mind, "Do, examiner is very strict, *bête*!"

". . . . . I'm doing sir, I said."

"Here, no student is gonna get more than twenty marks today." He said, stepping ahead, presumptuously. All it can be said is, he wanted to scare us.

I looked around as he went away from me. Most of us looked wiping the faces, a cold sweat. Here, I was fully confident and ready to face any unpleasant occurrence— an idea struck my mind.

I reached *bête-bête*. "Sir, may I go down?" I asked him for permission, "I have a call of nature!

I had a pretext.

He sulked his face but let me go, due to his compulsion.

I became a gun shot.

There directly I searched the key to his—the *Shakshi ma'am* was that.

By chance, she was alone, in the staff room. "What happened? Why are you wondering here?" She spoke rudely, as I reached her.

"Nothing, actually I wanna show you something!" I said with awe.

"What?"

I took out a chip, the ***b.f.*** of hers with ***bête-bête***— the same b.f. which I shoot at *bête-bête's* place.

"What is this?" She sharpened her eyes when I put the chip before her, on the table.

She lifted it.

"You have a multimedia hand-set. Take out your chip and put it inside." I said.

She gave me a strange look. She did the same I said. For the time, I made some distance from her. She switched on the cell and went up to make it functional.

"What the hell is this?" She cried as she found her darling and herself, together—the secret opened!

"It is that that you did!" I used a hard language "And don't cry. I have many others than it. I can show them every one!" I said, turning my face in an annoying way.

"What do you want?" She lisped her fear unable to be describe—one scared of, directly comes to the point, a special thank for STICK.

"There, in the practical hall, my fellows are weeping, the practical being very hard! And, moreover your *bête-bête* is poking his noise . . . . . !" I spoke roughly. "I want my all class to be given full marks!" I said, my voice strong.

"What can I do in it?"

"Don't do! I'm gonna show your this great doing!"

"*Butterua*, believe me, I can't do anything— the examiner is very rude!"

"I don't know anything!" I cried, "I won't my purpose to get solved— that's it!

"I'm compelled, *Butterua*!"

"I too may be!" I press-ganged her.

"Okay, call the Sir!"

"Sound's good, a quality of good people!" I smiled. I reached the practical hall and called him.

"What's the reason she is calling for?" He looked at me as we both entered the staff room.

"Don't know, ask her self." I shrugged.

She pored everything into his ears and showed the b.f. also on his asking.

He got bamboozled at this. "So, you know everything, hey?" He asked me, his voice very low.

"To enough extent!" I smiled.

"Okay!" He took a long sigh, "Do your practical, you will be given full marks!"

"Thank you, sir!" I said and backed to the practical hall. I didn't tell any one, any thing. He had to bribe the examiner with twenty thousand into getting us full marks— the problem was solved!

The chemistry practical came. But, there also the b.f. worked and we got full marks.

# 26

Now, our exams were not much far—there was farewell for us, by the juniors.

"Hey, *Butterua*!" I heard a familiar voice as I reached the exact place. I turned my face; *Pharat* was there. "Stop, *yaar*!" He said.

I got collared.

I was in a fancy black suit-pants with three buttons in suit, a cream-coloured shirt, a zebra-colour-tie and a pair of black shoes along. One could deeply notice five pointed but bright, diamond-like stars on folded collars in each of the two sides—the collars somewhat long.

"Cutting! Really, no star like you!" He gave me a compliment as he neared me.

We shook hands. "*Yaar*, where were you so long?" He asked. "I've been looking for you a long time since!"

"Sorry, *yaar*!" I spoke, my voice oozing ownity.

"Butterua, I have a word with you. . . . ." He said as we stepped towards the stage while we were in the *Pandal*, where the all programme was gonna going to take place. It was very big and decorated *Pandal* with peacock and rose like figures on it. There were 500 serried-scattered chairs, in an apple pie order; seventeen rows, thirty chairs in each. I was noting everything.

"Eh?"

"You really don't love her?"

"Her, whom?" I spoke as innocently as I could.

"Don't be so naive!" He said with the eloquence of his smile. "Tell, by your heart, you don't love *Mani7ha*?"

“I don’t know!” I said sans making eye contact. Actually, a confused mix of emotion stewed in me.

“Don’t know what?” He elucidated the feelings of my heart, “I tell you, you love her; you heartily love her!”

“Yea !!!” I accepted, “I love her!”

“Yes; I know it!” He spoke loud, cheerful and full of energy, a hearty voice, “Congratulation, my dude; congratulation!”

“Pharat you . . . ?” I held my head up with a sudden shock. You know he was after her, how much?

He smiled and then paused for a sigh. He said—

*“If one ain’t yours*
*Do compromise, I say.*
*At least you’re in good book, then;*
*Or else. . . .*
*Here, she loves you beyond;*
*Dies for you—*
*Can’t for me, all trying no use.*
*So, she is yours— I say.”*

I couldn’t speak anything, but was with emotion enough to hug him.

And, after a little pause, we stepped ahead, towards the stage.

The stage was one and a quarter mtrs. up from the ground and covered with the green carpet and its staircase with that of white.

I noticed all the chairs also were on a black coloured carpet.

Aiece and many others, particularly juniors were there on the stage, garlanding it. “Aye, *Butterua*! Where were you?” She asked, the same question as she glimpsed me.

I didn’t answer, on the contrary I questioned, “She didn’t come?”

“She, who?”

“That idiot girl; *Mani7ha*!”

"Nice one!" She cried with pleasure!

"After all the heart gone!"

"Oh, shut up! You're always just yanking on!" I smiled, the inwards pleasure insisted.

"Any way you are so typical— the oozing pain in your heart but no feelings no voice. You are an onyx, a great boy!" She garlanded me with the flowers of praise kidding.

I could do nothing except smiling.

". . . . . . How she came on your tongue, today?" *Pharat* pulled my leg, exulting.

"Actually. . . . ."

"Hey, one second." Aiece stopped me? "No, yarn, hey?"

"Aiece, I think I missed her very much!"

"Means, still you think— you are not sure!"

"I did. I'm sure."

"Then, why you broke her heart?"

I hung my head. I didn't speak.

"Butterua, you know, she doesn't eat properly; she doesn't sleep properly; she doesn't do any thing properly and remains always weeping!"

I could not stop my tears dropping down my eyes. I was almost sad, "Now, what about her, please tell." I requested her, "I'm dying to see her!"

"Sorry, she won't come now!"

"How come!!!" I cried, "She would; her pop would come." I cried even more. I closed my both hands, shut up the eyes and prayed, hey God, please . . . . .!

"I can't believe it!" *Aiece* cried joyfully, as she glimpsed at *Mani7ha* near to the exit—a surprise!

I opened my eyes. I saw. I clearly saw her rubbing my eyes. She entered the *pandal*. She had a hand basket, some flowers in it and two boxes of alpines in her hands.

She was in her black skirt that I love like any thing. "Hey, miss. *Monitor*! "How are you?" I caught her hand as she ambled from me.

"I don't want any one to touch me." She stole her sight, an inward smile along.

"My *she-lion* is crossed with me?" I peeped into her eyes.

Her smile broke all the boundaries.

"Sorry!" I caught my ears, "I climb down over that!"

"Good drama!" She sent me to coventry, smiling and acting naughtily.

"What?" I laughed with the proviso, as smoothie. "You sexy girl!" I forcely lifted her in arms. I went up to her lips and had a strong kiss—all the guys cried and clapped with joy.

She got shied!

Two hours later all the *pandal* crowded with students, teachers and guest, the programme started.

I sang a song, the song for *Mani7ha*—

Too hi meri sans hai
Too hi meri jindgi
Too hi mera khawab
Too hi meri har khushi
Too aajaa, too aajaa
Dil lagta nahin aajaa
Aajaa na. . . . . . . .
Too hi meri sans hai. . .
Harpal har lamha, jeeta hoon kaise
Pal-pal marta hoon, jugnoo kai jaise
Kate nahin kat-te, kanto se ye din
Raheta hoon tan-ha, tan-ha sa tere bin
Too hi meri man-i7ha. . . .
Too hi meri man–i7ha
Too hi meri raat hai,
Too hi ek khas hai,
Baki bakwas hai.
Too aajaa, too aajaa.

Dil lagta nahin aajaa.
Aajaa na. . . . . .
Too hi meri sans hai. . . . . . .

I received a lot of clappings, and a lot of praise in that din.

"You know how much I love you?" *Mani7ha* got weeping with a protension of innocence as we both met next day—an important tryst.

"You think only you love, I don't— idiot!" I said, "You know how much I missed you? I couldn't celebrate *Diwali* even—I was wondering in the jungle all the time!"

She didn't speak.

"*Mani7ha*, you girls always project it on to us; you never have faith!" I averred a guarded reply. Yea, of course, girl is the kind of thing that keeps you guessing right end.

"Hey, stop it, now! We are here after a long time, just to have romance!" She said, "Already, it's long time since, I have practically touched you."

"You want that?" I smiled roguishly

"That, what?" She asked, willigly.

"That. . . . That!" I went into her eyes with my dishonest passion.

"Shut up!" She punched me on my chest coming close. She hugged me, "*Butterua,* don't do so, next, otherwise I will not be alive!"

I became silent.

# 27

The exams came. The exams went. And the day also came when our results were going to be declared on the Net.

I perched myself on the edge of that tiny wall where I put rest my bottom always—actually, it was the chance of our congregating at the room. It was too hot and I was there in the open-spot; trying to have an eye-contact *with Sun* while my all fellows were inside the room.

*"Butterua,* are you mad? What are doing this, a silly joke?" *Pharat* came out from the room; moved towards me crying and almost with a to-do, as he noticed me on my tod, there.

"Nothing! I was just. . ." I looked at him tortuously.

The entire floor was as hot as an oven. Moreover, he was barefooted. I could notice his feet were burning there.

"Hey, what happened?" I smiled; caught his hand just to tease, while he started getting inside the shade, like a duck.

"It's chilly here. I feel cold. I'm getting inside the room, a toasty place. There at least I can shelter in quilt or can use a *Heater*, understand!" He pulled his hand free and ran off into the shade and then into the room.

"What about result?" I laughed casually.

"It's just in hand." He dribbled his voice into my laughing noise, panting due to the climbdown of innumerable steps there.

Haooo haaa. . . ! Suddenly a lot of hollering noise began in the room and I had to step into. Actually, the result of *Udit* was there — he got 73 per cent.

"*Congratulations!"* I placed my hand over his shoulder and gave a blend of smile and happy feelings.

"Thank you!" He smiled in response.

Soon, *Sindhi* surfed our results as well. I tell you it was the most pleasant day of our life. *Sindhi* himself scored 78 per cent, *Pharat* 77 per cent and me, full marks in PCM while total alongwith the rest two subjects aggregated to a top notch percentage 94.4 per cent.

In ***U.P. Board,*** it is too tough to achieve these sort of percentages. We congratulated each other. We hugged each-other and fed sweets each-other.

"Let's surf hers!" *Pharat* soughed as the resounding success of room went some cool.

"Hers whose?" I said so innocently that I had no idea about what he meant.

"Of our *Broyee. . .*" *Sindhi* laughed delightfully with his sottovace voice.

I smiled. "Why do you say so for anyone's daughter? She is not my wife anyway." I toed the mark.

".....So she would be any day." He chuckled while his fingers were on the keyboard.

*Hip, hip- - - ; hurray!* The noise resounded through the room once again as her result was displayed on the screen; they like mad-elephants lifted me and started bouncing in their arms.

"Hey, please. . . . ; please get me down!" I cried, huffed but almost with a mere twitch of inward pleasure.

Thank god, those wild animals had mercy on me and they left me.

I held my breath. And then, I went through her result. Sounds surprising! My naughty girl friend proved herself, any way. She beat me by one mark. Here, certainly I was proud of my luck that the sort of girl who loves me and who is almost bombshell is next to me all the more — *I'm into you God!*

A little later, as *Sindhi* toggled various across the results, we came to know that *Mani7ha* had beaten all students of U.P., not to speak of me. She was ***U.P. Topper*** now and I, her damn lucky boys was after her, on second position. Congratulations, *Mani7ha,* my heart spoke for her.

After some time, we packed our bags and bade good night to that 18th century building. Of course, there was a kind of sadness; I walked with my eyes dreary through that chuffing study centre which was our theatre, our fulmar- nest, the *G-spot* and every thing else.

*Dadi ji*— our rented room owner who was an old lady started weeping as we bent down to touch her feet. "Don't forget me children; keep coming!" She spoke, almost wailing as she wrapped us all in her boney arms.

"Don't weep *Dadi ji*; we would come. Of course we would keep coming....!" I said holding my emotions and casually making her cool.

After that 'filmy' group hug, we stepped down the street, promising her to keep coming in future.

She came up to doorway so as to wave a see-off.

*"Batterura*, what's your future planning any way?" *Pharat* asked me while we fell silent during walking forward.

***"IIT, my way to Kota....."*** I said excitedly and then felt the inward pleasure, "Kota I'm coming! Wait, now I would tell what a bloody villager can do!"

"Any way, I'm also planning to hold your tail." He grumbled looking at me.

"Good!" A toffee-nosed boy in me, smiled.

Likewise, we all were discussing and vowing to be friend forever and ever. Suddenly, don't know what happened, I had some tears into my eyes.

"Hey, what happened now?" Pharat said while *Udit* and *Sindni* were laughing; treating it as a filmy farewell. "Shut up you both." He scolded them as I was in more tears.

I was toey any way. "*Pharat*, I'm tormented very badly. Although, I never told you and also never let you know, but it is. . . . . my elder brother is very much after me. He is toppling me always." I faltered while my voice was enamelled with deep emotions.

"Why?"

"Don't know. But I know his fucking desire. All I say, his will is to see me behind any kiosk or in any fucking school." I bared my soul to him.

"Why?"

"Don't know."

"And your father; he doesn't say any thing?" *Sindhi* said.

"Nope!"

"Why?"

"Actually, he is henpecked, under his thumb or not a father enough!"

"Why? Any reason?"

"Actually. More than half of property belongs to him. He is the owner of almost all the lands." I elucidated them everything.

"Sorry!" They fell silent for some time and then *Sindhi* spoke, "Actually, he is the sort of old-fashioned father. As in past, the fathers used to love one the most and used to give him all the property, while about other all, they never cared."

While talking, when we neared to the flyover, didn't know. I wiped my tears. "Hey, let's go to *Aian- Aian*?" I toyed with the mood of paying the last year's fees.

"As you wish!" *Sindhi* nodded and then they both also okayed the proposal.

We bought a *sweet-box* and moved to ***'aian- aian's*** place.

I rang the door bell as we reached his house.

*Illa* aunty, came out from inside. She was in her light blue night gown.

We wished her but she didn't respond on the contrary kept looking at us doubtfully.

"Sir is there?" I roused her when she stood like a still statue.

"Any work?" She rumbled gruffly.

"Sweets... "Sindhi showed the box.

"Hey, are you audible?" She knocked our chemistry teacher, "Students have come. . . ."

"Send upstairs." He called in from distance.

"Good evening, sir!" We all ad-libbed in unison, as we climbed up the stairs and reached there on the roof.

I tell you there was a really good sort of garden on his roof. All area was covered with red flowers of Busy Lizzy. At the time we reached there, he was watering the plants— I noticed a watering can in his hand. He looked completely a villager in his simple white coloured *kurta-dhoti*. He was barefooted and his relaxo slippers were far in a side.

"Good evening!" He looked at us, almost with surprise, "*Aian–aian,* how come today . . . .. .. ?"

". . . . . Sweets!" I whispered whilst my friends could not dare to speak before him.

"You got passed?" He stopped watering as he held the sweet box in *Sindhi's* hand with his sharp eyes—while I noticed him stealing his sight.

He led us to the shade of the room which he would tutor in. He sat on a swing while we stood before him, leaving some space.

"Yes, sir . . . !" I cracked a jubilant expression, "With superb percentage. . ."

"Good!" He smiled alongside continuing to take the steps of swinging.

"Sir, he has become the 2nd topper in all U.P.; scored 94.4 per cent. *Pharat* excitedly said, towering over.

*"Aian-aian* ?" He stopped swinging, "Show me the result!"

*Sindhi* unzipped his green colour bag and took out his laptop. He showed him our results.

"I can't believe it!" His eyes went wide and remained opened with shock. *"Aian–aian,* make my mouth sweet. Soon, yaar....; my mouth is watering." He spoke childishly, exchanging banter with us.

*Sindhi* opened the sweet box and offered him a piece.

*"Illa... !"* He called his wife, "*Illa,* just see this boy has won the 2nd position in whole state!" He spoke full toss as she appeared before us a little later. Was that real or reason of any thing else?

*Sindhi* gave that sweet box to her.

"Sorry, sir!" I said with collywobbles out embarrassment while he was no sense of my words.

"For what?"

"Sir, all the time we kept teasing you. We did wrong. We are really very bad. . . ." I said finessingly and then started weeping, shedding pearls-like tears.

*"Aian- aian,* what is this? What is this, toe-caringly awful remark for?" He wriggled the matter, getting uncertain with his manner, "Why are you weeping? *Bolo-bolo,* what wrong you did? Nothing... .."

We wept more bitterly.

*"Aian-aian,* this is really bad; very bad! Don't weep. Otherwise, I will also start weeping!" He wiped our tears but almost with wetness in his own eyes. He wrapped us in his arms.

"Sir, we will remember you a lot!" *Sindhi* said grunting with an entreaty, as we broke the group hug.

"Sorry, but I won't .....!" he surprised us with his cunning words.

"Yea, any way we are for this." I said in a maudling voice—my style matey. "We must get the result of our bad doings also."

*"Aian-aian,* I didn't mean to say this. Actually, ***how can we remember those who can never be forgotten."*** He chuckled and then came out with laughter.

*Illa* aunty stood near us but with no words till now.

"Sir . . . !" I fumbled, groping in my jeans and took out three notes of thousand rupee each, as I remembered the main reason of visiting there. I tried to put them in his palm

"*Aian-aian,* this is what?"

". . . The fees of your last year, sir!"

"*Aian-aian*, I won't take! You are my boys. Go and be something. Then give me. . . . !" He shrugged us back while *Udit,* Sindhi and *Phara*t also were trying to give their fees.

We insisted a lot but he didn't take.

"Go, go my boys! Go, come out with flying colours!" He spoke in his dewy voice.

Our faces were rasped, any way. We all touched his and ***Illa aunty's*** feet; and then climbed down the stairs, waving bye-bye.

# 28

***Six year ago***

Helter-skelter, I parked my cycle and moved towards the assembly-line wasting no time—I was already late. I forgot my chintzy green bag on the carrier of my *ampala khatara.*

It rained the previous day, so all the ground looked damp, still.

*Chhapak! Chhapak!* I reached a boys' queue swiftly and stood in its end as if the last compartment of any train.

"Hey prayer got over?" I asked the boy just ahead of me.

"Yea," He said.

"And national anthem?" I asked again.

"That also." He spoke irritatingly.

"Don't get irritated, *yaar*!" I slapped my right palm on his right shoulder, lightly, "It's too late!"

"Yea," He threw a sudden smile.

I noticed-forty guys and only sixty girls in the ground — girls' counting was low. All the students wore their uniform — the guys white shirt and navy blue pants along with blue tie; and school named shing tin batz, and the girls wore blue suit and white *salvar* with no tie and no batz. The head master was very strict. All the seven teachers were in all the queues of students to maintain the apple pie order.

"Dear students! You are ruely told that the pride of our country *Kalpna Chawla* who had gone to the moon some days before, yesterday, while coming back her ***Spacecraft*** got destroyed and she became the victim of death along with other crew. We are verily sorry that she, the first space visitor lady of our country couldn't see the earth again after leaving it." Our head master came on stage and threw a sad news, "Dear students, it's a rueful subject that she is not among us now. She struggled hellishly and spread the name of our country all over the world. For her works, she will remain enshrined in our hearts forever. Accolades to her! Accolades to her struggle!"

He got down the stage and came again spending couple of twenty or so seconds. He had a page in his hand.

"Dear students, for tomorrow and for the next three days, school will be closed. On Monday, all the students are to come at the same time." He announced the holidays and quiped, "And deposit your fees as soon as possible. Your exams are to be held."

All the students behaved as if they were coming from some jail. They started running. But some students wore patience. I was with them.

"Oh, fuck! the exams are on the verge and they. . . . ; they are hopping in dying!" A school potato thought his that day to be throttled— he was a book warm.

"What happened?" I looked at him.

"*Yaar, w*hy they fuck die in our study time? Why not in leisure? Whole June is there! A list of fifty two Sundays is there! Why they don't die during them." He murmured, "Ownself they have achieved, but to us, are not letting do, ***bloody . . . . !"***

"Let it be, *yaar*! It goes!" I laughed.

"You are to do nothing but I'm to do. I'm to touch the sky!" He got serious.

"How many ladders will you use?" One of my friend asked laughing.

"You are always laughing. You never understand anything. What should you know about study? It is any joke for you."

We all laughed and he left us murmuring.

We all were coming hogging all the road; discussing how would we spend the time, many holidays there. Ten minutes later they all tat ties left me because they were from different villages, not from mine—actually I was alone from my village.

I was having fun while riding, leaving both the hands and shaking my booty up and down. My long attractive coiffure was teasing me again and again. It seemed as an awning. I had to ruffle them time to time.

There was a brook. I got down the cycle and crossed it, through a bridge, being on foot very mutely. It was somewhat weak; was managed to get costructed by wooden plates.

*"Ajju Bhaiya!"* I cried.

He came two minutes later. He was the owner of that bridge. Every one had to pay a single coin, if he passed through the bridge.

I took out a coin of rupee and put it on his palm. I crawled further.

My dorm was two kms stone from here.

"*Butterua,* how so soon?" *Ajju Bhaiya* stopped me as I was going to get on my *ampala.*

"Nothing, some body died!" I parked my cycle. And went into the dark hibiscus—I had a call of nature.

"The weather is so pleasant!" I threw a reasonless dialogue as a filler.

"Yea, it is a desire of God!" *Ajju Bhaiya* said. He was the elder brother of *Raju Bhaiya.* They belonged to my village.

Here, he had a *pakori shop.*

"Take *pakoris*!" He looked at me.

"No, yaar! Tank is full!" I said looking at him, "Actually, in morning I took two *rotties* along with some raspy *chatni* — I don't feel like taking anything now."

"Radio . . . . . ?" I whispered as I noticed a *Jolly Company Radio* there on the bench which was made by keeping some wooden plates on some bricks.

"Yea, yesterday, I bought it." He said.

"How sweet!" I said in a piercing voice that showed its own the real *Me' Coy* what pinioned me so soundly that being mauled, I stepped towards it.

“Of how much?” I asked holding the *Radio*.

“A familiar person was there, so some cheap!” He showed that he was truly a villager—actually, it happens with villagers; they never speak directly.

“Even then?” I enquired insisting it.

“It cost me 300”

“It’s good!” I started changing its *band* without asking—he didn’t mind to it.

He gave me a luxuriantly smile. He was black complexioned, some what plump and sweet voiced. On his face, smile writ large.

“Take seat” He nudged me with a mojo voice to sit there where already two old men, around 60-65 age, were sitting. Some hot discussion was going on between them. They were waiting for *pakories.*

“No thanks!” I said lugubriously.

I took a brick and sat on it. “Yaar, you didn’t come yesterday?”

“I went to Rampur to buy it.” He took out the *pakories* from the pan and busied himself cornering the fries and removing aside.

“Oh, sorry! You just mentioned!”

“Pass it, please!” *Ajju Bhaiya* asked me to pass the *pakories* to both the old men.

“Who is he?” One old man spoke to *Ajju Bhaiya.*”

“This boy . . . . ?” *Ajju Bhaiya* looked at me and paused for smile. He said, “He is the only studying boy from our dorm. He is very intelligent.”

“Mind is a God-gifted thing!” The old man spoke.

“No, it’s a self-created thing”. A young chick around 18, spoke in my back— she was. A private teacher of a nearby village, beautiful enough.

"No, *ma'am* you are thoroughly mistaken!" I turned back. I noticed she had a *five-rupee leaf* in her hand and intention to have *pakories*, "Ma'am, I have two pens in my hand. One writes fairly but second one roughly. You know why?" I took out both pens from my pocket and said showing them— I knocked her.

She looked at me curiously. "Because there is good quality ink in first pen and poor quality ink in second pen." She answered.

"Point should be noted, ma'am!" I said, "Ma'am we are just like these pens. In some, there is good quality ink and in some poor quality. . . And this ink is filled by God, not by us."

*Ajju Bhaiya* started clapping, "Just see, what I said!" He offered the *pakories* to her. "Madam, he is the master of our village."

"Good boy! What class are you in?" She asked me.

"In 8th", I answered and then busied myself in changing the Bands.

"Hey, stop here! There is something about ***Kalpna Chawla***." She suddenly spoke out as she heard some voice regarding *Kalpna Chawla* in Radio.

I fixed it on her request.

*The attainment of* **Kalpna Didi's** *dream is still a dream. We would make that true. We are arsey that she studied here in our college and lofted the name of our college, all over, up to the sky. She struggled hard. She did this that and blah blah blah....* there was a lot of noise; many more students from her college, were there.

For some time, I was not serious, but soon, suddenly, I went in deep emotions. I didn't know what had happened to me. All the hit-and-run hwyl regarding that matter started impelling me into deep water of madness. *Jack Robinson*, I felt in insinuating like any she-snake in me. My body started twisting very badly. I started pulling my attire. My clumpy eyes got red, and suddenly—

. . . .The radio which I clutched, fell down. I was supine on the earth. I started huffing and puffing—my breaths serious and long-long.

They all got flabbergasted. They had no intuitive sense of me.

*"Butterua*, what happened?" *Ajju Bhaiya* asked.

I could hear him but was unable to speak; so no answer there.

"Hey, what happened?" He shook all my body and threw all the dirty ***besan-using yellow*** water on me.

"Nothing!" I whispered two minutes later, "I would do that! I would do .. . .!"

My all body was in sweat. *Ajju Bhaiya* made me sit properly.

"Hey, what would you do?" The lady teacher asked surprising.

"Oh, sorry!" I spoke in low voice, and looked at that lady teacher.

"Hey, what would you do?" She asked again.

"I don't know!" I answered.

My all body was paining. I looked at the *radio* and mourned for it. It had been broken into many titchy pieces like a glass.

"Are you okay?" *Ajju Bhaiya* asked holding me with my shoulder.

"Yea, I'm okay!" I answered.

"Okay— enough to go?" He asked me again when I stood up to move from there.

I smiled.

# 29

Whatever, by a happy coincidence, I reached my dorm at 9.10. All the atmosphere was covered in smoke and mentholated fresh air—a menthol factory there, near the road.

*"Oh, bhaiya!* Go easy!" I spoke, my voice some loud. Actually, someone was throwing the toxic menthol substance.

"Oye, *pade likkhe!* At this time? From where?" One person spoke from the roof of that factory. He was at night duty. He was busy with chain block.

"From Rampur."

"All is ok?"

"By God's favour!" I said and moved ahead, smiling.

"Why so late?" My mother got all steamed up over my coming late, "Is it any time to come?"

"Actually, friends . . . .!" I spoke slowly.

I noticed all the family members were on the dining table except me.

"*Beta,* take care of time!" My father looked at me seriously.

"Sorry, *papa*! Actually, with friends, I couldn't pay attention!" I threw the bag in one side and shoes on another side taking off. I took off my T. shirt and jeans as well.

"Oh, so hot!" I entered into my room. I switched on the fan and sat under it, on the edge of my bed.

*"Beta,* dinner?" My mother called at me from table.

"No, *mummy*! I don't feel like!"

"Have you eaten any where?" *Manoj* said.

"No." I came out of the room.

"Then. . . . ?"

"I don't feel like right now!"

"You will eat at night?"

"No, I won't eat."

"Just eat, for company shake." *Kittu bhaiya* said, "*Poori-kachori* are there!"

"*Poori-Kachori*?" I smiled getting surprised, "In what joyous happening?"

"In the happing of your result!" He pushed me in an involved mud.

"You know my result?" I got totally surprised.

"Of course you have got $2^{nd}$ position in all U.P." He loafed iridescently, his right *armpit* on the top edge of his chair and head towards me.

"But how did you come to know? There is no cafe in this village!"

"*Bhaiya*, don't take it easy! India is progressing! Else, it is a managing country!" He said, "Mobile is there!"

I smiled. I was believed in.

"No, he is making you!" My mother said, serving the *bhindi masala* in Kittu *Bhaiya's* plate.

"Is there any need? He is already readymade!" "He jumped in again."

*"Manoj. . . .* !" My mother stared at him.

"Isn't, it? *Bhaiya?*" He commented, ignoring her completely.

"Eat properly!" I said with an iota of an inward smile.

"Shut up, *Manoj*!" She scolded him and told me, "Two media people came by a motor cycle!"

"From *Dainik Jagran*?"

"I think, from *Dainik Jagran* and *Amar Ujala*, both!" She looked at my father to clear her doubt.

My father nodded affirmatively.

"*Bhaiya*, they had a *Soni Camera,* the same that I wanted to buy."

"So?"

"They clicked many photos of our house and asked many questions, "He childized," You know what I said?"

"What?"

"I said *Butterua Bhaiya* is very *Buddhu*. It is me who pulled him up to this achievement."

"And?," I stole a mouthfull bite from his *kachori*.

"*Bhaiya,...!*" He irked at my flippant manner "Wash your hands sometimes!"

"Sorry, *yaar*!"

All laughed.

"It's a bad habit, bhaiya! Shun it!" He lectured irascibly, "You are a good boy! You are not supposed to do so!"

"Sorry!" I came close to him, "How often should I say?"

"It's ok!" He grinned mixing the rice in *dhoba dal* of *moong* with a spoon– *dhoba dal,* the rest of noon.

As his attention got diverted, I lifted his plate and ran away with it.

"*Mummy...!*" He clamored. He started stamping his feet.

I sat on another chair, not close to him and started taking the food served to him.

A gust of laughter blew the silence off.

My mother got him another plate served with all the dishes.

"Dirty boy!" *Manoj* clanged— his wrath expressed.

I looked at him a shameless— laughing face. "You were telling something". I said.

"No, I'm not to tell anything". He said rudely.

For two minute there was a absolute silence.

"Papa, I want to do IIT." Suddenly, I proclaimed breaking the silence— I possess an inward-IIT qualities.

"What is that?" My father, a roust about, pitched a gentle smile.

It is an four year prestigious engineering course. It has the apex position in all country. There are only five colleges in all of India—***IIT Roorkee, IIT Kanpur, IIT Varanasi, IIT Delhi and IIT Bombay.***

He was silent.

I looked his face with a ravenous hope.

"It's a swamping subject." *Kittu bhaiya* raked his tongue in the matter.

"Okay, let the time come! I shall think it over!" His answer threw me in razzle-dazzle.

"Thank you, *Papa*!" I rattled my voice, racy and style raving.

"*Beta*, anything else?" My mother asked me.

"Only one *poori*." I spoke, with a morsel in my mouth.

"...*Poori*, not *aadhi*?" *Manoj* pulled my leg, "How much would you eat? *Yaar*, already you have emptied the plate."

"*Mummy*, two pooris!" I threw him in a mixed-up puzzle.

"Oh, my pop!" He laughed and laughed, "Without feeling hungry, you are eating so much, how much will you eat in hunger?"

"At least 50 *roties*!" I said.

"Oh, my god!" He got mad and said laughing, "Colleges will increase the charge of hostel."

"Let it be, so!" I showed my villagehood, "Let me eat, a good quantity today!"

Next morning, I got up at six. My mother was in kitchen. After getting up, I directly entered the kitchen. At the time, she was preparing tea.

I stood near the door with the head resting on the door. I saw a pan was kept on the oven and *mummy* was pouring milk in it.

"What happened?" She peeped into my eyes, "You look sleepy; didn't have a proper one?"

"No!"

"Why?" She asked the reason.

"*Mummy*, I'm too obsessed in becoming an ***IITian.*** I feel like nothing elsi to do, my desire is deep!" I penciled, "I'm to be a great scientist. I'm to go on the moon!"

"Don't spool it in to your mind, so much!" She smiled.

I also gave a fake smile.

"Get me tray." She whispered pouring the tea into two cups. She put them alongwith a plate of fried *moongphali namkeen* in that flat utensil to what we coined the word— tray.

My father was sitting on a *sofa*, in the corridor, very close to kitchen. I noticed he was deeply engrossed in the paper.

"Tea . . . .!" I knocked him putting the tray on the table and sat on another couch facing him.

"Oh, thanks!" He put the newspaper on the table and took the cup in his hand.

"*Papa*, my photo!" I remarked, looking at my photo on cover page. I took the newspaper in my hand and ran my right hand's fingers on my picture. For some time, I was under narcissism. I felt proud of my achievement.

"We have seen already." My mother spoke at my back. She came to us wiping the sweat from her forehead. Her light black *saree* was moistened with the rubbish of the kitchen. She sat near my father, on the same *sofa*— the *sofa* big enough.

"Papa, at night, I saw a dream." I smirked.

"What?" He put off his spectacles and put it in a black cover, his eye brows lifted.

"Of IIT?" My brother guessed. I looked at him. He was coming from morning walk. He had a smooth stick in his hand and wore a white loose T-shirt and a black cafery.

"How do you know!" I put the newspaper.

"*Beta*, we are your guardians; your elders. We know you by your blood." He ribbed and they both supported.

He fumbled through his pockets and took out a lot of wild *mukais*. He threw on the paper—now, my face barely visible under them.

"Oh, . . . . .*mukais*! My eating horse!" My mouth watered. I filled my fist with them.

"Go easy, *beta*! These are not going any where! Take tea, first!" My mother stretched her hand to snatch them but I pulled it away from her reach.

My father laughed.

"Mummy, however nice you train a donkey, but he won't be horse— he will remain same, donkey." My brother laughed at my behaviour.

"What do you mean? Am I any donkey?"

"I didn't say. But if you understand, then may be."

"*Bhaiya*!" I shouted.

He gave a smile and went to get freshened up.

My mother served the *namkeen* to my father and also took the taste herself . He asked me but I denied.

"*Bhaiya*, what time for office?" I unwrapped a *mukai* and placed it on my lower teeth, stealing a glance at my brother. He busied himself in brushing the teeth.

"At ten." He spate the bubbles.

"Will you carry your lunch?" My mother asked.

"Of course."

"No, yesterday you didn't carry— That is why I asked."

"Yesterday . . .! I didn't have mood!" He spate the bubbles one more time.

"What? You ate nothing?" My father put his cup down, in the tray.

"I ate!"

"Where?" My mother looked at him.

"In office; *Deepika* insisted–she carried *bharvan turai*!"

"Oh... it is *bharvan turai* that you like the most." I smiled cunningly.

"*Butterua* ...!" My mother shushed me, "Take tea soon–stop eating these bloody *wild-mukai*." She snatched the *mukais* from my hands.

"*Mummy*!" I cried.

"*Beta*!" She smiled in the same way.

"*Mummy*, what's wrong with you? Why are you after my *mukais*?" I hacked my voice comically.

"I'm to remove all this mess." She answered.

"*Seetal*, this is the simplicity of our country" My father took a *deep sigh*. He lifted my favourite fruit and unwrapped it.

"What?" She laughed, "To eat these bloody *mukais*?"

"No! Not to forget their previous value; not to forget their childishness. To give the same importance to the things which you loved in your tough times however wealth you get, but never be a *pansari* with a haldi ki gantth." He taught her—while I looked at my mother smiling.

"You are mad and your father also!" She chinked.

"What?" I gave wind to the fire, "Papa, you are mad?"

"Leave it, beta! ***Jisko nahi buddhi, guru gyan kya kare.*** "My father passed the comment on her, "Actually, It happens to illiterate."

"You . . . . !" my mother chimed in. She got angry and stood up to leave the *sofa*.

"Don't get angry, *yaar*! I'm just kidding!" My father gripped her left hand and pulled her to sit. He cupped her in his arms and jumped into action.

"Hey, boys are sitting." My mother cried as my father tightened his grip.

"No, *papa*! We are not looking—carry on!" I covered my face with the news paper.

My father freed her. She gave a grimace of shyness, shifting herself some far from him.

"*Kittu*, what for your lunch?" My mother looked at *Kittu Bhaiya* with her sharp eyes.

"*Bharvan turai*!" I high balled with my tongue her question.

"Shut up, *Butterua*!" My mother cried again. Her face was suffused with laugh.

My father wondered our mysterious conversation, keeping shtum. He could not get it. "What is the matter? Someone tell me." He spoke ten seconds later.

My brother shuddered at this. He was staring at me. "Nothing, you will not be able to pick up!" My mother croaked archly.

"*Pandit Ji*....!" Someone called at the door.

"*Butterua*, see! Who is there?" My father said to me.

I minced up to the door and unbolted it— there was an old bugger huffing and puffing, papery and not good looking; he was wearing a scruffy and unpleasant *dhoti- kurta*:

"Medicine?" I looked at him.

"Yes," He mimed, "Since I got up, my breath is not in control—a grave problem!"

"Papa, any patient!" I rolled my tongue orotund.

"Just make him sit— I'm coming". He said.

My father was an M.B.B.S. but with no degree, without any*Diploma*, the people had given him this position; he was a temporary public servant—a permanent country doctor.

I opened the sitting room which was his clinic as well. It was not so big— one *takhat*, one cot, some space between them and a wall-fixed *cupboard.* I did the broom in all the room and made him sit on *takhat.*

My father came five minutes later. He had a tin–box and stethoscope in his hand and an *angochha* on his shoulders. He opened the cupboard, i.e. his *clinic* and seated himself nearby–– on the same *takhat* where the old bugger was sitting.

I pleasantly gazed at my prize of $10^{th}$, kept in a corner of the cupboard.

Suddenly like *Narad ji*, *Manoj* appeared with five rowdy-like people before us. He had a sweet box on the news paper in his hand, with a bright smile across his face—there were only two pieces in the box.

He gave one of the piece to the old, remained there for two minutes and went away noisly.

My good luck that God blessed me with such a brother. He made me talk of the town. All day, he distributed the sweets and showed my photo to every one with an article alongside. Hundreds of people were astonished after seeing my photo in news paper—they spread this news in all the village.

"What is this happiness for?" The old mewled.

Oh, no! My father forgot giving him medicine and got praising about my achievement. Five minutes after, *Manoj* also left him, acclaiming still.

I moved back to the dwelling portion of our place. I sat before my brother on the same sofa I sat earlier, reading the watch. "Bhaiya, so soon! It's only eight." I spoke calmly but cunningly as well.

He sat there, nearby my father. He was completely ready for his office. He was clad in corporate dress—a navy blue shirt, a dark blue tie, a black pants and a pair of black shoes— he was adorned with.

I only had a smattering of him. He was manager in some *Automotive Company*. But I was sure that he got an attractive salary plus incentives and an affair with receptionist named *Deepika*, the most beautiful girl in his office.

"I'm to go soon. I get late daily." He said. He was busy with his breakfast— *aaloo*-stuffed *paranthas* and a bowl of curd, with no other thing.

"Mhm. . . . . .?" I looked at him.

"I'm to go somewhere else too." He gave the reason.

"Ah, so this is the matter!" I buffed up the topic with my gestures naughty.

"Any way, when are you bringing my *Broyee*. . . ."

"Shut up, this guff!" He burst out, "Get me my lunch box and my bag as well."

I noticed his style seemed that of one who is newly fallen in love—a soft smile across his face and all movement clumsy.

He finished his break fast and moved towards his *Hero Honda* bike.

"*Bhiaya*. . . . !" I cried as he was going to kick the bike.

At the time, my mother stood near me, only one-and-half metres away from him. She had his lunch box in one hand and the bag in another one.

"What?" *Kittu Bhaia* lifted his head and looked at me and then at my mother.

"Nothing!" I ate what I meant—

But he understood my cunning idea; he laughed.

He hung his office bag on his shoulder and placed the lunch box on petrol tank and later in the dicky. He wore the helmet and kicked his bike—It was 8.20 in morning.

# 30

*"Fatso!"* I cried , entering my sleeping room. I was coming from out side; after meeting one of my chum. "Ouf, It's too suffocating!" I switched on the ceiling fan and stood under it— power supply was continuing.

"Don't hog the box, *yaar*!" *Manoj* cried.

"Where did you got remote?" I took the remote from his hand and played on the ***etc.*** channel, in which an interview of ***Amitabh Bachhan*** was being telecast. I sat on the edge of the bed some what near, above than *Manoj* and started watching the interview.

"Behind the box." He said

"Has the buffalo taken water?" I asked being deeply engrossed in the interview.

"Yea," He answered lazily.

The fan was circulating chinook. I unfolded my collar and undid the buttons of my T-shirt.

"*Hey fatso,* fetch a bottle please."

"Why? Can't you?" He spoke chivalrously.

"Yaar, please . . . . !" I persuaded him, "I would tell you one thing, then."

"What?"

"Just go, bring a bottle first."

"You are very clever *sooke bhai*!" He went out to bring the bottle. There were three rooms in our house—one for my parents, one for *Kittu bhaiya* and one for me and *Manoj*. The fridge was kept in the parent's room.

"*Hey*, blue shirt! Just come soon; the lunch is ready. And

convey to him also." My mother chuckled when he was going to enter the room—I couldn't hear it properly.

*Manoj* was putting on a blue T. shirt and black shorts. Therefor, he was given this name.

I took the bottle from his hand and chugged all the water in it.

"Hey, how many of years have you been thirsty for?"

I came across amusing.

"You were saying something!" He sat on the same place.

"What?" I looked at him.

"I know?" He said, "If I had known, why I would have asked?"

"Oh, that!" I gave him the remote alongwith the bottle.

"Last night, I saw a dream."

"Dream?"

"A heart-amusing dream, having many tinge moments—a very gorgeous and colossal house in ***Mumbai*** facing ***Antalia***, with many servants in it and . . . .!" I romanced every syllable of my sentence.

"And what?" He got excited.

". . . . And many beautiful girls around me."

"Hey! Hey, *bhaiya*! Get me one!"

"What?"

"A girl, the most beautiful one!" He spoke making smile appear on my face— looked active, just as a dog after a bitch. I noticed the innocentness that colorized his whitish hue face was gleaned with a comic look.

"What will you do?" I asked reading his gestures.

"What is done?" He used his eye brows," I will romance—long drive; dance; love."

I laughed, "*Beta,* still you are a child. She will lay you in her lap and subject you to listening a lullaby—— lalla-lalla rori, doodh ki katori . . . . . . ."

"So what? That place also is not bad!" He showed his shameless look, a very funny boy. He artificially insisted, *Bhaiya*, please! One . . . !"

"No," I said casually. "You will be spoiled."

"Who is not spoiled, all are...?" He spoke point to point.

"They are big, not a child like you!"

"And *Krishna,* he was teasing the *Gopies* always, while he was my age." He tried to defend himself.

"He was God!" I said.

"I'm also God" He said, "*Bhaiya* please...!"

I laughed. Actually, I loved him very much and treated him like a friend. Still, he was a child of 12. This year he had passed 8th. In leisure, we used to kid like this.

"No," I said again, "No, means no!"

"Go. Now, mind your business." He changed the channel.

"Hey, listen further!"

"What?"

"First of all, revert back to my channel."

"*Okay— wokay*!" He flicked through the channels and finally fixed it on ***etc.,*** the channel I like the most.

"You know, there were many buffalos, cows and other pets also in that great building?" I said.

He laughed and laughed. He mocked, "*Kunje bhai*, you will not change, never, whether you go to the moon or any where else— you will remain a complete villager always!"

"There is about you too."

"What?" He asked, "Any good?"

"Not very good!"

"Then by all means.... !" He said.

"*Yaar,* I feel tireness. Let me lie first" I stretched my body on left side, "Could you press my legs?"

"Get down the bed!" He said rudely, "At least do the bed-sheet gentle some times."

I didn't leave the bed but he busied himself in his ownself, murmuring.

"Sorry, yaar!" I was laughing to tee him off. In het-up, he threw a white colour pillow on me and did the pillow colour bed sheet ok. I took it on my back and placed my both shoulders on it—my back leaning with the wall.

"Nowadays people are very lazy. They can't do even a tiny work." He sat where he sat earlier.

"Not lazy, cunning?"

"And lazy too!" He pinched on my thing.

***"Ooo!"*** I cried involuntarily, "So much pain!"

"Don't fuss around! Tell, what next?" He queried.

"Don't ask, *yaar*! You will go crazy!"

"So, tell!" He got excited, "Stop this blathering."

"You know who was patting my animals?"

"Who?" He laughed showing more excitement, "***Mukesh Ambani,*** the owner of ***Antalia***?"

"No, some body else; you will go hundred per cent crazy after listening."

"You tell, don't think about me!" He touched my chin.

"Okay" I gave a righto, "You were there!"

"*Kunje Bhai. . . . . .* ; I have this position? You will be among girls and me . . . . . . . !" He jumped upon me, throwing the remote in one side "*Yaar,* you have destroyed all my position!"

"You have any position?"

"*kunje Bhai...*!" He lamed into me twisting my both hands crossing them over my chest.

He was on me. I was laughing. He too was laughing; hitting up in a kidding way— our noise at the time was more than the the volume of the T.V. volume and it started emanating out.

"*Butterua*!" My mother cried "Take lunch."

He freed me and switched off both— T.V. and fan. We both moved towards the dining table.

We all sat properly, following the table etiquettes. I sat in the middle of *Kittu bhaiya* and *Manoj,* facing my mother.

"You are being somewhat more pampered!" She heaped my plate with *Bhindi*.

We both gave a smile.

"*Ma'am shahib,* is the electricity there?" My father asked to my mother.

We all laughed.

"*Beerbal* had correctly remarked—***there are ninety percent blind in the society."*** My mother commented switching on the fan. The switch of the fan was on her back, at an arms length.

"*Seetal* . . . .!" My father laughed at my mother, his face amusing.

"*Papa,* I want to have a word with you" I took up the topic.

"What?" He whispered.

"Papa, it has been ten days since my result was declared, but you haven't made your mind yet to send me *kota*."

"So?" My brother interrupted.

"So, what? Am I not to do *IIT*?" I said and looked at my father. "***Papa, for IIT JEE***, I will have to do coaching and its time is coming to close day by day. After some days, there will be no seat in any coaching institute."

"*Beta*, I'm thinking on it."

"Till how long will you think? There is notmuch time." I further added, "*Papa*, it's my dream to do *IIT*—— in reality, not a mere infatuation."

"I know."

"So?"

"*Beta,* you know he is in wed lock; people are teasing me?" He said turning away his eyes towards *Kittu bhaiya,* "Somehow his marriage is to be done, either today or two days later."

"So?"

"*Beta*, his marriage is not any cakewalk—It requires money."

"So?"

"*Beta,* we are not rich enough—only this house and some forty ***Beegha*** land, you know! Nothing is hidden from you."

"*Yea*, I know but why are you talking so?"

"Beta, now you are not a new-born child. You know each and every thing. "His tongue spelled parsimony. "His marriage will need six or seven lakh amount, at least."

"So?"

"His marriage and your *IIT*. . . . ., both? How I can afford both things in a single time." My father re-affirmed, "Last year your mother got operated and before that your sister's marriage took place. After all that all consumed money. Moreover, the extra burden of this family. And now, this house also requires some money for refurbishment."

"Never mind, don't spend six or seven lakh in ***bhaiya ji's*** marriage—four or five lakh would be enough."

"*Beta*, our family has a reputable position. It's another thing that no one knows the rigours of its. How our family is managed, you know better but the others don't. They have respect towards us." My father pointed the importance, "This marriage will be the first marriage of a son in our house. So, four-five lakh are not enough. After all it is a matter of prestige."

"And my IIT; isn't that?"

No one spoke. For one minute there was a stoic silence. I kept looking at the face of every one.

"***You can do B.Sc.***" *Kittu Bhaiya* precipitated his idea considerably.

"What?"

"Yes, there are many options in teaching."

"Me. . . . .; do the teaching, not possible!"

"Not any sillyteacher—you can do *Ph.D.* and can be a erudite professor. Nowadays professors are also earning nice salary, nice repo." My brother said with an element of blandishment.

"No, neither I'm to be any professor, and nor to do the teaching in any case" I came outside.

"*Butterua*, why do you forget that professors like you, are the need of this time? Nowadays all the colleges are recruiting intelligent and hard working people like you. They are forced to bear many selfish and lazy professors. Just go and show yourself!" *Kittu bhaiya* tried to persuade me.

"Sorry, I'm not getting your mind."

"*Beta*, try to read the time. We have no adequate money. His marriage is a great deal."

"So, postpone the marriage!"

"It isn't possible—*Deepika's* parents are coming on Sunday." *Kittu bhaiya* spoke.

"Why can't it be? Her parents are yet to come. They haven't come so far. They can be denied in this regard."

"As you say!" "*Kittu bhaiya* sulked his face."

"Bhaiya, I don't know anything. I'm to do IIT and only IIT. I won't do B.Sc." I was chuffed with IIT.

"So! Leave your study and do any job."

"What? What you said?"

"That you listened; leave your study".

"Why?"

***"Because we have no money for your IIT."***

"Oh, for your marriage you have, but for my study not!" I retorted— in fact, I was bitterly enraged. For two minutes, I hashed out with him rigorously.

"*Butterua*!" My mother looked at me.

"*What Butterua?*" I got tears into my eyes, "He is saying to me to leave the study; to go away from the books. You know, how much I love my books? I can't be alive without them. *Mummy,* **books are my breaths.**"

"*Mhm*!" My father nibbed at my emotions.

"*Papa,* I never asked you for any thing except books. At least, these shouldn't be snatched from my hand. You don't get me food; don't get me clothes— nothing, I want. But get me *IIT* done. Please . . . ., I'm begging!"

"*Beta*, how will I manage this much amount?"

"*Papa*, send me to K*ota* somehow. It needs only one lakh or so. For the course, any bank will lend the education loan."

"Who will pay that loan?" *Kittu bhaiya* pre-empted again bleakly, "There you will elope with any *Maudhri Dixit*. And here, we will be paying the debt."

"I'll pay." I said, "And don't worry I won't do what you are thinking."

"Every one says so but forgets soon after, always." *Kittu bhaiya* gave me a hideous face.

I got flipped, "*Papa,* ask him not to speak. I'm not talking to him." I sharpened bitter tongue, ***"I don't like one who wants other's future to be spoiled."***

"*Kittu*...!" My father shushed *Kittu bhaiya* and spoke to me ten seconds after, "*Beta*, what's harm in doing *B.Sc.*"

"No harm, But I can't compromise with study. I'll do IIT,... IIT and only IIT— that's it." I insisted.

"*Ouf!* Why are you after IIT?" My brother held his forehead.

"*Papa*, I tell you. He has a dream to be a scientist— a tuff task! It needs good study, good motivation, that he can't get in these *degree colleges*." Now, *Manoj* opened his mouth for the first time in whole conversation, "*Papa*, he wants to go to the moon; and wants to complete the work which *Kalpna Chavla* left half."

"So many like you...." *Kittu bhaiya* poked his nose again.

"Of course, may be that I am!"

"Papa, he has become loopy. His mind is out of order. Nothing can change his mind. It is sheer wastage of time and energy both, to talk to him." *Kittu bhaiya, the villain of the scene* said leaving his chair.

My father looked around. He had no idea to solve this difficult puzzle.

"*Papa,* please send me *Kota*. Please.. . . . . .!" I caught a corner of his *kurta* as he was going to leave his seat.

He had a look-see but didn't care of my feelings and left me with no voice.

I was no mind. I felt very helpless and sad.

"Mummy, you have kept me in your stomach for nine months. At least you can under stand my loopiness. Please, send me *Kota*." I fixated my eyes on my mother appealingly—my eyes as if those of any ***bali ka bakra***.

She also had a look-see and left the table as my father left. It was a great set back for me. I got churned. I put my both hands crossing each other on the edge of the table and forehead on it. I started weeping bitterly.

***They had no sympathy!***

# 31

My mind was middle-of-the-road but still a bee was in it. I felt there was any kidding going on with me. I had changed the sides ten times.

There was no sleepy in my eyes.

Suddenly, I hopped out of bed and went up stairs. It was around ten. The moon was getting up in the east.

I started counting the stars.

I wore a white T. shirt and a lower. All the three buttons in my T. shirt were undone. My hair were not gentle. They were spoiled and uncombed. My curren robes also got dirty. For three days, my clothes remained exposed to nothing except sweat. During this period, there was no bathing, no eating, no talking.

"So, you won't eat?" I heard a voice in my back— the voice of *Manoj,* my well wisher.

"No!" I ruefully squealed, my voice raspy. I didn't turn my face.

"Why?" He touched my shoulder, "You didn't eat yesterday and a day before also."

I turned back. I saw he had a plate in his left hand. There were four *paranthas* and some *sabji* of *bharvan turai*, the choice of *Kittu bhaiya.*

"So?" I cracked an acidulous voice, "I don't feel like."

"Just see your health—so much deteriorated!" He spoke loudly.

"There, my all life is in stake, you are looking at my health." I whispered, drearily.

*"Bhaiya,* never be crossed with food. It is ...., only for it, all the world is doing everything. People are dying. People are

killing. They are ditching each other, are after the blood of each other— every one is doing this for food only!" He lectured.

"Have you?" I said my voice dignified.

"Tell, what the food has got to do with your matter?" He cried, "How long you won't eat; one day, two days, three days...., how long?"

I looked at him, no voice.

"Don't look at me like this. Just eat it, soon." He put the plate before me on a tiny wall.

"I won't eat. Just remove it."

"If I say.....?"

I went up at his naughty tricks with my eye brows. "You are my darling. How won't I. But don't insist me at this time." I said my words in his own way.

"Why?" He came in front of me, his both hands holding the plate. He took the plate in his left hand and served me a bite of *parantha* along with *bharvan turai sabji* into my mouth with his right hand.

I broke into tears.

"*Bhaiya!*" He whispered with sympathy, "No tears! No, no weeping! You are my brother, the suigeneris boy!"

**"*Manoj,* I'm dying to be an *IITian.*** But no one holds; no brief for it. All are selfish. They are becoming cruel. And their brutality is cariaturing my dream. Brother, my bad time is caressing my tomorrow!" I said diffidently, "It's a killing set back. I can't stand it any more! I will die; will kill myself!"

"Aye, why do you think so?"

"It's looking like my life heading for a collapse!"

"Shut up, *bhayia!* How this thought occurred to you? You know who commits suicide?" He cried, "***Ram dev,*** bloody coward, who can't face the problem! Are you like them?"

I didn't speak.

"*Bhaiya,* this beautiful human life occurs after 33 millions births. It is the greatest achievement of the result of our good doings, in past. It is not for committing suicide—god does not like it!."

"So?"

"Just see, the *Bollywood Shahansh Amitabh Bachchan* wanted to go in media , but he couldn't go. He didn't commit suicide. And where he is today, it is not hidden from anyone, you know?." He invoked ***Big B sir*** sort of actor to back up his argument.

I didn't speak but kept on looking at the stars, ignoring him.

"You know he has done only B.Sc., nothing else?"

"That was the time of B.Sc."

"So, it doesn't exist now?" He caught a chink in my armour, "Many students are perusing B.Sc., today also."

"B.Sc. is not for me sort of students! I'm the second topper all over U.P."

The cat got his tongue. He looked running with his exiguous mind in the mid-air of deep thinking.

"Of course, that is not for you but you know ***Maharana Pratap***? He had to eat the ***chapatties of grass***. Were those *chapatties* for him?" He spoke thirty seconds later, his words a bitter truth tuff, "He was a great emperor...."

Now the cat got my tongue.

"Bhaiya, these are the vicissitudes and you will have to fight with them." He placed his hand on my shoulder gently. "And anyway, you are good at writing. Just brush up it. You can be a competent good writer—take a try!" He exhorted, trying to exhilarate me.

I looked at him.

"*Bhaiya,* education doesn't matter for the people who are tough— only excitement is enough."

***"Education does matter!"*** I cried with a sudden pain. My all inward anger broke on it. I took deep sighs, "Education does matter! Education does matter!"

He got switched off. His tongue got fused before my eleven thousand voltage current. Whatever, he was in a deurmekaar. He never noticed this much anger on my face in all the days since birth.

***"Only, this is the crux, the noxious thinking of our Indian parents. They prefer commitment to marriage than other duties. They love their own hollow respect. The education of their children has no value for them."*** I expatiated on education for two minutes.

"*Bhaiya*, they have many ***HAVE TOs***! There is a miasma of compulsions hanging over them always. What should they do?"

"They should not get sliced. Then no family, no children and no else do they need to have. Very easy way— must be ***Baba***." I pontificated acrimoniously, "At least this much they can do!"

"*Bhaiya,* you are too much!" He smiled a flinty look.

"What I am too much? Who forced them to get married; and have children . .?" I expended upon.

"*Chil* up, *bhaiya*! It's not the end. You know the dry seasons in life not last, the spring rain comes again." He commented "And *yaar,* it's the life of all great people! It goes!"

"But they don't face any study problem. They face another sort of!"

"So, what? May be, there was no another sort of problem in the possession of God which he would have thrust upon."

"Don't bother! Go down! My mind is getting out of order!" I cried in disgust, creating some distance with him, "And take this plate too!"

I got wondering all around the roof, with no voice, silently. Although, he was desperate to communicate with me but I ignored him at all.

Ten minutes later he went down, the plate in his hands.

"Why? Why this all is happening to me?" I came up with a lot of tears in my eyes and kept weeping all the time. I was talking to moon. I was talking to stars. I was talking to sky. I was talking to God. I was talking to myself.

"*Bhaiya*, there is a phone for you!" *Manoj* cried 10 minutes later, at some distance.

I ignored him completely and pretended not to listen.

"*Bhaiya,* there is a phone for you!" he cried again but I was on the same mode.

He came up stairs. He had a very lovely white colour *GTS* 3300. Samsung mobile with slide facility, in his hand. It was the gift from friends which they gave forty seven days before, after the last exam as a forsake.

It was ringing.

"Are you hard of hearing? How long I've been crying? You know, your phone is there? He accosted receiving it, "Any Mani7ha is there!"

"Hello!" I put the cell on my shell-like.

"Hey, lady bird! Congratulation!"

"Thanks."

"By the way, you didn't congratulate me!"

"Mani7ha. . . ?" I whispered quietly. I was actually, *ipso facto*, sad but didn't want to involve her in it— by god!!!

"Thanks, you sexy boy! You know nowadays I'm in air. I'm very happy inwardly."

"I know."

"So, tell why?"

". . . . .. . You have beaten me!"

"No!" She had a chinwag, "I have won my love. I have won you. Now, you are mine—my property!"

I spoke nothing.

"*Aye,* are you listing?"

"*Yea*, speak!"

"One secret, nowadays, I'm becoming some more sultry. You know for two days I'm alone at place. Last night I slept naked with two milkypillows—one in my arms and one on my hot zone and dreamt unlimitedly about you. You know as I got up in morning, I went through my figure before mirror—*ouch*! It is no answer!"

Actually, it happens if any girl truly loves some one, she feels soft and a bed becomes more beautiful.

I spoke nothing. And what could I've spoken? So serious problem and my girl in mood. . . . !

"*Hey*, I'm excited! When we are meeting?"

"In next life."

"What?" She laughed.

"I'm serious!"

"*Hey*, the son of seriousness. Here, I'm on the hot oven and you are saying to wait. . . . . . ! No, no! I can't do it! And, by the way I'm not *Devi Parvati*. I can't wait for the next life." She dilated with her naughtiness, "May be I were a princess in next life and you any slum dog, then how can I talk to you?— the question of my repo!"

"Then, forget me."

"Shut up!" Shut up! Shut up!" She diffused commenting, "You ***Girgit***, don't change your colour now. Don't be so rude. I'll get crying. *Yaar*, I'm a baby—so innocent!"

I spoke nothing.

"Whatever, tomorrow I want you in ***Ambedkar Park*** by the evening, any how— I'm waiting."

"I won't come."

"Yet, I'll wait."

"I can't come, *yaar*!"

"Okay, then I'm detouring to your village."

"What?"

"*Yea*, I'm coming and then everything shall lie exposed."

"What all?"

"Our affair, or what?"

"Stupid, this is a village, not your any city. Here, there will be an issue." I behaved doltishly.

"So let is be. Who cares?"

"Don't be deuced mad."

"*Oh, my dildo*! You are a HE, not any SHE. I wonder, you fear as a girl in spite of being a boy. If I fear, it goes, but if you—what sort of a he-man, yaar!"

I spoke nothing.

"*Hey*, be serious! I'm coming!"

"No, you are not coming; I said, you are not coming— my swear!"

"Then come. I'm waiting!"

I DISCONNECTED THE CALL.

In some seconds it rang again.

I didn't receive.

It kept ringing.

"Why don't you receive it?" *Manoj* said strangely— he was standing some far from me.

The phone was ringing and ringing endlessly. I was compelled to receive it when it kept ringing for fifteen minutes. I lifted it without speaking anything on it.

"*Butterua*, I love you. I truly love you. If you don't have mood to talk to me, you can say only. There is no need to give your swear—your words are enough." She was weeping and weeping.

"*Mani7ha*, don't weep! Please, don't weep! Otherwise I will also be in tears!"

"*Butterua*, remember I'm yours! I can wait for you not for the next life only but for many other births ***Li***— more than ***Devi Parvati***!" She sobbed saccharinely.

"I know."

"No, you don't know. You boys are so. You have no feelings, no heart. You are teasing the girls always."

"Mea culpa, I'm really sorry!" I wore sack cloth and ashes—in all two years, today, I was smitten by her, "Just see, I'm catching my shell-likes!"

"I'm not seeing." She laughed almost weeping.

"Believe, I'm really catching. . . ."

"Ok, fuck it!" She digressed, "What institute are you going to choose; *Bansal*, Resonance or Insight."

I spoke nothing.

"Hey, tell soon. I'm also to take admission."

"I'm not going to do IIT." I spoke, my voice quenched in seriousness.

"Aye, again . . . .?"

"No, it's sure!"

"Any financial problem?"

"No, I have changed my mind. I'm thinking about B.Sc."

"Why?"

"Just like that"

". . . .Yea, it's also not bad. Many students are doing." She said, "Well, I'm also changing my mind."

"No, you must do IIT. I love *IITians*."

"You love me?"

"If you do IIT."

"And now?"

"*Mani7ha*, let's talk later." I said, "Good night!"

"Kiss you!" She disconnected.

I took out the battery from the cell, so that it should not ring again. I put it on the palm of the talkative boy.

He went down smiling; I assumed my same disposition.

At three, I came down and sacked out.

Actually, if you have any bad time, you have scaring dreams as a portent. It occurs. The thing is secret.

I also had a dream, a very horrible one. I saw a *corpse in the stinking mud near the road. Many mangy dogs were skirmishing each other for it. They had hogged his face, any guess about him was quite impossible. The blood-hounding hungry dogs were eating him. They were biting his skin. They were tugging his stung body as if it was made of some rubber or plastic. What a abhorrent situation! There was a sachet of wooden-like powder at the place of this body after some days with very bad smell skirting around the road. People had to pass that place covering their nose with a hanky.*

"Eeee..." I cried out suddenly and was perspiring profusely. I had long-long breaths and a lot of fear loomed in my eyes—

It was me in the dream, with my mark sheets scattered around.

# 32

My all mates had gone to ***Kota*** five nights ago. *Udit* and Aiece took their admissions in *Resonance, Sindhi* and *Pharat* in *Career Point* and *Mani7ha* in *Bansal*. But I was now here not even in any degree college. Else, I didn't receive my marks sheet even.

Any way, it was the *Ring Ceremony* of *Kittu bhaiya*, today. His affair morphing fine-tuned into marriage, exogamy. There were two generators on, glinting lights covered all my place and nearby area as well. My all house was stuffed with the guests and with some friends of *Kittu bhaiya*—I didn't invite any of my friends, and also didn't participate myself.

I was on the roof, alone.

The sagai function of his was arranged in ***Seven Tree Vishnu Mandir.*** It was next to our personage. The place was large enough to accomodate all programme. There in left, in a particular row of the boundary of the temple, are seven trees of ***SWEET NEEMS***, the same are around the ***Kutia*** of ***Guru Jhilmila***, some up the ***Neelkanth***—the temple of *God Vishnu*, due to this, it is called '*Seven Tree Vishnu Mandir.*' My grandfather planted those trees having brought them from their place of origin. One peculiarity, one can prepare *pakories*, using the leafs as *beson*, with the mouth watering taste!

Almost all the guests from girl's side had come— I had a look-see from there, where I was. They came by seven *Scorpio cars*, eight people in each, nine lovely samples or mouth-watering hoisin of around sixteen-twenty and five dholes along. They all had arrived from the city of *Priyanka Chopra*—from Bareilly.

All were alamode, the girls more foppish.

Searching, Manoj came up to me on the roof. Here, he also looked the synonym of **MANOJ**. In his yellow T-shirt and Dude company Nevy blue jeans, he was rivalling the beauty of moon.

I was in my old dress with no else upkeep—familiar white T-shirt on same colour lowers.

"Bhaiya, what drama is this? All people are down and you . . . !" He huffed and hoicked my right hand, "Let's go down!"

"Off you go!" Huffily, I slapped him hard on his alabaster left cheek and hummed and hawed, "Go, don't get on my nerves!"

Albeit many tears in his eyes, but no weeping, however. He stood straight on my face.

"However much you beat, but come down." He said, with no tears or sobs but in a voice with a huff, "*Yaar*, it's his *sagai,* never will come again in future. Many new guests are there—what will they think?"

"Whatever, I'm not to go!"

"*Yaar*, you are not like him you are a wise person! Whatever happened, keep that in your heart, you will get chance to hit. What's the use you get after showing off?" He parleyed, "All people will have complaints or blames against you . . . .! You will be wrong in their sight."

"So, let it be; let them have complaints or blames or whatever they want. I'm not to go." I said, "And please don't be after this topic. You are to enjoy, so do—I'm not denying you... !"

He ignored my remark totally. He kept standing as any statue.

"Just go. . . . . !" I had a hullabaloo.

"I'm also not to go." He insisted.

"Please. . . . . , by my swear!" I said hokeyly.

After all he, a boy— emotionally black mailer— had to go with his mood off, the paroxysm of tension about me.

There of course, my matter parochial, but . . . . .

Anyway, I was totally in the world of my own, once again. I was thinking and became depressed enough to think of lying on the railway track or other ways of committing suicide—a vexed question.

Don't know after how long, I heard Pandit ji saying, *My yajman* ***Mr. Kittu Giri Goswami****, the son of Mr. Shanker Swaroop Giri Goswami has received a key to vaganar, one lakh cash, one golden watch, a golden ring of two tola pure gold and many gifts separate, total wealth of eight lakhs as the dowry from Mr. Deva Giri Goswami, the father of the girl named Depika— thank you.* And I rubbed my eyes then. For some time, don't know what vetoed my idea of killing myself.

A little later, the D.J. was on— a lot of noise of clapping, crackers and fires, a rapturous applause for him. In a little while, the vibrant noise started speaking all around in the vicinity, an acrobatical dance must be on the floor—against all odds, an attractive iridescence on the floor.

Suddenly, by some reason, there was a rigorous Aussle on the floor. *Pavan*, a friend of *Kittu bhayia* was responsible for it; he dances randomly, carelessly throwing his legs into others— I could hear the noise.

Here, the matter became fiery, very hot. Now, an abusive language was being used on the dancing floor, but, somehow, the matter got solved—actually, my mother pondered formulaically to my *nani ji* and she sent some girls on the floor and went her self also. How nice, with cute girls!

My mother's formula worked wonder but soon it became a greater problem—all the wolf whistlers looked as if they would prey on those sexy.

The problem became even tougher, bloody hungry the hoipollois!

*Achcha!* No alarmed, the D.J. stopped all stopped. Guess...?

**"Botal Mein Meera Dard Hai, Isme Nahi Sharab,**

**Moti Sare Bikhar Gye, Mala Hui Kharab!"**

Suddenly, the sort of soulful voice covered all the hall resonantly. All got surprised as they came to hear a familiar voice; they looked back. Yes, me it was!

Blue shirt, light chocolaty tie on it and black pants on the same colour *lee trophy loafers*, I was decorated with. I had a mike in my one hand and a bottle of vodka in another one, the bottle half-empty.

My voice cast a spell. All got gathering around me along with new guests, hearing my voice—*Manoj* no word!

I was there a complete drunkard on the floor.

I saw the hall was divided partially into two parts, one for ladies and one for gents. The D.J. was on gents' side, near the stage.

I saw *Kittu Bhaiya* had broken all the records— looking more handsome than Sahid Kapoor, in his plain green tie on blue shirt and *badami*-coloured formal pants. And on his coiffure, almost all the in-age girls must have carried away. He looked very happy, his feelings subtle.

I saw my mother wore her favourite green colour printed sari with many light-jellied eels, with a bright and dark black border in it, light black blouse, a pair of low healed mules and a lot of gold jewellery. She looked not less than *Jaya Bachchan*, the wife of *Big B*—my father's luck!

I saw my father embellished in *kurta-pajamas*, devoid of any fashion. Ach, my mother fancy, my father simple!

Girls side people also had put on nice clothes some of them sat facing *Pandit Ji,* some facing *Kittu bhaiya* and *Kittu bhaiya* facing the public on the stage.

My eyes moved towards the *Pandit ji* also. He was not much old, not much young, middle aged. He had all the qualities of an able *Brahmin*— a white colour neat and clean *dhoti*, a *janeu*, and a thick tail in his hair and some *chandan* on his forehead with no *kameej*.

How cheerful all were! But me; I was vexatiously crying inwardly. Oh, God what could not have been done? What was my father unable to do?

Commercial viability— no way, it was just only an excuse.

Worse-worse-worse, I crushed the bottle, having a vicious hit of it against my chest.

I danced as any sozzled-boy dances falling again and again on the floor while I would be a wall flower—

"Kya khawab khoob Jhoole

Khawabon ke Jhoole Mein

Deke Jhonka Chhoda

Mere Naseeb Nein.

. . . . .. . . . . . .

. . .. . . . . . . . . . . . . . . . . .."

All guessed I'm acting but ——

Soon my father peeped into me and got the truth. Now, all were thinking ill ideas about me. He and my all family had to suffer the insult and humiliation of being criticized in public. *Kittu bhaiya* pulled me up to the house and threw me on my bed as any rubbish—my both legs stretched, both hands stretched and all the body stretched.

My mean not *hocus-pocus*!

Next day, I was not there, a moon light flitted boy!

# 33

***Jhakad-Pakad; Jhakad, Pakad-Pakad***

***Jhakad-Pakad; Jhakad, Pakad–Pakad***

Tooo. . .

*Dadar Express,* a pacy train from New Delhi to *Dadar (Mumbai)* carried on squeezing the neck of the distance; swooshing, tooting and crying and flying a cloud like patchy-smoke.

I was there inside the train, on a single seat near by an emergency lintel, quite calm and a not speaking boy. I had a simple villageric bag with me with my documents and some clothes in it.

I leaned my head on the window and had been watching every thing, the running trees, the rivers, the lush green Shangri-La fields along the thistles, and the big-big buildings—truly a real piece of natural beauty!

I stood up from seat and having left my bag on it as a sign of seat deservedly mine, traipsed to the *loo.*

The compartment was badly stuffed with passengers. I reached the *loo.* Fuck! It was latched from inside. I knocked it three times but no response. I knocked again fourth time, with a gap of twenty seconds.

"Why are you after this? Use another one!" I heard a low male-voice.

I had a sharp sight on another one loo. It was without door, moreover very dirty too. "It is door less. How can I?"

No answer.

"*Hey,* are you coming out or not?" I cried.

"Why?" The buzzing voice said.

"Why not?" I squealed.

No answer again.

I cried many times, but all the times the result was the same. Finally, I had to back to my seat. Why was he inside the loo for so long?

Some station came and the train took halted for two minutes. Many people got in. During this, a lusty nymph around 20-21, adorned by natural colours and amazing beauty, decorated in an attractive *badami* jeans, dhani poloneck along an anorak on it, and a pair of shiny black mules, appeared before me.

"Can I sit here, if you make some room?" She spoke to me, when, while waiting she spent three minutes standing up and found no place to sit.

"Why?" I stared at her.

"You have no manners?"

"Where the manners live?" I said, having a watery smile across my face.

A boy, sitting in front of me had some empathy towards her, "Sit here, if you want. I can go standing up!" He said and left his seat for her. Wow, for a girl every one has sympathy!

". . . .Uncouth shyless!" She gave me a dirty look while sitting ". . . Don't know what kinds of guys are nowadays; a girl is standing up but. . . . !" She murmured.

I wanted to interrupt, but I didn't. She kept speaking menacingly whereas I remained silent, smiling inwardly.

She had a back pack with her. She kept it under the seat, which she sat on. I noticed her cap a pie. The egg shaped lovely face of this girl had a florid complexion, a pair of sly eyes and the lips stupefying, sexing-up her image. Her glossy hair were sleeked over her back and flying like an eddy. They looked back-combed and appeared quite thick.

After ten minutes, she felt thirsty. Her aesthetically naughty lips looked chapped. She took her backpack out from under the seat and kept it on her thighs. She unzipped it and reached inside with her right hand to take out the bottle, the news paper along.

*Gatak-gatak-gatak*! She having uncorked the bottle had some water with a little distance from her mouth, in a line. Still, the back pack was on her thighs and the rolled news paper in her same hand with which she clutched the bottle. Suddenly, the line of water missed its way and wet her.

*Aye- hi!* The water-drops were glistening on her glassy neck, making the girl more bright, more ravishing!

She hurled the water.

I looked around. As for me, it was hard to have control on piss. I stood up and stepped towards the loo again.

I became banana when I found it closed again. "Hey, why are you there so long? Any prob?" I cried and used some slangs as well.

"No, nuffin! Everything fine! What wrong would be?" He flared like a murmuring flubbing.

"Then, why are you hogging this follicle? Don't you have nose?" I said, "How bad smell is there! How are you standing it?"

"I felt, but so what? I can't stand the rowdy crowd. So, it is better to be here!"

"But it is wrong. We are suffering!" I said.

"What's wrong? There are many others; they can be used!" He made a fumbling answer.

"I don't know anything; come out, otherwise...!" I cried.

"Otherwise what?"

"I'm calling T.T."

He didn't blow his tongue; gave no response.

"Please come out; I can't control. It is too hard...!" With a lot of imploration, I dragooned him politely, closing my both palms into coming out, "Please, have mercy on me!"

"*Okay*...., but I don't have ticket and nor any money too.

What if. . .?" A died and embarrassing voice flicked the reason.

"Don't worry. Come out for only two minutes— after that, hog it again!" I said

The voice gave no answer. But, thank God! The door got opened! A codger almost 60, coughing and itching his keister came out. He was on the tip of poisoned thrones; feeling neurosis he looked around.

I offered him many thanks. And then, I trampled into the rest room.

I shut it hardly with a bang; he narrowly escaped from fallen down, and might have licked the dust if a person standing nearby washbasin hadn't clutched him.

I came out from the *john* after three minutes.

Really, it looked he was breathless until I came out. He sat crouched nearby wash basin, waiting for me with in an perplexed manner.

He was nervous and feeling himself in the tub of boiling oil.

"*Hey*, now take it!" I forbore to nudge him.

It was bound to happen; with watery smile he nodded and as a nit-wit went inside the toilet.

I washed my hands and came to my seat.

# 34

I noticed the girl opposite me was going through the news paper; two youngsters at her side, along the seat, cracking nasty jokes on the hot item with a boy who sat facing them.

On the attic, over their heads, two lovers were as blind in the world of romance, as if they both were on a pebble peek, buttered with long–lush-green fields. She, the naughty fox was in the chief zone of his body; a multi-tasking couple, mulling over! No hesitation, no shyness—an open affrontery! They were having a lovey-dovey talk. For the cemented future, the annas were putting the bricks of oaths, along decorating with the puckish hot dreams, a cool mulligatawny picture!

They were feeling each other.

They were kissing each other

They had nothing to do with the people around and were busy with their act unhesitatingly . . . .!

Below, for some time that three-people-group carried on with the topic on education. Everyone among them was perfect in frying the conversation. My side boy was levering the discussion up by mocking them who loathe the present-struggle and lobotomize the future in consequence of. He was a live wire; lobbing high idea for getting success with a great vim.

Next time, the topic of cricket caught up with theme—with bravados of *Sachin* and *Dhoni* on their tongues.

And finally, that hellish conversation veered into politics—*Anna Hazare,* as if the hero of theirs! They had a heated discussion.

*Pooo. . . o. . .n!* In the mean time, some one among them farted, how dirty!

The atmosphere of the zone possibly remained not withstandable for sometime. Every one looked having their hankies on their noses. "What the hell is this? Who is farting?" The boy in my side who was in livery matched jacket of rain, cried, "*Yaar*, don't do this–it better to see the *loo!* Just go!" He said, exquisitely.

No one spoke at this.

Here, the girl-seated facing me and I too had to stand it, a tough task! I turned my face towards the window and had the breaths in fresh air.

*Paaaa.. . . a. . .n!* A loud weeping-voice entered my ears, in the mean while.

I changed the direction of my face, an ugly crying-rug-rat about five, there! I noticed many tears rolling down on his black and heavy face. His clothes were tangled and shabby. Both cuffs of his torn-black–sweater were in the nose running up to the mouth. *Eee . . . e!* He was tonguing it, how giddy!

He was bare footed.

"Hey, see your mate there!" Tongue-in-cheek, the boy, in my side went off at a tangent to the one suspected to be farting when he passed through there.

"Hey, darling! You are weeping? A bad habit! What happened?" One boy caught him, frivolously.

*Paaa. . . . .a. . . n!* The boy intensified his crying, the noise really annoying.

"No, baby-no!" He persuaded him.

*Paaa a a a. . . . . . . nn. . .!* He cried even more acutely.

"Oh, shut up! Shut up, your horn!" He scaled him when he didn't stop weeping. He shook him vigorously.

*Pa a a a a. .. . nn n . . nn. . . n!* Now, his crying became more thunderous!

"Hey, one second; let me . . . .!" That girl facing me chipped in the affair, "It's a bad habit! No weeping, you are a good boy!" She handled the boy politely. The child as if understood everything, his loudness of weeping came down. But, still, his sobbing continued!

"Shut up, shut up your mouth! You idiot popless boy! Just buzz off!" In the poignant period, one on an elucidation about him, shouted. He had become irritated at his poky weeping

*Paa a a ann. . . . nnnnn..n.nn.n*! His crying continued, now— he filled the full compartment with noise.

"Shut up, man! What blunder you committed?" She fobbed him off. She patted the child affectionately, emasculating him, "After all, he is his mate, you don't know?"

"Oh, yes! Sorry!" He lampooned and patted the child, ". . . . . There is a good boy, a good boy, hey!" He foisted on. He was on the arm-twisting.

The targeted boy stared at every one.

All were giggling all the time.

*"Gholoo. . . . aye Gholoo. . . .. o!"* Suddenly, a fatty woman, calling out her child appeared; a bizarre entry!

Every one became silent, with their pleasure marred.

She was a menial woman with dirty teeth— looked as if she had not brushed since birth— and heavy voice. I noticed a dirty-crumpled–red-colour sari on her, with ruffled long-long hair.

She came fleet-footed, squelching and squirming her hips, *"Lalla le kela khale . . . .le!"* She folded him in her arms and pacified him, offering a banana to him that she carried in her hands.

There every one had a heartily laugh.

The boy got foiled. He was silent, now. *"Na a a. . . a. . . !"* He denied and threw the banana on the floor.

*"Na, beta, kha le. . . . !"* She lifted that thrown-up banana and insisted him.

He got eating that, how abhorring!

She carried with him in her lap, ahead.

He who sat in my side, the most-talkative-boy took out a packet of biscuit. *"Lalla le biscuit khale. . .. le!"* He offered biscuit to another one, as she got disappeared from there.

He stared at him, all broke into laughter.

I noticed them and remembered the day of Antakshri that once we had at college in which I sang the song *haba likar gyi pya ki* and all got mad at this.

I was sad at all this.

# 35

My opposite side-sitting, bevy of beauties was cool. She swirled the bottle, else, as a child got feeling it on her cheeks. A crooked smile cropped upon her foxy lips, along her legs-crossed, style cunning. I would have gone far afar with the colorful thoughts, harboring, if *Mani7ha* had been here, in her shoes.

No emotion was there on my face. I was thoroughly in myself, not concerned with anyone else. I squinted all around but remained passive. Here, I was faced with the all oncoming dangerous probs in life. Frankly, I was gesturing the out side scene, the air very cool!

Suddenly, an engaging voice entered into the heart of the everybody in the coach.

Gosh, what a voice! I beheld back graciously. A thirteen-fourteen year guy, a beggar in unkempt clothes was singing and stealing the hearts of people in the process. His face hideously deformed and voice energic.

She and the others also darted as I did.

He was singing in a goofy grin manner. Very superbly, he amused the people and earned a nice amount. I gave him nothing, the girl opposite me as well.

"*Hey*, you good singing boy! What's your name?" A twenty seven year youngster stopped him when he came near by. That youngster along with one of his friends was sitting a bit far, in the side of girl facing me.

"Why are you frittering away; curling up, you great sir!" In a quavering voice, he said.

"You have the potential of becoming a good singer; a great tycoon. . ." He said, "Would you study if you are provided with?" He sat leg-crossed for comfy, taking a long breath.

". . . . *Lemme* stay at me! If you are to give anything, so please . . . . . ; or, don't humiliate!" He said fretfully, "Sir, I respect your exillency! But, I'm sorry! I can't study— it's a bloody sin for us!" He said emotionally.

That noble man took out a leaf of fifty from his pocket and buzzed him off.

"You are mad? It's their everyday job. They are beggars, the nasty odorous nuisance! They are not given heed!" His neighbour, opposite him opened his mouth when that boy went off.

"He was poor, *yaar*!" He showed his haughty teeth.

".... The bloody mistake he was, of his parents; the syncnym of an insect, gleaming in the stinking drain!" His same neighbour lisped; freighted as a red-hot energetically young flame.

"But,"

"But, what? You are much loaded?" The same neighbour reached his shuffling and lectured a long, "They are for this! This is their value— idiot!"

The matter became hot!

At the moment, his cell rang with the song *jalebi bai*, a nice tone. He sussed him. *"Hi*, chocolate! What's up?" He spoke in his cell as he received the call— he spoke in his cell hand free and I could barely hear the voice.

"Talking, with you!" She laughed, no fabrication— the voice was loud enough to reach my ears.

"You, sexy ....!"

She didn't speak, a girl almost shying.

"Hey, what happened to my AC?"

"It's exhaustively cool without your heat!" She said gurgling, "My long-long clouds, my eyes are erotically dying for you. So, c'mon, na!" She sighed.

"Don't worry, I'm there soon!" He said, "Any way, an AC is so cool so effecting— sounds good!"

"What the hell is good? Here, I'm dying and you . . . !" An irritating voice came to my ears via him.

"You, what?"

"You know how long has it been since, you touched me?" She threw a beery voice.

". . . . . . Just two days since!" He said.

"Not two days, 172800 seconds. . . ." she befogged, an answer befitting.

He laughed, "Okay, I'm coming. . . . ."

"Come soon— I'm waiting, right?"

"Right!" He disconnected the line when she bade him good bye.

"Who was there?" His same neighbour asked.

"Girl friend!" He bitched.

*"Oh*, good! Mind exiting!" His neighbour looked excited. He looked me true, not fabricated. "You didn't tell me." He complained.

"Chance didn't beckon!"

"Yea," He agreed, "How does she look like?"

"Quintessentially, a thing very boisterous!" He bedecked her features with a lot more hot words.

"I wish I could have . . . . . .!"

"You know what happened once?"

"What? His neighbour showed deep interest while—

"May, you touch the sky! May, you go beyond the sky, *babu ji*!" A beggar around forty, and with unpleasant figure appeared there betwixt and in between their dicussion, he opened his mouth to speak, "*Babu ji,* this blind beggar will bless you always. For God sake, get him something!"

"Now, meet him!" The same chap looked at his

neighbour's face, being irritated by that nuisance. He had a sharp 'don't-bother–me' sight on the beggar.

The beggar was shabbily dressed and had a dark glass on his eyes. He, of course looked blind. But truly he was, or befooling the people, don't know!

He had a chipped steel bowl in his right hand. The man noticed the bowl—one ten ps. coin, one that of five and one that of two. He stole all the money from his bowl.

The beggar felt tight.

But he couldn't do anything, the fear of getting his secret open— he silently stepped ahead. Some station came and he got down. Here this side, my neighbourly-girl also moved towards the *loo* to get herself fresh.

A lot of bedlam!!!

"Samosa–samosa, piping hot samosa!" A vendor with loud noise, hanging a basket in right forearm, punctually clad in vendor's ruled velvet, passed through there with a lot of energy.

"Yes, sir?" he whimpered audibly when that man stopped him.

"These are hot?" he confirmed with a bizarre face gesture, vibrating biblically.

"Yea, how many?" He uttered.

"Four!" He nudged, taking out three bucks from the pocket. He added them with the money that he stole, complete twenty.

"Here you are, sir!" The vendor smiled and earnestly gave four *samosas*. He received twenty, checked the amount and crawled ahead.

He offered two *samosas* to his opposite-side sitting friend. They both took the dainty little bites of their samosas, talking on spiralled-up inflation and harking back to the same things valued low in the past.

***"Wow! What aroma!"*** His friend showered the praises for the samosas.

I remembered the day of my college when I along with Pharat sipped the espressos which were being fetched for teachers by us.

I had to at least smile, having protem!

# 36

“What happened, uncle? C’mon, na!” My neighbouring girl who was backing from loo, turned her fuzzy face back. “Why you stopped?” She uttered looking back. Hospitality and opulence glinted in her eyes, all the time, no fury blazed.

I looked back wiping my tears. There was a codger, the same one who met me in loo. She was insisting him on following her—why without any futile reason?

He fudged the answer. I noticed he was a hunchbacked, a raunchy old man with long beard. He was agitated with the hullabaloo in the bogie. “Don’t prolong the agony, please!” Stoic, the old stooped a request; all agility of his mind burnt by the atmosphere—aflame.

“You don’t need to curb your fear. I’m here....” She assured him.

I reamed him out. There, he stood stock-still, silent, razzed and put zing around. He was compelled to follow her. Later a long, quailing and quaking, he drifted before her.

He was unable to withstand the stinging rebuke of people, almost. “Sit here!” Stonily, she nudged him to sit on the seat in her right—the seat already overfilled.

“It is fauxpas. Now what if T.T. comes? I don’t have . . . !” With several foreboding he worried. He was fairly embarrassed and serious due to not having ticket.

“Don’t worry, uncle! Sit properly!” She glimpsed at him levelly as she hogged her seat.

He also took the seat. His side-passenger sulked the face when he sat—the one, who gave her his seat to sit, had already gone. She looked around quixotically. And, having taken out the newspaper, she started frittering away, frivolously.

"Be heaven yours, all the time! *Beta*, may you go beyond the sky!" He blessed her, a quirky sense of humour.

She smiled. "Would you take water?" She gave him bottle. Was he any of her known?

He murmured something but that got lost in the raucous noise of the train.

"Where are you going?" She asked turning her sight on to the recto. She turned the page idly the next minute.

"There . .; where the time pulls!"

"What?" She closed the newspaper shocking.

"*Beta*, there is no one to care about me!" He said with an ignominious end.

"You have no family?"

"No."

"Any children?"

"My bad luck, *beta*! Seventeen children are there but no one can feed even a single soul. I did all for them but they . . . . . . .!" He wept quivering his lips, "I gave them food to eat. I gave them clothes to wear. However, it could be made possible, I gave them all that they desired."

*....And books? Did you give them books to study?* I wanted to ask but I didn't. I remained silent. In fact, I was in great harbinger. I wanted to kick him out and wanted to do anything I could.

"Don't weep, uncle! Have faith on God! He does every thing! Everything will be ok." She sympathized with him, keeping her back pack on her thighs, again. She hurled a torrent of abuse on guys.

The old kept on speaking.

She sat putting her both elbows apart on the backpack and the chin along with bottom jaw within the easy reach of a ravishing base, prepared by both palms dovetailing the fingers into each other.

"Any way, what are they; your children?" She asked as she got chance.

"Nothing, some are working as the labourers in the fields of others and some are roaming aimlessly." He said.

"They are married?"

"Yea, only three are left."

"And your wife?"

"She is no more!" He spoke very slowly, grief- stricken.

Here, she became silent. "Uncle, it is actually your own folly that you are there. You did seventeen but provided the education to none." She said, ***"You know one is wild with out education!"***

"Cher! Time teaches the experience. It is an elephant's foot to earn only square meal for this much big family." He quipped with an emotive tone.

"Then, why you did so many?" She smiled loathingly. "You must have done one or two or three to the maximum extent. But you must have provided them with education." She opined.

The old man was a perfect listener. He was listening to her patiently.

"At least they won't have been working like animals as they are doing today. Now, here they are already hands to mouth, what should they do for you?" She was livened up.

"*Beta,* children are not in our hands. They are the giving by ***Allahh... h!"*** He said.

"No. . .., they are not the giving of *Allah*!. They are the giving of stupidity." I, all of a sudden, entered into their discussion, while I didn't want to. Actually, I was already so much gingered up to gift-wrap someone with my anger. Here, all of my anger that I had inwardly, caught the neck of his.

The cacophony of discussion spiralled up and arrested the attention of others bysitters, atmosphere botched up. All others, gathered cupping around. Now, the hunchbacked lost his balance.

She stared at me.

I ignored her at all. ***"If you had done one, that would have become a lion and would have been roaring. But now your seventeen will always cry dhenchoo-dhenchoo!"***

No one could stop their laughter, even my neighbourly girl as well. The tantalizing aroma or the thoracic amusement of my funny and tortuous statement was wafting a fun fair towards all, a lot of *hoo–ha!*

"Here, actually, your recreation includes it. You want to stand a ***team-India."*** I looked at him with quasi-lemony expression, not recovering from my anger. It was of course a situation, I got mad and humiliated someone in my life this much using my bitter tongue, recriminatorily.

He became silent.

I, in fact, towed him badly, treating like a fritz vehicle. Why, I don't know the reason.

However, the matter ended. But, suddenly, after five minutes, he ran his mind. "In starting, I sent them to school, but they didn't study. In that case, what I could have done? They fell in bad company, and. . . ..." He said emotionally.

As if, he threw a spade, filled with coal, into the dying fire— I couldn't tolerate. "Now, your kite is away. Go and haul in your twine righteously, otherwise it too will be looted. The naughty-wild-kids have made you bald as a coot. They are very dangerous, you know?" I said smiling, an animus along.

For some time, the matter turned back discussion weather perfunctorily. It looked my lexical item explosively furrowed the dying matter and demolished its back bone nicely.

"*Beta* . . . ." He wanted to speak something but——

"Shut uppp. . . .. .pp. ..... . P!" I cried as loudly as I could, standing from my seat. "Shut up, you hunchbacked, otherwise . . . . . . !" My face got red with anger.

"What is this man?" The girl opposite me scolded me. So far, she was not there in the conversation, since I dropped myself in.

"Shut uppp. . . . .p. . .. . p!" I shouted at her also but—

"Sorry!" I cut my tongue as I possly descried a booklet of Resonance in her hand. Automatically, my lips quivered and I broke into tears. I tried hard to stop the tears but I couldn't. Why it happened so?

All were surprised at this.

"Uncle, please go away. I can't stand you here!" I, as a lamebrain caught my head and said already wiping my tears. My expressions were rich enough to explain the lamentation of my heart.

"Aye, hero! What happened?" She looked at me shocked. She actually couldn't understand anything. She pushed my hands off from my face and caught my chin.

"Nothing . . ." I said, trying hard to keep the reality under the carpet. I wrenched the bag of mine and left that place, ignoring all, good grief!

# 37

The electric locomotive gave a loud horn—distant creaks and groans echoed eerily along the all station. In the next three minutes, slowly-slowly, it stopped.

*Mumbai,* the most colourful city of India is lying in alongside *Arab Sagar*. There is a lot of fashion, passion and are many daring dos in it, with amazing designs, a very beautifuly city! ***Nov. 2009 8 P.M.*** I descended on it; at ***Dadar Railway*** station.

The train was many hours late by its time.

This, the land of ***Bollywood*** is very busy city and remains in hurry twenty four hours. There is lot of cruelty in it. No one has no time for others, a very selfish city, afar from my village!

I was completely new to this city, every one new— no friend and no relative! All I could do was believe my pocket while I was with no much money—only 547 bucks—that was all that I had to do. I noticed everything, standing at a place as a statue. For half an hour, I was there watching the all the crowded station, many shoe-makers cobbling and many people in hurry; many ceiling-mounted fan lazily rotating and many photographs of the spians with heroines as well.

I was very sourpuss.

I came out of the junction weeping and wiping the tears at 9:10 PM, with no particular way to follow.

I was on the road, wondering aimlessly.

Many cars, many buses and chauffeur-driven limousines were revving before my eyes—I was weeping.

Many multi-storey buildings were there in the each of my side. I kept weeping.

There were many couples roaming on the footpaths taking liltingly and motoring on the roads.

Here actually, all those things were pinching me and I was weeping at things, which I would love always; I felt some jealousy towards them, now—any way, no hunger, no cry!

By all means, I had no more wish to remain alive. So, I just wanted to have a glance of this great city, before dying. I wondered around many places; saw many things and their reality. It is ambivalently filled with both, good and bad aspects. Somewhere, I noticed a lot of vulgarity existing on the roads freely; the city in dishabille. And, some where it looked as a bride in veil—so shying!

I went around ***Maha Laxmi Mandir,*** the oldest temple of *Mumbai*; situated along the bank of sea, in the north of ***Malabar Hill***. There are three large images of ***Maha Laxmi, Maha Kali*** and ***Saraswati***. One can see the ***Dargaha*** of ***Hazi Ali***, placed on a stone in the water from there.

I went to *Preteexa*, 10th road, *Juhoo*, the residence of ***Amitabh Bachchan***— without any subjective reason, only just to see the resident of the ***Shahansha*** of ***Bollywood***. For a long time, I kept gazing at it. Why, I didn't know the reason. I was wondering in front of it, having the tears in already dry eyes. I noticed an open plot against that beautiful nest. I kept on looking at it— if I were an owner of the *banguala*, at that place!

There also, under a tree on the roadside near the garden in east of that place, I passed a night— the red ants bit me all the night, really very dangerous ants!

Next, my slumber got broken at six when a black colour *maruti* car stopped near me, my eyes not properly limpid. I freshened my eyelashes and restored my sense. A girl around twenty, a beautiful bachelorette in an official dress got down the car. She had an apple company handset. She dialled some number and started talking to the person at the other end, a very fluent speaking girl!

"Hey, my hots!" A handsome young almost 25, came there. He wrapped her in his arms and they both, a dolled up couple flee away from there. Is there any office at this time, so soon?

What the luck of theirs, I thought!

My day started with tears once more. Here, I was sinking into the slough of despondency. I was weeping and weeping and only weeping, but with no voice. Why my father did that; spoiled my life?

From there, I moseyed on over to *filmistan*, *film city* and then *Chhota Kashmeer*, my spirit took me over there. But no use of anything. People say here, destiny gets changed overnight but I never found it true. I kept wondering many days on the strange roads of this *Maya Nagri*. One thing that I have to say is that **the dogs of *Mumbai* never harm you unless you tease them.**

Finally, I felt limp and exhausted. My dermis went dry. Now, I was not rich enough to take even a plate of food, a poor boy with only seven rupees.

I had no will to do anything.

I stopped walking. ***I wanted to commit suicide***, to be exact.

I stood there on the fly over, at ***Shiva Ji Rao Terminal***, a very large and curvedly made viaduct. I stood silent and staring at the buildings to the extent possible; it was 2 O' clock at night. Everything was bright. How happy the world was!

. . . . . And me; I had only hot tears in my eyes, without any delineation. All the sky was gloomily covered with clouds, the atmosphere reveling and scary.

"*Hey,* what are you doing here?" I suddenly heard a hard threatening male voice around me. I moved my head. Two cops black complexioned, quite healthy and in proper uniform stopped their *Yamaha* bike near me. "What is in this bag?" A cop enquired, getting down the bike— at the time ***Taj Mahal Hotel-Bomb blast issue hot.***

***Bomb***, I wanted to speak but remained silent.

"Hey, don't you have tongue? Why don't you speak?" Another cop also having parked the bike in a side, came to me. He was very rude.

I didn't speak, but kept staring at both of them.

"Just see, how is he staring? Let's take him to the police station. There he would vomit everything." One who parked the bike, the senior to another one, said. They put me pillion in the middle.

I remained silent all the time.

They asked many questions. But I didn't open my mouth. Afterwards, they took me for a mad person and so threw me in the way and got lost in the dark.

For some time, I continued walking. But soon I dropped down to my knees, my body giving up. During this time, the rain started, a very thundering rain! I could get no place to be sheltered. Resultantly, I got unconscious and then.. . . .

# 38

It is the most important and the most surprising fact that, in your life, if one way is closed, many others will obviously be opened—be sure! If it doesn't happen any time, for all practical purposes I say then there it will be the last station of your life.

Well, the nature had mercy on me, and—

The gurgling sound of someone throwing me up in the bathroom aroused me. *Where I am? Whose house is this? And, how could I be here? Ah, who carried me here?* I murmured own self when I found myself on a bed, in a room.

I tried to get off the bed, but a sudden shot of pain seared through my head and I could not be freed from the confines of the bed; I was really very tired. Soon, I had to decide to lie down again.

After sometime, don't know after how long, the door of the bathroom opened, and I was awake already! Though groggy with tiredness, I somehow managed to figure out a black complexioned strong young man around 26, dressed in his under wear. Any way, he was not going to hurt me.

"Now, you're okay?" He came over to the other side of the bed and gulped down a bottle of water while I waited for him to offer an explanation of his own.

With some emotional arousal, I wondered in his eyes, trying what to speak to him. At the time, the clock on the wall showed 1 O' clock at noon. "This is your house?" I had to work my arse off, just to ask this little question.

He waved his head in positive, but didn't speak.

"And, you have fetched me here?" I threw another one question before him, with rapid expressions on my face without any pause.

He smiled with ecstatic gestures across his face. "*Yea*, you were there on the road, thoroughly unconscious and helpless. So, I thought and...." He satisfied me while his cool-cool palm ran up and down on my forehead, "You have too much fever. Anyway, rest, I will just come."

It was impossible for me to offer the sort of thank for him. I could do nothing; all I could do was to see everything happening in my life patiently, and accordingly, I was doing. He went and came back in short while with a glass of warm ginger milk.

He stripped off some tablets and put them on my palm. He supported me from my back with his shoulder and made me swallow the medicine, milk as well.

Oh, god! What good I did in my past so I was getting this, I thought. That scene could have been quite filmy if he had asked me about my past but...; he didn't ask me my name even.

I got well soon and then we had stuck a conversation. He was *Amit;* would drive a car of someone in *Gore-Gaon*. In true words, here, in *Vile-Parle* he lived in a house which was not his own and was not rented also, on the contrary, it was given to him to live from his owner's side. Before me, he lived alone but from no where I had dropped and became his family.

Surprising! He never asked me about my life and also never showed any interest too. It puzzled me what sort of person he was. Without knowing anything he gave me everything to use.

Whatever I requested him and with the help of his owner, he got me a nice job in an English spoken institute. But soon, I had to leave that beautiful job; and reason, he never asked.

You know I detest teaching? But there I had to do. I had to do the compromise; and that was what I never wanted to do. Because I think, ***if you compromise, you can't get that which you actually wish to—no argument, you enjoy the every vibrancy of your life.***

Needless to say, I finally made my mood to destroy my life. I secretly carried a jar of poison. Actually, I had a plan that I would kill myself but before it, I would leave something just to tell the world what had happened to me.

And, during one night, as I got chance, I planted my all life-story on a white paper.

I read it.

When I was reading it, don't know what pulled me, I suddenly changed my mind— the letter looked something else rather than a letter. Don't know how an idea to write any novel struck in my mind and at the same time I started working on it.

There I brushed up my knowledge and became a tutor; started teaching the tuitions.

Slowly-slowly, I became the most wanted teacher all around the area. Now, many more students were coming to me, and I was minting money. Now, all the day I would teach and all the night I would write— life became so busy and tough!

It was Tuesday, Nov. 23rd 2010. I didn't write that day and that's why went to bed soon. As usual, *Amit* used to kip with me, that day also he was there on the same couch on which I was; I had a dream—

I was mysteriously glad and happy and cherry with the blithesome waves of emotions waving or hanging in the pages I rubbernecked, *one, two, three . . . eighty, eighty one; oh, means I'm writing a novel, becoming an author! Thank you very much God! Be with your this sight in my luck always, please! You are really very great!*

*Aaank-chhee!* At the time I was in garden green, I heard a voice of sneezing; don't know where it came from and who the bloody bastard did this bad omen. I got sniggled and started throwing ill words to the person whoever must have sneezed.

As it is said that the anger is just like ebb and flow; as it goes high, it comes down also. My mind rested and slowly-slowly it went cool and then I ignored all.

I set all the things, my jug and glass already there on the table. I had the point of my pen into my mouth and went in deep in order to get new thought.

Balle! Balle! Suddenly, I got a cornucopia of very nice-nice thoughts. But as I put the point of my pen on the page to write, my cell mystified me; trrrn-trrrn, trrrn-trrrn......

I lifted my cell phone and peeped in to its screen. *Manoj*. ...! Suddenly, I cried out and my heart filled with a lot of joy; feet were not resting on the earth.

"Hello!" I received the call.

"Nameste Bhaiya!"

"Hey, Nameste Ke Bchche! How are you? And yes, it's how long since you talked?"

"Sorry!" He said, his voice low, "Bhaiya.. . ." He wanted to speak something but—

"What?" I stop in middle.

"Bhaiya, I want to have a word with you."

"Huh?" I cried.

"Bhaiya, it sounds execrable."

"What the blazes are you saying?" I cried even more energically.

"Loan. . . ." He whispered.

"Loan . . .; of what?" I took it in fun— actually, he was a boy of deep habits in my dictionary, his words were like the hard grams for me to swallow. "Hey, don't spoil my mood, yaar! Hardly, it is garden-garden; for in the desert, it is always".0

"I'm serious, Bhaiya; not kidding!".

"Where is *Kittu bhaiya*?"

"I don't know, but he is not at place. After the marriage, he took broyee alongwith and fleed away from the family." He said

"And, how about papa ji?"

"He is hardly watching–boy"

"And, Mummy?"

"She is hard of hearing. Bhaiya after you left the place; our family is in hot water. "He wept sorrow-stricken–heart–tears.

"How you guessed, I'm still alive?"

"Nothing bad can happen to my brother till he gets his target. Although, here all people think that you have died but me. ... "He sighed deep, "And you would usually say, if no one listens to me, you would listen. That's why I tried and . . . . ."

How cunning my this brother had become, I had to smile, at his witty talk. "Ok, tell in brief. What's your matter?" I said.

"I got admission in B.Tech. in SSVIT, Bareilly."

"You've crashed 12th?"

"Yea, with 83 per cent marks, three distinctions along." His voice hutted up as he went on describing.

"Good!" I said, my way of saying pleasant, "Which branch you have chosen in B.Tech.?

"ME; mechanical engineering."

"So what about loan?"

"The form of education loan hasn't been submitted in the Bank so for." He said in a ser9ious tone, "The Director sir has clearly said to me that if the form of loan is not submitted before 19th of December, I wouldn't be able to sit in the exams. Otherwise, all the fees would have to be deposited."

"What bank have you applied in?"

"In P.N.B.; our college ties up with this bank!"

"Then, what is the problem?"

"I gave the form after carrying out all the formalities to Upadhayaya Sir, the chief officer who also has the echelon related to education loan affairs of the college. But now he told me, the form that I gave him, was carried to the P.N.B. Branch nearby us, by a man of the college but the Bank denied saying the dorm is not in its service area."

"Then?"

"Then what? He put the blank form back on my palm and asked to get it submitted any how before the date."

"You went to Bank?"

"Yea; I went." He worried, "Similarly, I was replied; the manager denied me in clear words. I'm very worried, Bhaiya. What if . . . . . ?"

"Still, I'm alive. I'm not died. You leave being worried. Study hard and be merry. I would handle all. Nothing can harm you in my presence—be sure!" I cooled him; spoke with all heart, "And, get me the cell no. of your Upadhayaya Sir—— I would talk."

"Nine seven five six two seven seven nine four nine." He recited his cell phone number in two minutes—and I memorised it already.

"Okay, now don't worry. Hold fast to my words. I'm here, there is nothing you to fear." I said, "I would fair handle everything, cheer up!"

"Bhaiya, one more thing." He spoke when he felt I was going to disconnect the call.

"What?" I said; was more worried at this.

"Where are you speaking from?"

"From mouth!" I laughed.

"That I know. . ."

"So?"

"I mean, where are you now adays?" He showed his cunningness.

"It's none of your business!" I said and disconnected the call. Bhaiya-Bhaiya..... as expected, he was crying and crying. I could feel he kept crying all the time.

My dream got broken. I arose suddenly, a lot of sweat on my face. *Nine seven five six two seven eight no not eight seven.....* I tried to remember the digits, I asked *Manoj* in dream.

Amit also got disturbed; he woke up with a sudden jerk, murmuring.

"Hey, brother! Would you kill me? What is this; nine seven five six and blah-blah?" *Amit* looked at me with surprise. He was noting me for a long time—he would sleep near me, you know better!

"My Manoj is in danger! I must go!" I spoke childishly; was excited in worried manner all the time.

"Who *Manoj*?" And, where are you talking to go?

"My, brother!"

"You have any family?" He asked startling and waited for a pause so that he could get his answer.

". . . .Listen, I tell you all that happened one to me." I whispered with delirious expression after half a minute, he had asked that which he was never interested in.

He came close to me, nothing if not curious about my story-words. He straightened himself and nudged me to be on.

*Pronto*, I had a stormy look at the stored up past of mine and started the story.

# 39

I got lost in my past and got silent while the all chapters of my life had been narrated to him—I was as still as a stone.

"And then, what?" Amit shook me, when he found me for more than forty seconds silent.

"And then, you picked me up; I opened me eyes here, in your room!" I spoke with in–depth praise for him. I offered him many thanks.

"I can't believe it!" He let an indrawn breath fill-up his lungs." "A boy in love with study so much, mind blowing! Really, mind blowing!" He patted my shoulder.

"I have incurred my dog-life!" I said, my voice emotively weeping; soon. I broke into tears as he tried to cool me.

"Hey, you are weeping!"

"No, I just. . . . . ." I rubbed my eyes with an indolence, and more tears rolling down, "*Yaar*, what wrong had I done? Why my father incommoded me?"

"*Hey,* you know a topper is always topper; dark nights can nothing effect him— no indoctrination. He is just like a star. And, I see that star in you!" He massaged my e , "I have every confidence that the decision of yours will be fully vindicated—one day your father will have to think it over."

"Amit, only you are the one who understands me. You have rekindled my values; reanimated to go ahead, otherwise..., all fucking bloody duffer doffed me always!" I spoke querulously.

He smiled.

I also gave him a company. I quelled my all confusing thoughts.

"Butterua, I don't understand one thing."

"What?"

"You are a bright boy; very hard working, an intelligent person, of good character and no fault boy. How can you be fired from anywhere?" He queried with a little surprise, "I wonder . . . ; can't piece it together!"

"The redemptive power of love. . . ." I looked into his eyes, a quasi-cunning glance with.

"What?" he went loopy as he heard it, a phrase very strange and beyond his mind.

"*Yea.....*" I proved, "You know *Mani7ha* is in my every breath. I am hers; can't be dishonest towards her at any rate!"

"I understand. But, how she came here? What has your love got to do with this matter?"

"It has." I was revisited with all that incident in my mind, "I tell you, but just let me see the *loo*, first."

He looked at me smiling. I got down the bed and visited the *loo*. I came back in seven minutes. During the absence of mine, *Amit* prepared the tea, a nice one.

"*Yea*, you were speaking something." He said, pausing only to offer the tea; the time almost that of the morning.

I held the handle of my cup. "However, when you fixed me in that spoken institute, there, I went with all heart. I worked hard. I remained honest all the time. And, with a great perseverance, I continued stepping ahead. Every one was impressed with me, my boss *Ravi Rastogi* or my other colleagues, but *Swati Ma'am* one of my seniors was some more." I had a sip, slurping.

"That's good!" He cried with a fun.

"Just listen!" I slurred as I took another sip, "The story didn't stop here, but took a twist. She was always up to trying this or that— however, it could be— for me; she looked at with a different sight. And. . . ." I was going to speak further while he stopped me—

"Stop-stop, how old was she?" He said.

"I didn't ask."

He doubled up with laughter.

"Looked that of mine!" I said, "Yes, once I was alone in the office; lunch period went on. *Swati Ma'am* was taking her lunch in girls' room and all others were out.

Widely, I fluttered my eyes in the room as some one trying to count the stars. It was a big room painted in milky colour. There were three colour-matched curtains; one for main gate and two for windows. Two sofas facing each other, two-three chairs, a table with a swivel chair was kept in a side and an aquarium-cum-hogged an another corner situated very near, being attached. They all were beautifying the office by their own presence. The aquarium was worth watching thing, bubbling water, many swimming fishes of different colours and they along with the aquifer looking artificially made.

It enamoured me.

I moved up to that lovely point.

With the feeling zonked and wet, I ran my fingers on the glassy wall of the aquarium. For some time, I got lost in it.

There was a teddy bear kept on the fridge, middle-sized and sky blue coloured. The teddy bear was very light and very soft and in golden colour, the same colour as that of most of the fishes in the aquarium. I lifted that lovely article, and felt it as the girls do.

"Hey, sexy boy! What is going on there?" *Swati ma'am* entered the office with a Note Book ASUS NX 90, the double touch-pad and her slightly red colour tiffin, decorated with many white stars, in her hand.

"What?" I spoke surprisingly as I turned my face, her first statement confusing.

"Nothing" She smiled at this. She put her tiffin in a side and sat on a couch, "What is there, *yaar*? Just come, I want to have a word with you." She said; looked in mischievous mood.

I sat facing her, on another one sofa; a sticky wicket. I didn't leave the teddy bear there and, it was in my hands still.

"Oh, teddy bear!" She tried to be in conversation with me. She took it in her hands, "You know why the girls usually love teddy bears like things?" She gazed at me steadily.

"No!" I replied.

"Actually, it's a big fact that the boys and the girls have equal desire for love. Now, it's up to them, how they express it. What I think is that the girls, up to some extent, search their love in natural things such as birds, flowers, butterflies or rabbits etc. Some of the girls like the teddy bear or doll-like things and some of fashion. Resultantly, they are free from all evil effects." She said with quiet confidence, "And here, the boys—poor creatures—have no interest in these nice things; are always glutton; following the girls!"

"But, I have seen many girls roaming around the guys...!" I pointed out the fault in her statement.

"It would, but the girls are in the position of guys with all respect, then." She explained me.

"Good comment! But I don't think so." I said opposing her.

"Why?" Her breath stank of garlic.

"You love these things?" I asked nudging towards the teddy bear.

"*Yea,* very much!" She spoke with an excitement.

*Then, why are you after me,* I wanted to say but I didn't. A cunning smile came across my face. How can her this explanation be acceptable?

"What happened?" She blew velvety voice as she noticed me smiling.

"Nothing, mind went some where else." I excused hiding the main reason.

She was silent. For the next 50 seconds, there was no business of words between us. She was a quite serious girl with deep thinking, "*Butterua*, you don't take lunch; aren't you ever hungry?" She said.

I didn't speak.

"You remain so sad, why?"

I didn't speak.

"Is it a girl?" She asked the question which actually she wanted to ask since I came here. She was some nauseous and lost her confidence.

"*Ma'am* please!" I said politely.

"I don't mean to stick beak; I just asked." She said.

I sat cupping my face and peeping into her eyes. She was a sexy-figured girl with sloe eyes and voluptuous body, a girl very nice and sweet. Why didn't I think about her?

"What is that, there in your hands?" I intelligently changed the track of conversation.

"*Oh,* I forget to tell you. It's double touch-pad note book *ASUS NX 90;* the slimmest note book all over the world with the facility to show the 2D movie in 3D and games along." She threw a lengthy description, extending her right hand.

"Good!" I smiled and went ahead with my hand to catch the *note book.*

"You know, I bought this note book when ASUS, the biggest mother board maker and note book selling company launched its very first exclusive store." She sanded her side down, the *ravan* in her sapphire eyes.

I peeped into her master cudgel.

Still, the note book was in her stretched hand—one could see a diamond ring in her right hand's *middle-butter-soft* finger, easily.

"Take it, it's very sexy!" She used her eye-caching brows, the cudgel very dangerous.

I looked at her as much as I felt.

I took the note book in my hand and frolicked with my fingers on the pitch of it, for a minute.

Yea, its body was fiendishly smooth, "It's nice!" I whispered.

"And, what I said?" She gazed at me once more.

*Tosh*! For a moment don't know what happened to me, the free spirit of my risqué frisson stayed at her torried lips and thirsted to play with the temperate zone of hers.

"Never!" I suddenly knocked her nerve with an exotic tongue.

She lifted her eyes up, her face like the goddess of sex fire. She was almost shocked at my way of speaking; had an inward pleasure naughty "You are speaking so?" she asked shockingly, sly shyness along.

"I think so!" I also continued with the topic.

"What?" I gave a nasal and naughty smile.

She couldn't tolerate the pleasure. For two minutes she did nothing except teasing her lips and notching the sheet of sofa which she sat on. I noticed her eyes greedy and breaths tight.

I was looking her all madness, her feelings heady concoction of passion and emotions—with excitement aroused. She wriggled a little and—

Surprise! Suddenly without any alarm she stalked me, cupped my both cheeks and planated a suprise kiss.

I could understand nothing. It knocked me out on the sofa, my both hands straight, my back on the coach and me tasting the egg-nag like beer of her lips.

For one minute, she remained on me, a girl very thirsty all along the life.

I became nervous.

"*Ma'am* !" I nasalized, the pit-a-pit of some one's coming, there.

"Sorry!" She left me shying.

Oh, my lips so warm!

She made her hair up and slunk out of the room. With the plesure of kiss, she looked feeling herself very soft.

The eyes of mine were bating a gragful sight wrylyly on her every further step.

"Hey, one second!" I cried suddenly, as she neared the door, an outburst of my doghood active.

At my very first word, she stopped with her slittos. I noticed an untied sheaf of her effulgent hair springing up and down, an action sought after.

"Eh?" She soughed turning her milky neck. It seemed she couldn't take the correct reading of my that soppy act.

"You look so. . . . !" I groped.

"What?"

"Nothing."

She groked. She in fact had understood my sense. "You, a naughty boy!" She waved her index-finger before my eyes, the style slinky. Cracking a smile, she slid out the room twenty seconds later.

Now, I was alone, in a state of flux with many more otiose emotions. I touched bed of my upper lip in middle. For thirty seconds, I gawpped at the finger. I noticed the naughty lips of mine had snatched some lip gloss from her lips lissome which one could see on my finger.

I was playing with the feeling lovey-dovey.

# 40

"Oh, once again, a new get-up!" A girl sprang up on her space as she glimpsed Lady Gaga, a thrilling dancer on the TV—while I was on flicking though the channels. I turned my neck towards her and zeroed in on.

An eighteen old girl, good looking and so cute— acutely, the spiting image of *Juhi Chawala*—sat on a bed with some girls. She hogged the place what the *Brahmins* usually deserve, a fly girl!

It was the chance of the marriage of *Ravi Sir's* daughter. All faculty of the institute was invited, me too. On this marriage, he was spending more than 30 lakhs; so the party superb!

At the time, we were watching the idiot box, in the ante room at *Ravi Sir's* place. The room, in which we sat, was constructed expensively; built for secret meetings and to talk with important people. There were mushroom-like panels, that is, sound observers to reduce the reverberation on the ceiling of the concert hall; the sound from this room could not go out.

I was sitting in the middle of *Mahesh Negi,* one of my colleagues and *Hari Shanker* uncle, the brother-in-law of *Ravi Sir*, on a long blue colour sofa, besides a double-glazed window.

"Please, set it here!" She requested me to pause on the channel, she liked. Her voice subjugated; I got splashed and gave her remote.

She fixed the channel.

"Who is she?" I elbowed *Mahesh Negi* in his stomach while he sat to my right.

"A girl! You don't know?" He looked my face.

"This I know but who is she?" I spoke again smiling.

He gestured as if he was thinking deeply, "I got, she is a girl! Hundred per cent, she is girl; or ask her!" Suddenly, he spoke few seconds later.

All the girls got guffawing at me, my face comic!

"Oh, I know this!" I cried.

"Then what?" He smiled.

". . . . Her name?"

"Ask her; she is there, not far a field!"

I felt embarrassed.

There was a room full of laughter. I looked at my brown shoes; coyfully, I didn't lift my head up for next two-three minutes.

"She is my niece; *Chulbuli*. She is pursuing IIT from *Kanpur*." *Hari Shankar* uncle spoke with pride.

". . .*Chulbuli*?" She sulked her face, "No, I'm not any *Chulbuli*. It's *Sahana; Sahana Rastogi*." She remarked back naughtily.

*Mahesh Negi* looked at me slyly.

"You're doing IIT?" I asked some seconds later, ventilating my feelings.

"Any doubt?"

"No, actually after a long time I'm hearing this word!" I opened the book of my former desire.

"You wanted to do it?" She said impatiently.

"Its mania was on my head, but . . ." I bit my lip, down one.

"But what?"

"Some problem occurred; and couldn't do." I said bathing in the emotions. I got lost in my golden past with the desires green on and soon my body got wet in sweat.

"Then, what are you doing now?"

"Only, job!" I gurgled with an ill voice.

Thus, our conversation went on for some time and soon stopped at the point of *Lady Gaga.* A lot of eldritch noise was there in the show in which she was invited as a chief guest during a night show of hers. Many people were giving her an affronted expression.

The eyes of the all people in the room were on TV.

*Lady Gaga*, the great pop star, young chick was on screen, her figure sexy and hair white. There was a very affluent and fit red colour long dress on her body; with some jewellery around her neck, a bracelet in her left hand along.

Actually, she had totally done her stomach and looked pregnant there on the TV in her famous song *warn this way* while, already there were many rumours flying about her affairs—some that of her bed romance and some relating to getting her porn clicked with her boy friend along the shoreline.

All of us also got shocked.

Very soon, the book opened; a new get up of hers this was, nothing else.

*Aiyo*! All became her own once more, fanatically fit. A nice formula she used to put her presence in the heart of her fans, really surprising!

I noted the point for the future.

A smashing time! Suddenly, *Ramkali Dadi*, the mother of *Ravi Sir* entered the room and here, all of us got silent.

She had an old- fashioned glass with black frame and two big-big holes in it, on her speaking—but not bulging out, nor hidden inside, middle aged. A simple sky blue sari was put on her money-cared 83 year-old body, her height around 5 fit-2 inches.

"*Nameste, Dadi*!" I wished her.

"Nameste!" She smiled with a bless.

All others also wished and she blessed everyone.

"Oh, children are you not going to eat?" With a wave of freshness, she slurped in the hotchpotch of namastes.

"The *barat* has come?" *Sahana* looked sidelong at her, breaking the silence.

"A long time since!" She said, "Just go; the bazaar is taking place. Eat soon and . . . .. ." Knocking all of us, she turned back after two minutes; left a subject of amusement— bazaar!

"What bazaar?" I asked *Mahesh Negi*, as she went out.

". . . . . . Don't know!" He shrugged.

"I think the dining arrangement in *Buffet system*." She spoke on her own, while I was about to ask her.

"I think so!" I had a shufti at her answer.

"Let's move?" I asked, Mahesh Negi with an expression.

"Yea." He articulated. "Otherwise people would be thinking what we have been invited for— to watch movie or to attend the party?"

"Let them think, programme is nice!" She said and increased the volume of the box.

"*Sahana,* you are a very insisting girl." One of her friend, sitting near her, bunged up her hand.

"That I am!" She smiled, "What's there to say?"

"....*Yaar*, you don't let anyone go before you." She murmured.

"Of course; after all I am an *IITian*, the proud of my country!" She teased her speaking with pride that she didn't like.

She felt very uncomely. Some lines of anxiousness were glinting in her arid gestures, "Ouf! If you are to watch, keep watching. But I feel pangs of hunger; am going!" She replied.

I was about to laugh, but could check it somehow.

"Don't get niggled, *yaar*! We are also going!" She said laughing.

"Then, Be on."

"One second, *yaar*."

"What a strange thing—party is going on and we bloody asinine are here marring the chance." She boiled all of us, murmuring own self. "If nix there, go then for doing the broom!"

"It's not going to be finish so soon." She threw her tongue, carelessly.

"No, it will wait for you!" She spoke with opposite sense.

"Obviously, after all I'm an *IITian!*" She smiled again. How much proud she had?

"How arrogant you are!" She said in irritating voice.

"That, I am; don't say again and again." She said, teasing her.

She fell down prone on the pitch of talking, "Ouf. . . . !" She sighed tightly, looking the ceiling.

"Okay, *baba!* let's go!" she gave the remote to me and patting her step-cut hair with her right hand's fingers, got going out; rest of girls followed her.

I noticed her pride and tallied it with my past—how much proud I used to have!

"Hey, where have you got lost? You are not to go?" *Mahesh Negi* shook me, when he found me still.

"Oh, yes, let's go!" I said flabbergastedly. I saw he was standing just near me and *Hari Shankar* uncle; a splint tied with his right leg tried to stand up carefully. All the room was empty now.

I looked up and down; the remote was in my hand. What a thing, I burnt the fire and they cooked their food!

I switched off the box and put the remote on the bed, the TV wall-fixed and with no place to keep the remote on.

We also came out of the room.

# 41

The whole marriage ceremony was organized in *Suriya Banquet Hall*, very near to the place where *Ravi Sir* lived. It was big enough and decorated amazingly. I noticed many cars parked in the parking zone a lot of noise of the D.J. inside the cluttered building.

Those all girls who were in the room with us, just some time before, met again on the stairs—the eating arrangement on the first floor.

"Butterua, I'm just coming." *Mahesh Negi* said, gruntly as we climbed up some stairs.

"Where are you going?" I asked.

"I'm just coming!" He spoke puzzling and without telling the reason, coasted down.

"But come soon!" I emphasized waving my hands.

"OK." He agreed and walked away.

"You look friendly, an interesting boy!" *Sahana*, looked at me smiling. And we all started climbing the stairs again.

I spoke nothing, but smiled in expression, "It's not too tough!"

"What?"

"To impress a girl!"

She laughed, "*Yea*, it's too easy! If you wanna see any girl in your arms, praise her and be friendly with her group— that's it!" She clowned, "The formula works wonder. . ......."

"You look experienced!" I looked at her with the coasts of my eyes smiling.

"Of course, after all I'm an *IITian*." She cocked her head to one side and spoke inordinately with her eye brows up.

"It goes there?" I glanced up surprising. We shifted ourselves aside, in a corner so that we could not be disturbed, the place girdled in noise.

"What doesn't go?" She spoke with sarcasm naughty, *"Eve teasing, Adam teasing. . ..,* everything; everything is fair." She opened the book of *IIT*, an institute great!

"What are you saying?" My eyes stayed opened with a great shock.

"... *Yea*! That's a big institute, not any small college. Don't talk girls, or don't talk guys, do it and don't do that—— these archaic things play in small schools, or in the allies of inchoate villages, not in *IIT* sort of big institute. There all goes; all is fair!" She let the cat out of the bag.

"And what about study?"

"That also goes."

"But?"

"There is no but!" she said with the expression on her face, a dead give way, "You can see the result."

"Oh, I wonder! How is it?" I wondered, thinking how so much high value *IIT* has. "Is the faculty very good?"

"*Kaddu!*" She smiled irritatingly and using some slangs.

Oh, over the moon! I would have liked her always as an irritating girl, if I were a boy friend of hers. I couldn't stop myself from cracking a laughter.

She smiled, "I tell you. Today, what ever position *IIT* stands at, it is just because of students. They don't expect to be spoon-fed. They are so hardy; the faculty bloody-hell, is good for nothing!" She threw a growled-tongue speech.

"Yea?" I got puzzled in her words and couldn't satisfy myself, the gestures of my face connoted the confusion going on in my mind.

Other girls, the friends of hers were getting bored with us. They were looking their faces.

"Don't be so much confused. I would explain you everything!" She said as she read my trouble, "Anyway, let's go to eat. Otherwise, they will start eating us!" She spoke smiling with a glance on the other girls.

"He hasn't come so far!" I just grunted.

"He will come. It's not any *Kumbh Ka Mela;* let's go!" She said pulling my hands.

There was good arrangement. The hall was big enough to cover two thousands people at a single occasion. It was decked out in flower shaped bull. Many different sort of food stalls and nine hundred-people crowd.

I took some *sahi panneer*, *pulao* and *salad* in a steel-plate; searched a corner to stand properly. That new girl, *Sahana* leaving her other friends also came to me and stood in before me.

"*Yea*, I was telling you the arcane of the result of *IIT*." She spoke on her own, as she took a sigh of relief, in that stuffed atmosphere, "Actually its credit goes to girls!"

"How" suddenly, some rice came out of my mouth as I spoke getting shocked—the rice were going to fall in her plate but, thank God; they didn't.

"Go easy!" She said smiling and coming at a side.

"Sorry!" I whispered, feeling embarrassment.

"It's OK!" she said, "You know the guys have taken *Spanish fly*. To blog the girls they have to sweat out in study. And there, in the coexistence, the girls take the guys as a challenge and they try to conquer them. Thus, there is hard competition, and the result is before us!" She explained, feeling cock-a hoop.

"Yes, it is!" I agreed, "Of course, a girl is great; the root of all smiles. She is like an earth, which absorbs all the evils of boy and provides him with the atmosphere best. She is the only soul who teaches a boy how to live a life; shows the right path—otherwise they are wild creatures. . . . !" I buoyed her, showering a lot of praises for the girls.

"But the guys are also not bad; they are of course the moon struck!" She took the side of guys, "Actually, it's not their mistake— they are so by blood!"

I smiled as I noticed her finessingly-speaking.

"Do you think cock a Mamie it is?" She stopped her spoon with rice and curry in it, near her mouth, when she found me cunning.

"No, actually. . !" I gave it a second thought before speaking, "You have any partner?" I asked her with the cunning corners of my eyes, the cordiality in voice.

Cock-a–doodle-do! She smiled and only smiled. Was she really spoken for?

# 42

"Excuse me!" She paused and moved aside to take water. I noticed a boy of 24, stripped to the waist was pouring the filtered water into *'use and throw'* glasses, there.

She lifted a glass, drunk the water and came back to join the company, throwing the glass in the tub. "You know about ***Thomas-10***?" Biting a salad, she asked me.

"*Thomas*-10?" I paused and turned away as if I tried to remember. "Yea, once I read in a news paper." I said.

"It's a sort of competition in which . . . . ?"

"One second!" I stopped her and was lost into crowd. I served some *razma-chawal* in my plate and came back to her.

It seemed as if she felt somewhat non-descript alone; was wondering at the ceiling, counting the stars.

"Sorry!" I gave a placatory smile as I found her not looking at me.

"It's Ok." She whispered, giving me a nonchalant smile.

"You were telling something about ***Thomas-10***" I nudged her to start the topic again.

"Yea . . , it's a kind of competition in which a guy has to put the lipstick on the lips of any girl, he likes, with no use of hands, holding it with his mouth." She explained.

Pizzazz! I cried as if it was a pivotal view-exchange that I found first time, ever since, I dropped in Mumbai. Here, you must remember I was never a reciprocating spot for the loafing. I always deemed it ***do everything whatever you want but be strong at your position.***

"It took place at our college; a boy any class fellow of mine, very handsome with long-long hair like *Salman Khan* in *Tere*

*Naam"* She couldn't stop herself from laughing, ". . . selected me for the competition purpose. He was very cunning and won my heart in first go, along the competition."

"How?" I grinned.

"Actually, I wanted to just fool him. As the competition got over, I neared him and spoke to catch me at *Gopi-Kishan Park* in evening..." She only laughed and stopped her tongue for the time, she completed her mean, "You know than, what happened?"

". . . .You didn't tell!" I threw a pleasant smile, my gaze stern.

Here, she was giggling all the time; telling less, laughing much, "I didn't reach there. . !"

"What?"

"Yea . . . , he kept waiting for me for the day and for many other days; for seven days. He didn't meet me neither in class, nor in *IIT*-mess. I got afraid and moved to the point. There, I found him lying on a bench, in a zazevo in the pool." She described everything giving equal importance. "It cast a spell on me. For a long time, I kept gazing at him; my feelings nebulous Suddenly. I broke into tears."

"It happens!" I felt great as she gave a heart touching description, "And....?" I said.

"He woke up, hearing the voice of my sobbing."

"Huh?" I behaved friendly.

She laughed at my strange manner. *"You are still waiting for me, idiot,* I gave him a nice I-love-you scolding and hugged him, howsoever tightly I could."

"And thus your love story got a *hari jhandi, right?"* I spoke before her.

"*Yea.*" She nodded in expression, "But don't tell any one that I told you; no one knows about my affair!" She said.

"*Okay*!" I gave her a faithful glance.

"*Hey*, *Sahana*, you are here! And we have been in all party for you!" All of a sudden, a group of girls, some of those who were watching box with us and some new ones, came to us, as if to attack on our secluded conversation.

They were holding their plates in their hands.

I got thrilled for a moment.

"Shall we go? *Dulha-Dulhan* may have reached the stage." I spoke to that particular girl, putting my plate in the tub.

"You have taken?" she looked at me.

"Yea . . ." I nodded positively.

"Don't mind, you guys are really pigs, eat so fast. But we are girls, at least we should eat properly!" she joked.

"You are commenting?" I said with an informal smile.

"No, I'm just saying; a truth!" She shrugged.

"Any way, just see the time!" I passed her a cunning remark.

"Oye! Its 12:30!!!" One of her friend cried, reading the black colour watch in her left hand.

". .. I've also taken to my fill!" She, the *IITian* blew a low voice, and put her plate down in the tub.

"No-no, eat properly!" I laughed.

She also gave me a pleasant glance.

Now, all of us took some water and one-one white *rasgulla* one after other.

"Hey, you have any *setting?"* She blinked her eyes towards me, with a straight question as we came up to stairs to climb down.

"Setting what?" I spoke pretending as if really I didn't know what that meant.

"Ho! He doesn't know *setting*!" She smiled looking at her friends.

"Any girl friend, you have or not, she is asking that!" One of her friend said waving her right hand.

"No, I'm complete chaste boy; the *bal brahmachari. . . . .*" I smiled.

"In this after noon?" She fluttered her eyes suspiciously and with surprise, "How come it is possible; burning-aged boy has no girl friend!" She slipped in to a tumult; her friends turfed with turmoil as well.

"But it is here!" I showed a fake confidence, stepping down.

Ayn! Ayn...! Ayn...! Ayn....! A different sort of pleasure started bucketing down in side me. I got bubbled over with the kind of strange feelings. I had been arrested by something— I felt so.

"You must go!" My tongue twitched with some jittery that one feels before a girl; a signal of love.

"Why? You are not coming?" She turned her milky neck back.

"No, actually . . . . , actually, I feel like eating something more!" I groped, "You must go; I'm just coming!"

"What? You will eat again?" She asked with a suprise and laugh; caught my first sentence.

But, I had no word to answer. I was silent and looking up and down. Actually, *Swati ma'am*, my *Joohi Chawla* was coming up. She had neared the landing, her right hand on the banister.

We were on the last tread, very near to the landing.

"Hey, Butterau! How are you?" She glad-handed as we came close to each other.

"Aiyo. .. . !" The girl, Sahana tugged at my sleeve reading the feelings which bubbled beneath my surface. "Okay, Mr. *Bal Brahmchri*, Good Bye; let's meet in *Jai- Mala*!"

I looked at them smiling.

## 43

I noticed light chocolaty, beery lipstick on her fleshy lips, sexy enough to increase my heart beats. She was stepping up and her net tippet was swaying on her one shoulder, a breathless fairy in her simple *salvar-suit.*

"You look gorgeous!" I spoke to her in her ears as we climbed the stairs and placed ourselves in the corridor along the grill; they all had already tripped off along the stairs, down.

"*Pow!*" she spanked me an artificial punch in my chest, feeling a tickle.

"Ouch" I showed an artistry of guys, "Really, you are a neplusultra of natural pulchritude". "Just see, your waist and...." I said trying to stroke her curved snake-like swaying body.

"Shut up!" she pushed me with my hand, feeling shy, "How smart you guys are at fluttering!" Her lips curled together as she gave a grimace of killing smile.

I laughed, "Yea.... I can bet there is nothing hotter around than your....."

"Than your what?" She did her eye brows up.

"Than your long-long hair; than your locket; than your dangly earrings; and than your twinkling charming bracelet. These all are really lethal weapon of yours, a perfect back around for seduction!" I could inhale the fragrance emerging from her hair as I pulled her along her waist.

"Ouf, you guys ...!" she fluttered her fluffier arms trying to go out from the joint that I had prepared folding my hands around her but—

With the entire strength, I pushed her against the grill. She bent with her waist and I sucked the freshness of her damn slippery lips.

"*Butterua*, you look spoiled by your mood, a dishonest boy! You need some rest!" she murmured making her hair when I freed her.

"So give me, na! I'm longing…!" "I said innocently, peeping into her eyes."

"You know how long I have been waiting for you here?"

"If I hadn't come then….?"

"I would've been waiting…."

"How long?"

"Unless you would have come; for months, for years, for lifes and for……" I said; all the feelings were directly coming out from the heart.

"How mad you are!" she laughed as she noticed my craziness knowing no limits.

"All the guys are mad, ma'am ji! But you girls don't care for our feelings; bloody sadists bent upon teasing us!" I said with emotions deep and pure.

"Sorry!" she exclaimed cunningly without any loose feeling.

"It's OK." I consoled.

"So…… let's go to eat?" She breathed long; actually, her mother, a smart lady of 44 in a green *sari*, with many gewgaw stars in it, was on the stairs climbing up.

"Butterua, meet her; my mother!" she introduced her with me as she came to us.

"Nameste, aunty ji!" I offered her a wish, closing my both palms.

"Mummy, he works with me; my colleague!" she spoke to her.

Her mother gave me a pleasant smile. "From village?" She asked and waited for, what my answer would be.

"Yea." I nodded.

"Then, don't call me aunty!!!" she said to me straight forward.

I got confused.

*Swati ma'am* also could take no reaction.

"Why?" Suddenly, I spoke out.

"Because, there is no love, no respect in this word" She said, "You can call me *chachi ji*. It's our native word and has a lot more love, a lot more respect."

"Oh...... that!" I waved my head. "Then Nameste, *chachi ji*!" I wished her again.

"Namaste!" she smiled and trundled for the dinner with both of us, my *Joohi Chawla* in middle of her mother and me.

"Just see your mother is more-better; at least understands the value of our own things and you...." I winked as her mother was lost in the party.

"Then, follow her. Why are you after me?" She laughed trampling over my feelings.

"Yea....? You wouldn't mind?" I said keeping my both hands in the pockets of my her lipstick colured pants; the all three buttons of my suit were undone, the green tie silent on the plain blue shirt.

"No." she beautified her face with a vacuous expressions.

"Sure. . .?"

"Yea.. ."

"Don't be a vacillating girl later." I said with all the acting.

"Why the hell will I be?" she replied almost a question.

"Then ok..." I crawled away from her, looking around to see her mother to follow.

"Hyeee. . . e. . . !" She cried; caught my left hand and smiled with a denying gesture. "She is the property of my father; don't keep your greedy eyes on her!" she said as she came out from the rush, decking her plate with bhindi masala, paneer along some good-quality *basmati* rice which I saw never before.

"And what about me?" I was cunning all the time; in the garden of flowers. I sat on a blade of tub, biting the end of my tie . . . before her.

She was eating and I was gazing at her . . . ; gazing at her simplicity and her activeness, how formal she was!

"Hey, *Mr. Majnoo!* Now, stop gazing at me. Go and take your plate otherwise . . ." She spoke it so erotically, that—

I couldn't control myself. "Just go naked and let me be on!" I suddenly left the tub and caught her tippet, not caring the people, my passion brimming.

"What?" She turned her neck astounding; pulled the tippet with her right hand—what the hell I was doing?

"Nothing!" I left her flabbergastedly as I came in my sense. Why the girls have so sexy tongue?

She stood still, silent and with a smiling face, biting the tomato-salad. Here, her killer style and bayonet looked equal.

I was on the tufted carpet, looking around and making my mood to get into the party once more.

"Hey, one second!" She called me as I turned towards the crowd, "What's there on your back?"

Fuck! There was a 'map of India' on the back of my suit, drawn up with yellow *curry* and rice. Who the bloody hell had done that? Perhaps, someone would have thought me a tub when I sat on it, and that's why would have done that 'decoration'.

I mouthed a couple of abuses to that bastard. I put the suit off. I gave it to her to hold and jumped into the gathered *wananchi.*

"Whose suit is this?" All of a sudden, her father popped as if the rain with no clouds—I was some far but could hear them accurately.

"It's . . ." She got twitchy and felt as if there was no earth for her feet to stand on.

"Sir, its mine!" At the moment, I reached and essayed to control the situation, taking the coat from her hand.

"Who is this character?" He asked her very rudely doubting. Why are the parents so skeptical?

"Papa, this is Butterua, my colleague; works with me in INSTITUTE." She answered with an awe.

"It's Ok!" he amended, "Where is your mother?"

"She must be there with the ladies."

"Eat fast and say to your mother also; we are to back just now!" He said,

"Why so soon?"

"*Hari Shankar* is going. And we can get lift in his car." he said baying, "Otherwise, we will have to hire any other vehicle."

"That's good. But, you also should eat something!" She said

"No, I've taken snacks!"

"Where?"

"Down stairs; with some guest—*Hari Shankar* forced." he said going down.

*Aiyo*, how bulky he was! If he had slapped me once, I would have taken more than hundred rounds as one takes in space, his personality macho.

"That was your father— bloody elephant!" I spoke suddenly, "I wonder how your mother stands him in bed?"

"Butterua . . . .!" she cried.

"I'm just joking, yaar!" I laughed.

"What a bawdy joke it is!" She bawled out.

"Sorry!"

"Sorry what?" She murmured, "You guys have no manners of speaking; whatever occurs in your mind, you spit it out, idiot!"

I laughed.

In fact, if one is besotted with any girl, he is a batty. His reactions are the pages of an open book. What to do what not to do, he doesn't know; his tongue dances. Yea, people in love sometimes don't realize how stupid they look to the world.

"Stop it, Butterua!" She stared at me, putting her plate off in the tub.

"Don't infantilize me, yaar!" I said practically. I also put the plate in the tub.

She gave a smile and pouting went away.

". . . .So you are going?" I asked with all innocence as I followed her up to the staircase. I felt like a voyeur standing there. This was not how I wanted to meet her.

"Yea."

"Would you do me a favour, please?"

"What?"

"Ask your mother. . ."

"What?"

". . . How she stands your father?"

"Butterua. . .!" she showed me her angry but cunning and blue eyes once more— I loved them. "You can never be serious or can you?" she smiled.

I laughed and laughed. And she along her mother got disappeared from there.

# 44

After two-three days of the party at Ravi Sir's Place, we got a chance to do it. *Swati ma'am* was alone. Her parents went to her village; some closely related had died there— the God great!

She called me in. And I rendezvoused with her at her place.

She lived near by a local railway station in Andheri, a very dark and dirty colony that I went to.

I found her on a chaise lounge, reclining; a table with two overfilled eggnogs, garnished with spicy dish like onion, *namkeen* and *mango-chatni* on it, nearby. Her icy-hot skin was decorated with a fixed coarse smooth stirring sexy and indecent dress. And she looked not less than *Shakuntla* or *Menka* or any other nymph.

She was in great tediousness; dolefully serious and looked awaiting me for long. Actually, I was some late by the time she asked.

Oh, brother! She became mad, her marbles lost as I appeared before her. "This is the time of your coming, hey?" She rocketed with long-long steps towards me.

Gutter! She was at that time; a hot flame of the red angry sun, annihilating anything or an atom-bomb, enough to reduces to ashes any one. She was an inferno, crying and complaining. She spoiled the atmosphere; looked difficult to assuage her!

I got frightened and stood at a side, a guy quite silent and as still as any statue. I let her keep speaking.

Actually, her heart got cracking; she took that all to her emotive zone.

"You, my angelic darling. . . . . ." I tried to grope her as she looked some cool, but—

"Don't touch me!" She threw my hand at once and cried even more, "Just buzz off from here! I'm not in need of any one!"

"Hey, you are angry?" I tried to grope her again.

"Don't touch me; I said, don't touch me!" She turned away to look away.

"So hot....!" I teased her smiling and waiting for the expression on her face to change.

"Shut up! And, go away!" She cried rudely and stamped her feet towards her boudoir, shaking her pliant body after that forth with, an obstreperous situation!

....Exciting! I also followed her picking up both egg-nags. There, she lay on her breasts, on the bed, having long face.

"Okay, Baba; sorry! It was my mistake; won't be in future! Now, let's enjoy. Just see the stems are waiting and the feelings are also in toing and froing." I said as I plunk both the drinks down kept on a stool, near her bed.

She didn't speak.

"Hey, it's not fair! Your hero is saying sorry and you are not speaking! Just see, I'm catching my ears! I'm doing sit-ups" I tried to persuade her thus.

"I'm not looking!" She said, her voice wet with playful smile.

"So, look at, no!" I groped her once more.

"You, naughty egg! It's your need. I know it! You are just playing some trick to net me. But be sure, I'm not gonna be caught!" She laughed conamore but didn't lift her head.

"Aye, at least once, please! Just see, I'm catching my ears, once more!" I sat near her and felt her milky shoulders.

Now, she was in control, "I'm not to see!" She said, naughtily.

"Okay then, I'm going!"

"On your bike!" She mock-allowed, looking at me.

"You won't stop me?" I stood up and plodded my way across the door.

"Go with great pleasure!" She cried while I had reached the door, "But I'm sure you won't go...!" She pulled her voice and stopped at the last word. How confident she was!

I came out and hid myself, some where in a tree, outside her house.

Actually, the girls are very soft from inside. They can't face the separation with their partners; no matter they are very stupid with their tongues.

She came out after half an hour when she didn't found me back, almost crying. "I'm not angry. I was just showing you...." She cried and cried.

But I didn't appear before her.

Oh, good-better-best! The fragrance of an eglantine started teeming down around me. I felt awesome; feeling free and joy unlimited! I found the morning-freshness devoured ventilating into my emotions.

She sat on a stone, near the railways track and got weeping, plopping the tears. "I had been waiting for so long and....., idiot!" She wept passively.

I was a boy with an obstreperous mood. "What happened ma'am ji?" I, with my face ambushed feeling her back, hung up side down, on a branch of the tree.

It shocked her.

"You sexy egg! Come down!" she spoke with an inward pleasure and stood up wiping her tears. "You can pass your night here with me. But don't antagozine me further!" She caressed my face.

I came down the tree.

She placed her head on my shoulder while I wrapped one arm round her. We both crawled towards the bed as couples usually roam here, in the Mumbai on the roads.

We reached the bed.

She played a b.f. with a pulsing rhythm of music, on the TV and carried a bowl of frozen ice from her fridge. She gave me a come-on. I stared at her with a wolfish grin. Finally, the chick was in my legs, quite surrendered; and now!!!

I threw a glass of eggnog on her, following the b.f. on TV.

*Psst!* Pulchritude of hers hogged the room. The Piri-piri alcoholic queasiness of the coming light of her milky ice-cream like skin pirouetted across the room; the music pipped at.

I put a piece of ice on her cleavage.

Chhsss-ss-ss! She behaved as if the hot oil subjected to fallen drops of water into it, while her beery wet body, glinted in the soft light of the room.

Now, the game was gonna be on. I used my lips to lick the eggnog and to carry the ice-piece up to her mouth, with the sparking and the cracking of a fire!

"Aye..." She spoke something in expression and stepped down the bed to carry a prophylactic after I left— it was kept somewhere in her books.

I was looking at her with my greedy eyes, sizing her up. Suddenly my mind went some where else—my observant eyes caught an oblong figure of ***Mani7ha*** around me in place of hers; the beautiful girl looked so cute; the black skirt, so many stars in it, three very fine black threads along bright pearl in her neck milky,— my *Mani7ha* bomb shell!.

*Oh, no! How I did that I shouldn't have done? I'm a great sinner; O' my heart, I'm your. . .! Please, pardon me; please!* I penetrated into the emotions penitent, my tongue sad and repenting.

"Hey, what's up? Here alone . . . . . , who are you talking to?" I heard a voice of *Swati ma'am*— I scoped her standing cross-handed near me. "Butterua..., is all Ok?" She spoke phobically as she saw an ocean of tears into my eyes.

Without speaking to her, I rubbed my tears.

She took half glass of eggnog and left half for me. She sat pliant closed to me. "Hey, baby! Be romantic, *yaar*! Just see, there is a sexy girl in your arms." She pulled my shoulder towards herself, the aphrodisiac—eggnog started speaking.

My body quaked. "No, please don't touch me!" I said keeping her hand away from my shoulder—my voice low.

"There is a chance baby! Just come on!" She caught the buckle of my belt to unfasten it.

"Ma'am ji, please! Don't do it! I can't do that...." I halted her when she reached down to unzip my jeans—while she had unbuttoned it already.

"What happened?" She sighed as a girl in your leg, "Are you that?" With her beery eyes she mock- smiled. Thats what, she was speaking about?

"Shut up! No sordid talk, please" I stared at her, "Sorry, ma'am, please don't insist me!"

"But what happened?" she insisted again.

"Sorry, I'm really very sorry!" Potentially, I groaned and sallied forth.

# 45

"Next day at the right time, I reached the institute but not for the purpose of doing job; I submitted my resignation letter on the desk of *Ravi sir*." I spoke low voice.

"It means you were not fired?" Amit turned his knob-like head on his neck as a wheel on its pole, shocking.

I didn't speak.

But he understood everything. Yes, the friend is around even when words aren't spoken.

"Just dial a number." I opened my mouth when four minutes silence passed.

"Whose?" He looked at me puzzling.

"The number, I'm telling." I said and the ten digits number of *Uppadhayay* sir which I was told in my dream just before two hours, trying to remember. I spoke to him to dial the number that I was mentioning.

He dialled. But number was wrong; the line couldn't be connected.

He questioned how I got the number and broke in to laughter as I told about my dream. But **a friend is some one who believes in you**—he kept dialling again and again.

Hoooo! He cried as the bell went, while my earlier efforts failed. He gave the phone to me.

I put it on my right ear and became quite still with a ruminating mind.

"Hello." A man spoke in an impressive tone from the the other side.

"Sir, am I talking to *Uppadhayay* sir, the liaison officer of SSVIT?" I asked as much formally as I could.

"Yes!"

".... The matters related to education loan are under your supervision, right?"

"Yea."

"Sir, this is Butterua; I am  the elder brother of *Manoj*." I said.

"Whose brother"?

"*Manoj's*."

"*Manoj* who?"

"Sir, he is a student at your college in B. Tech., Sem-I, in ME Branch." I said; was confident and full confident but only for the speaking. My heart got loosened at the question he asked just now. How funny I was arguing without being sure of myself!

"Oh, *Manoj Kumar Sharma* ..." He spoke with proud, "Very nice student he is!"

I felt my patience wearing thin; smiling from heart. "Sir, any loan matter regarding him is pending with you?" I asked pacifically while I had to control hard on my inward pleasure.

"Yes, dear, his education loan is to be done." He orated seriously, "We got the loan file from you and sent one of our men to the P.N.B at ***Chamrow;*** but...."

"But what?" I asked worriedly. My heart was beating fast.

"He came back hung-face."

"Why?"

"Your dorp is not under the bank's service area; actually—he was told so."

"So, now what?"

"Just take a try. I have handed the file back to your brother." He said more discreetly.

"Your Excellency, if you, the well endowed people couldn't get this work done, how would I?" I said with an undue excitement.

"Just try. He repeated his words", "And make me talk to the Manager if any need occurs."

"Sir, up to what date it must be submitted?" Once more, I proved the fussy foolishness of mine.

"What date, what?" He spoke getting irritated, "Do it as soon as possible. And Listen, otherwise the whole fees will have to be deposited. So hurry up!"

"Ok, I'll try my level best." I said lickety-split.

"Obviously."

"Sir, one thing...."

"What?"

"Sir, keep it secret that I'm handling this matter."

"Why?"

"Actually, sir. . ." I told him my all story in a nut shell. And thank God he could believe me. "So sir, take the file back that you have given to *Manoj*; I will take it from you."

"Ok." He agreed.

"So, what are you thinking?" Amit asked me as I disconnected that call and sat serious for a minute.

"Let's go?" I looked at him with keynote.

He nodded and for solving the loan problem, we both left the *Mumbai* before the evening.

We reached the Bank via *Uppadhaya sir*, taking back the loan file from him.

It was winter; very cold in U.P. at the time. So, I covered myself in an octopus pants and black coloured jacket. Amit also wore warm clothes.

"Hi, this is Butterua!" I shook hand with the Bank Manager, a formal dressed man in the pink, introducing myself.

I dragged a swivel chair a little backwards and got seated on it properly. Amit also placed himself along side.

I put the leather-bag that I hung in my right shoulder on the table and took out the loan file.

My eye started flattering as I pressed the file before the *Bank Manager;* not a good signal really, a nettlesome situation for me.

"This is what?" the Manager whispered a constituting tone of my already pitiful heart; he was sipping the tea at the time.

I looked at *Amit.* "Sir, we belong to an indigent family. We had one of our brothers at SSVIT in Bareilly. Just some months before, we got his admission done in B. Tech with the expectation that we would get education loan. But now. . ." He explained with a nice skill.

"But what?" The Bank Manager said with a very different glance.

"Sir, it has become a tough task now!" I spoke.

"Why?"

"Sir, everyone wants bribe and that we don't have" I fibbed. "Sir, my brother is a very sharp minded boy, just see....." I indicated emotively trying to show him the marks in the result card of my brother's 12$^{th}$ class— 83 per cent along with four distinctions!

"Sir, his B. Tech. exams are gonna start—19$^{th}$ December is the date. Amit held the conversation.

...... Phhh! *The Manager* dragged his chair back, putting his cup down. He stood up, went up to the cupboard by him and took out some files—the files very old, dusty and in poor bindings. He in a determined way turned the pages of a black–cover-cobra file; continued murmuring with a jolt in his mind.

He sat in his chair and became *rishee Balkmikee* with the file in his hands, a hermetically sealed container.

"Sir, my family is not strong enough to tackle this prob. We are very poor under debt and with no other solution." I spoke with an alto voice, "Sir please ...."

"I'm all ears!" He said some dryly and not giving the importance to us.

*Sir, how nice marks he has got, just see.....* I wanted to speak again but I didn't.

Now, he had half an eye on the marks sheets, whether fixed in file actually— not sure. Oh, God! Suddenly, there I found a delirious smile across his face—whoopee!

*Aloha,* every thing looked in my favour. I thought to make the most of that flower–bud, thinking nothing. "Sir, I'll be yours forever if you could come to my help, a great-kind hearted and bright creature of God!" I added some sugar of flattery.

"Where are you from?" He asked.

"From, *Mundia*." The man who came with me replied.

Hearing all, he put his right-hand master finger on the metronomic bell and pressed.

One minute later, a peon like a Michelin man entered the room.

"Where is this *Mundia*?" The *Manager Sahib* asked him.

"Around twenty stone in north-east." He replied in an energic voice.

"Just see, does it come in the Branch area?" He ordered him, putting the file in his hand.

"No sir, it doesn't come in our Branch." He spoke two minutes later.

"Show me!" The 'key to my lock' took the file in his hand.

He was serious now. "It is a matter of pity. It can't be possible to process your matter here in this Bank. I'm really very sorry—your village doesn't come in our service area." He gave the file to make me believe in—he was not conning into. He handed our file back; sopped out nothing useless. "Or, I would have felt great to do it for you— so good-merited boy is your brother!"

My all mettle was put to test there, I couldn't come to feel. "But sir..." I said hopefully, I was hung in middle, in microcosm.

"Dear, everything has its limit, you better know. We can't go out from the boundaries." He made us understand. "The matter of yours also pivots around the limit of the service area of this Branch." He put the Midas touch.

I felt no energy in me. We stood up from the chairs to leave the Bank.

"See any other Bank—I wish your work gets done." He showed sympathy.

# 46

"Hey, stop!" some one cried on our back while we had reached near the road.

We turned our head and stopped looking the peon— who met us in Bank—coming towards us.

"What happened; work couldn't be done?" He threw his question while coming to us.

"No." I spoke very slowly.

"The Manager is very bastard; doesn't do anything without money!" He spoke.

"Actually, our village doesn't come in the service area. So, what can he do?"

"Fucking!" he sulked his face, "Money is money, key to every lock!"

"What?"

He recited cunningly—

"Hot Na Aagya, Bin Paisa Rey;

Aaa, Phile Pe Kachhu, Daija Rey"

I was damned if I could count the pecks of my perseverance at that time. I stood straight, both hands in my pocket, head up and the eyes up in the foggy sky, a serious,determined and a ruminating boy.

*Hunnn.........!* A twenty year, with a slim-body, beautiful girl passed across my eyes on the road, her scooty speeded up.

So parky! Really, it was like 'Billy-o' to stand the cold. But the flying elf with flowing hair was in her form with no helmet and wearing a jacket, though unzipped.

I kept looking at her till she was lost in the fog. I compared her with the actress in ***Rab Ne Bana Di Jodi:***

Eureka! My mind moved; found my *Mani7ha* in her and there was a fresh thought in my bonnet.

"It's too cold. Would you like to take tea?" I asked the peon with an indolent tongue. "Actually, I wanna have a talk with you." I explained him when I noticed he couldn't understand what I actually meant.

"Why not?" He said with his mouth open and tongue coming out with greed, a bloody dog!

We moved towards a tea stall, a very simple *tripaal* covered shop with two simple benches, under a *pakar tree*. The complete tree was in the effect of drizzle.

The 30 old-young man, with a long nose an, unpleasantly six-fingered *rang root* was with us . . . . . .; covered in black jacket, muffler and poor-quality shoes.

We all three seated ourselves on the benches. A puff of white smoke billowed from my mouth due to the chill.

"Hey, tea?" A 20-year grown-up, in a denim jacket gave a loud gurgling sound from five mtrs distance; from the place he would prepare tea.

I ordered for three.

In fifteen minutes, the tea-stall boy poured some chocolaty liquid—that we called tea—into three cups and handed us.

"So, where he comes from?" I asked the peon, as he took the first sip from his cup.

"Who; Manager Sahib?"

"Yea, the incumbent Manager of your Bank." I said but not harshly or rudely.

"From Rampur; from the teachers' colony." He answered with an excitement.

"He bikes to here?"

"Yea."

"Along this road?"

"Yea."

"What time he goes back?"

". . . Usually up to 5."

"*Yaar*, we are in hot water. Please, could you do anything for us?" I said, requesting so as not to let him be serious towards my previous questions.

"Why not? Why not? If you say, I will talk to *Manager Sahib,* today." He assured himself of the loan. "And don't worry; your work will be done. Get me your number. I will call you tomorrow." He vouched for the work; put the cup down after sipping the tea to its last drop—how glutton he was!

"Thank you, thank you very much!" I said only for sake of formality. I gave him our number and took his as well.

The tea-stall boy came and collected all the cups. I paid for the teas.

"Hey, where is your cell? Just take out!" I spoke to *Amit* when that peon went back to the Bank.

"Where will you call?" He asked in confusion, putting his 'wing' company cell phone on my palm.

I didn't respond.

I dialled a number. "Hello..... *Uppadhaya* sir speaking?" I confirmed as the call was received.

"Yea." The answer came from the other end.

"*Butterua* speaking, sir!"

"*Yea,* speak......!"

"Sir, please come. The bank is ready to do the loan." I said confidently.

Amit couldn't understand anything. He gave me a surprised look, as I noticed.

"The P.N.B is holding it?"

"Yea, the same Branch which denied you." I said, "So, come up to 12, on the morrow, right?"

"Ok." He said.

"And, yes . . . !"

"Speak."

". .... Bring my *Manoj* also with you, please." I requested him, "It has been long time since I saw him."

"Ok." He spoke with an assuring voice.

"Are you mad?" There he buzzed you off and here you are...." Amit fell on me just like any torrent as our conversation got over. How can it be possible?

"Just keep watching......" I smiled.

In the evening, as the Manager was going back to his home, we both stopped him in the way and.. .....

Next day, at 10:30, a white coloured *Maruti Van* stopped at the Bank premises. The formally dressed Manager got down. He, a 45 yrs, white complexioned man was covered with a medicated cleansing pads around the sensitive skin of his neck with a bandage around his head, a Band-Aid on one of the cheeks, left arm in sling and right leg plastered. The obvious reason of his this condition and of his coming by van....; we know.

We both were sitting under a mango tree, 30 mtrs far from the venue. The sky was fortunately becoming clear and fresh—the sun was arising and the fog was getting dispelled. We could see all that happening there from the distance.

The Manager stepped inside the Bank.

The same peon, who we talked to a day before came out and went back into the bank bringing his suit case and *Tiffin box*.

Two hours later, one another Van stopped there.

Bingo! A young handsome seventeen boy in his college uniform came out of the van as the door opened—I barely could see properly.

I had many tears in my eyes.

"Is he your brother?" Amit put his hand on my left shoulder as he heard me sobbing.

"Yea." I nodded wiping my tears. How grown up my brother had become!

Three other people also descended from the van.

I noticed them talking each other. "Just call that peon!" I looked at Amit; spoke with malicious eyes.

He dialled the number of that peon and gave me the cell as the line got connected.

"Hello." The peon was on line.

"... Lemme talk to your Manger." I spoke hard.

"One second."

"Hello" A low voice of that rascal came; I could hear clearly.

"Butterua speaking...."

"Butterua who?"

"Your pop!!! I wonder how you can forget me so soon". I spoke as I could, "Well, I can tell you once more."

"Yea; speak!" He said. I think he had recognized me— a good boy!

"Some people are coming to you. Do do the loan! I bulldogged him, "Otherwise, your idiot peon has told me your daughter, a twenty chick is at college every day. What can a bull do with a cow?— you can understand!"

"Please, don't do any thing. I'm not denying... I'm doing. I'm doing." He begged and begged. His tongue lisped with fear. Sometimes, of course it's good to be bad!

I dropped the connection.

All the people who came just now entered the Bank.

They all came out after forty minutes. They looked cheerful.

I made one more final call to *Uppadhaya sir* as they all sat in the van and disappeared from my sight.

"Hello." *Mr. Uppadhaya* spoke, his clear voice came to my ears.

"Sir, what happened there?"

"Where?" He said, "In Bank.......?"

"Yea."

"He is doing—a very noble man he is!" He put my praises for him, "Some of the formalities are done and some are left. In this month, he will do it."

Thank God! I felt elated and thanked my lucky stars taking long sigh of relief.

# 47

It was 3:40 at night and my novel got completed; a great news—hurrah!

Now, I was dancing and dancing. I was doing everything that I felt like. Actually, the pleasure drove me mad— I had lost my sense. "I'm alive India!!!" Suddenly, I cried out.

Jeepers! *Amit* got flabbergasted. He showed me his neurotic face from the blanket, three mtrs away from me. He smiled and nettling his jaw into his right hand's palm, kept smiling perceiving the change into my behaviour.

"Hey, one second!" I halted *Amit* in morning as he was gonna leave the place for his job, "Can you stay few more seconds?"

"Hmm......., why?" He asked when he found me going.

I didn't speak but landed on the road.

"......Those were your few seconds?" He spoke to me smiling as he noticed me at the door, coming back —I ate 20 minutes.

"Sorry!" I chirped asking him to stretch his hands.

"What is this?" He also chirruped as I put the parsad of God Shiv, in his hands.

I came up with an attractive smile across my face. "I'm coming from the *Shiv-temple,* after offering the *prasad;* my novel has been completed!!!"

".......You promised him?" He held his eyes up, of course a reported question.

"Yea ......!" I said in slow voice.

He smiled and went his way with pleasantly.

In evening he returned with some people; sooner than he would return usually. "Butterua, meet— this is Mr. Jitendra, from Mayure Publication." He said from few steps distance, coming inside the room.

I turned my head away from the shine board while I was writing something on it. There, as my job of AIEL got left, I picked some students of B.A. just for living sake and not to be a burden on Amit–I was tutoring!

"Hi, this is Butterua!" I shook hand with him along with others who came along with.

"We know you a simple, weak and papery boy; a box of knowledge!"A thirty five, fatty and somewhat dark complexioned lady looked at me smiling. "Our ears are stuffed with the praise of yours; he has told us everything." she sneaked upon Amit with her pleasant eyes.

He is he; what to say about him! "Nay, he sheltered me in this unknown city, but helped me in all respects." I became wet with emotions.

He smiled. "They are here just to talk to you regarding your Novel." He came on the main point, changing the topic.

"...Please, only for ten minutes." I indicated with a soft voice towards the students. "Ok, but...." he chivvied me along and carried them to the sitting room.

"....Sorry, I'm late!" I appeared before them with an apologetic but hammy tone, ten minutes later — as I left the students. At the time they were enjoying the snacks.

"It's Ok; I like it." Mr. Jitendra, a white skinned, tall and an attractive, around forty, young man had no stroke, "Gandhi ji also would be in your block, in any time. Once someone came to him while he was doing work, that person wished him. Gandhi Ji also held his head and wished in reply. But, the next moment, he busied himself into his work again without any pause. Only when his work got completed, he talked."

"Of course, the work is first!" The amiable lady said an aphoristic phrase in his support.

"Take your seat." Amit said giving the place for me, on the sofa.

"One second." I said and left them talking each other for carrying my novel.

I appeared before them once again later after three minutes.

"This is the book; that pulled you here." Amit took all the handwritten papers of my novel covered in a cobra file and extended towards them, while I sat beside him.

"Sir, I have written it with my all aplomb!" I said just to throw an impression, as he turned some pages.

"Good!" He smiled and went serious for some time. He complimented on my novel or the sentence I spoke just now?

I felt pleased.

"Awesome . . . ., really awesome!" Anyone can write so well, I can't believe it." He looked at me with no locomotion in his eyes. He went mad. "What's your name?" He asked a silly question; was a boy very loco.

"Show me!" The cat–eyed, observant lady took the novel in her hands—no respect to his question and also no chance for me to speak any word for the answer!

I kept quite. Every one kept quite. Another person, around 25, who also came with them, was also at my simple white polo shirt and black lower, with his 'I - can't – believe' eyes.

I fixed the locus of my sight on the cunning movements which she was making with her eyes while turning the pages. "Of course, a good try!" She whispered, "I can see a fine writer of India in you—no doubt!" She said practically as she closed the book.

Thanks, I wanted to say but—

"Although many mistakes are there, but no matter— they can be improved." *Mr. Jitendra* spoke during the time lag. I would have thanked her. "Well, what will you do of this? Will you get it published or sell it?"

"What shall we have to do for getting it published?" Amit became active.

"Many works are there. First of all it is to be copyrighted. And then..... blah–blah–blah!" He said, "But why do you worry? You can get a good amount of this, if you want. . . ."

"How?" Amit asked.

"You can sell it." He cleared his wicked mean.

We both, Amit and I lifted our eyes up, looked each other and kept looking for a while.

"Well, you can get ten lakhss" He gave a reminder as they waved a smiling bye – bye, ". . . . If you want!"

"What do you say?" Amit asked me when we were taking the dinner. "We are going to get ten lakhs."

"We will get it published!" I said pausing the spoon of rice and yellow *daal* near my mouth.

"But how?" He said with a chaos in his mind.

"How....!" I left my breath. Yea, we know nothing. I was silent but saved the 'HOW' in my mind.

At 11, I switched off the light of the room, we would sleep in. We both were sleeping; close to each other. But my soul was wondering here and there. Where, don't know; I found myself at my college in the cycle competition. I saw I'm standing like a statue near *Dhaka Sir*. I saw Pharat is laughing at me; everyone is laughing at me. I saw Mani7ha stepping towards me from the stairs, in the same way she actually came to me. "Mani7ha, please...... don't say to me the same stopping sorts again." I said.

".......Idiot, I love you; believe in you!" She smiled.

I appreciated it.

"If we don't have anything to prepare but the hunger supper, we can at least manage the broken rice; can prepare the khichri— all hunger over, that's it!" She threw a senseless lecture with her quizzical expression.

"What?" I wakened by the knock of 'WHAT' in dream; it was 3 O'clock in morning. I placed my back against the wall and went in depth with the dream. What was she wanted to say exactly?

Amit also got up to 4. We both left our bed for the morning walk. I was chaotic all the time because of the dream, I had in morning.

I caught a photograph on the wall of *Bit-tthoo Javdekar*, an actress and also an M.P. from the area we live in, with my eyes as we passed by some school. Wacky-wacky! Suddenly I stopped. I let my gaze wander towards the picture; smiley-smiley-smiley.

"What happened?" Amit came back to me from the distance which he added.

"Is there any sweet– shop?" I asked him, a funny question.

"What?"

"Tell, na!" I danced with my expressions. "My novel has been published!!!"

"Hey? Anything wrong . . . .?" He put his right palm on my shoulder with a doubt. Had really I took leave of my sense?

# 48

"Salutation naturally comes to me!" I said to him with renewed confidence, smiling while we got back the room. I told him not much but asked to leave *Mumbai* for his village.

He was in a fix. Yea! He had seen my task-solving skill recently-how I solved the loan prob—so his mind looked some more wondering. He praised me to a lot for my sharp intelligence as I told him the crack pot plan— actually, I had an idea to invite *M.P. Bit-tthoo Javdekar.*

Whatever, in ten days we walked up to his dorm, my students along. There, for the programme purpose, I selected an opened ground. It was out of the dorm, somewhat below the by-pass, pothole and a place useless for the people.

It needed a hard labour.

I looked at *Hanny,* the best student of mine; 9 o'clock. It was night. And the moon looked charming; was casting its milkish light.

"At this time?"

"So what?" My mouth blasted.

He became a kite, not respected the airwards, falling down. "No, I mean you....... you anything....morning." He stuttered with his comic face. What he wanted to speak, exactly?

"What?"

He got stupefied here. "Nothing, let's go guys." He said vibrantly leading all his folks, a heroic style boy!

Actually, we had no much time—the chief guest *M.P. Bit-tthoo Javdekar* was going to come around 12, next day— and there were many things to do.

My all boys scythed the grass and plained the ground. Amit and me were also with them all the time, helping.

It was 2, and the ground was ready for the programme.

By 4, the stage was ready.

At 7, that's it; in 12 hours everything was almost ready.

"Good morning sir!" I heard a familiar voice in my back while *Amit* was on the stage adjusting the mike on lectern and I was tying a covering with an iron pillar; one student was on the podium making the sofas and one was scattering the chairs.

I turned my head back.

A fumbling boy, not very healthy, in white check *T-shirt* and blue *jeans*, stood before my eyes. He was *Zeeshan*, one of my B.A students. I noticed a bag with him.

He was handicapped—with no good physique-and had to use crutches.

"Good morning!" I responded.

"Sir, there are some papers". He spoke hesitatingly.

"Papers......, of what?" I spluttered.

"Sir, day before yesterday I didn't come to tuition. So to know what you taught that day, yesterday morning I phoned *Hanny*. He told, you were busy with some programme. Yesterday evening, the next of kin of *Hanny*, told me each and every thing."

I fixed my gaze on his tongue.

He was fumbling at his legs and added "Sir, however, I could print these papers for advertising. These can be pasted on the walls and also can be distributed to the people."

He showed some papers also. These were pink, yellow and white.

"Sir, I have prepared the *laiyee* too to stick the papers on the walls." He spoke one minute later; tongue-tied voice hesitating but feelings excited.

He was wondering about the decoration of the programme with his eyes—the decoration was in an apple pie order; all the things were speaking lively.

Forty seconds after, a boy, an eighteen neared us.

He had put on a white levi's[tm] which had been flattered with two black lines in each pants end to end. A bucket was in his hand, the *laiyee* in it.

"Look at it, Sir!" *Zeeshan* brought my eyes upto the bucket.

A smile of inward pleasure slipped over my lips. "*Zeeshan*!" I looked at him lovingly.

"Sir, a teacher can ignore a student, as he has many others. But a student is nothing without a teacher. However, he can't forget him."

I peeped into his eyes and noticed the subcutaneous brightness of a student glinting in the words of his.

"No, my lovely leveret; no, it's not so, as you think! A teacher is also incomplete without a student." I skied a shot of words.

"Then, why?"

"*Zeeshan*, you are already.......!"

"So what, sir? Not more, but something I also can do. Why from the sublime to this ridiculous?"

"My son, why don't you understand? It is not your cup of tea." By the words, I made a plateau.

"Sir, I'm handicapped, for only this, can't I do any thing for my teacher. Can't I do even any tiny work?" he said emotionally, the pearls of tears twinkling on his eyelids.

My subconscious silent!

"Ok, go. I'm not stymieing you." I waved my head.

At the same moment, *Hanny* appeared with six *rickshaws* along with *rickshaw-puller-students*. Every *rickshaw* was completed with a sound-box and mike. All of they came practicing how to announce among the people.

"*Hanny*!" I called phlegmatically.

"Yes, sir!" he came upto me. His next of kin *Vipul, Bipin* and two other students also came along.

"Take him with yourself and teach everything."

"Okay, Sir!" He, the naughty boy, blunted the sharp blade of my eyes.

They all left that place. Crying and making noises eight minutes later, about 8.20.

Really, the student is a great levia than others. Nothing goes before it. How lucky I was that I got such sort of students who were ready to do anything for me! My heart wanted to touch the feet of the studentship of my pupils. I was upto soul in the suds of proud.

And there the announcement was being made.

May, I have your kind attention, please. Respected M.P, M.P. **Bit –tthoo Javdekar** . . . . . . to your village, via. . . . , is arriving today at 3.30"

Tin-tin-tin.

To have a walk in the programme, in a large number and to make it successful and beautiful, you all are requested and are welcomed heartily and solicitantly.

Tin-tin-tin.

We thank our lucky stars and elicit your support if you can take out some time to turn up in large numbers.

Jai hoi. . . . . !

Tin-tin-tin.

May I have your kind attention please . . . . . .

In an hour the orotund words were dancing; *rickshaws* were taking the rounds in the villages.

Relatively speaking, the people were stupefied with that sudden programme. Whoever heard, wondered.

The people all over were being gathered. I got the generator started and started the programme with my favourite song *Jai Hoi* from *Slum Dog Millionaire*, a movie, my most favourite.

Their Amit proved himself the best receptionist; welcomed every one heart fully; provided them with their seats.

The progamme looked fine, but my bad luck.....

Suddenly, not long after start of the programme, about 10.20, a big block of thunder clouds looked coming from the north-east. Soon it began to rain very hard. It was relentless and was getting more and more strong, and refused to stop—a maltreat and moi-eating thing.

People started running from there and very soon we were alone—all my students, *Amit* and myself. My head began to ache. One of the students stopped the generator.

I stood in the open rain–while all others were under the shade of *pandal*—staring at the wea ther God. My both hands were in the pockets of my jeans. I was hot-eyed; in double jeopardy.

The God must be an examiner of $10^{th}$—as pissed as a newt, I noticed all programme, my dream looked going in vain. No mercy on me!

Around one, the God looked to show pity; the rain stopped.

Now, there was no rain. Although the clouds were in same state as earlier, but no matter! I noticed a deluge of water everywhere, the incubus great!

All the chairs were submerged 5 cms in the water; I looked at helplessly. The stage was wet. The *pandal* was also wet. I noticed the generator barely showed its upper end-the potholes over flowing!

It made me indecisive, the pitch darkness around me. I remembered the day I was planning to go to *Kota* and my elder brother poked his nose; here the rain looked me similarly in his shoes. I was weeping silent tears!

"Butterua. . . . ; Butterua. . . !" *Amit* shook my all body as if he found me any ice stone. My all pupils were also with him.

I could hear his voice and could see others all around me but was not in position of replying; was sad like never before. *"Hmm. ...?"*

No one spoke. They looked at each-other.

"It's really bad!" *Hanny* whimpered with serious expression.

"Is she coming?" I asked Amit nostalgically on a more serious note, ignoring *Hanny*.

"*Yea*; in three hours!" He answered three minutes after confirming on phone. "She has two other programmes too to visit." He said.

"It means, still we have two hours!" *Hanny* spoke heftily; pulled every one's attention.

I wanted to speak something but—

"C'mon guys!" The boy full of beans, beckoned and went to beaver away with all his companions.

When going gets tuff;

Tuff gets the going!

I did nothing but kept looking at him as he was going. Today, I remembered everything; noticed everyone. I looked myself in him.

I looked at *Amit*; he alongwith some other students scoured out a hole in a side. Now, the water was moving towards it and they were emptying that with buckets which they collected from the village. I noticed, some other students untied the covering cloths and fixed as they were, wringing them. I saw they wrung the carpets of the ground and also of the stage. They placed them in their previous position; left no fault there.

Finally, they all hauled the generator out of the pothole and tried to start it. But beau coup efforts of theirs looked no use. I saw they were really trying hard. I closed my eyes and my *Mani7ha* was there padding towards me— smiling and shying— with her tippet tight around the backside of her waist while she held an end of it with her right hand. And, suddenly—

The generator was started—*Jai Ho!* I heard a thunderous, enthusiastic noise in my ears. I noticed they all were coming towards me with their squelching feet.

"Sir, still 15 minutes are left in 3." *Hanny* smiled with satisfaction.

I couldn't believe how wonderfully my all students mugged upon an idea very fantastic and without mulling! Psychologically, I had been hemmed in tickling from inside my body. How lucky I was!.

"So, be ready! The main work is left to do . . . ." I said smiling patting on his shoulder.

They went to improve their appearance. And here I climbed up the podium and held it. Now, the same noise of the announcement was there, once more. I noticed the people started coming again—they were evermore taken aback.

I saw every corner of the hall was heavily gathered before my eyes. I was speaking and they all were listening. Here, my all students, along with my friend proved themselves as good receptionists, once more.

I called in *Amit* on the podium; actually, I hadn't had anything since last two days so it felt me a little bit tough to carry on.

"However, now it looked, the weather god had mercy on us; the rain had stopped. Anyway, respected M.P. Smt. ***Bit- tthoo javdekar,*** the chief guest of this programme is gonna be very soon among us. You are requested to give a warm welcome for her. It will be the chance ....." He was calling out to them.

# 49

"Respected M.P. *Sahiba,* the chief guest of this programme, my all students my folk *Mr. Amit Yadav* and you all respected people, it is me *Butterua Giri Goswami* with a feelings of warm reception for you. At heart, I'm highly indebted to this remarkable support that you came and beautified this ceremony. And.... would like to place on record my gratitude and apologies also to *Buaa ji, the star* of this occurrence along with you all people that I pained you in this thunderous weather. I' will be of course very thankful to you for all life— your cooperation sacred!" I breathed calmly as I held the lectern after *Amit.* "Very often it happens that we get an opportunity to do some thing; people believe us. Well, optionally every one wants to do this or that. But it needs a chance. My opinion is that an opportunity is every thing! Here, as we all know that just some time ago *Buaa Ji* was not given the Ticket for contesting election, but now...." I continued speaking while—

The active lady located her eyes at me as she noticed me opening the pages of her election's epoch—actually a rumour spread that Azam *Khan,* any star leader, bloody wicked wolf of her own party wanted to colour his night with her but got angry when unsuccessful and was after her in the election as an befitting reply of the word smith women.

"At the time, some people from her own party were after her, many doubts there. In such situation, she needed a chance and that she was given. We did as much as we could do". And now we see. . . . . "I turned my head towards the centre of the function." *Buaa ji,* today I'm also in the same situation in which you were sometime before. *Buaa Ji*—

The sun eagerly hath all

Get the east, let go on;

You'll see the noon and more

No doubt; promise! I promise!
The east does morning; does all.
The nonchalant air – not ever shown.
It is the nook. No, other way to shore—
All sky hell. Promise! I promise!
Cool- Cool deadly you do call;
Do be proud, you heard the horn.
All I say is, it is the core.
If the east, the light at all
No morn, if not; it's over on.
I'm like all it for"
I threw an epigram.

I kept on speaking and she kept on listening. I told all about my life and moved curvedly towards my cunning mean. With a delay on mike, I gave a nudging look to *Hanny* and handed him the polythene in which my novel was, to press before my dark luck. *"Buaa ji,* this is the novel, I sweated for. And now it is completed. I wish you to get it published. *Buaa Ji,* I want only a chance. So, please........ please, come and say something; I'm waiting for your answer; expecting positive!" I said and descended the stairs.

I sat in a red colour chair, straight; doing diddly— squat except angling my eyes on her reaction.

She came to the lectern with a vote of thanks. "Dear, I'm very pleased looking at all this. I wonder you loved your study so much. I wish I would have been in your shoes!" She expressed the dictum, my praise made me smiling inwards. "About your novel I would think. I would try....." She said and paused to look at me.

Diddums! She was speaking on while I couldn't stand the words *would -think* and *would-try.* I screw the cap of a *tiny jar* open and **swallowed the all poison in it**—one last time, I was a lamb to the 'slaughter'.

I threw the jar.

*Ha!* The wind stopped. The clouds stopped. Everything stopped. The great lady could understand nothing, all people as well. Their breaths stopped. And here, the earth looked me circling around and very soon I started vomiting. I fell down from the chair.

I was vomiting and they all were hogging me around. I was falling into unconsciousness while I heard someone cried get–me-an–ambulance. Who would have called out? *Buaa Ji, no*?

"Butterua, hey . . . . . ?" Don't know after how long, a buzzing came in to my ears.

I was unable to move, energy level low. Moreover, my right arm was connected with a blood bottle through a fine rubber tubing while the smooth plastic pack was clamped with a stand and hung over my head. Was I in hospital?

I laboured away to notice the speaking person. *Buaa Ji* was there beside— I looked around. I noticed *Amit* and my students along with a team of specialists stood around me.

". . . .Are you ok?" She patted me on my forehead.

"My Novel . . .?" I laboured the point while I could blink only the expression, to use the lips next to impossible.

She smiled and nodded her head.

"I wonder, what are you?" *Amit* asked me with all surprise when we were going to attend an occasion on the publishing day of my novel. At the time, we sat in the state car while I was with *Buaa Ji,* near the driver and *Amit* along, my all pupils on back seat.

"Why?" I whispered peeping out from the side window—it was around ten, at night. The car was running along the sandy sea-side. I was gazing every thing—how beautiful was every thing!

"You spread your name all over the world within a *ziffy* while it takes all life to do it." He said, "You know, today everyone knows you. People are waiting for your novel."

"Yea, I know." I turned my head and looked at him smiling. "Of course, risk is a great think. I knew better the result of my propramme already, I thought. And , result came in my favour".

*"Butterua* you don't care for your life?" *Bua ji* asked me with a picturesque gesticulation.

"I care of nothing!" I spoke calmly in a serious tone. "I love my sweat. I can eat everything for it. I can die. I can kill. Every thing. . ."

She did not speak but kept figuring out my expressions.

In ten minutes, we stepped down the car, in the ground of *Iden Palace*, a famous five star Hotel in *Mumbai*. A fantabulous programme there!

"Butterua can not be any author. He is more than that; something else. I have noticed he is a completely different mood boy. He creates the ideas in so amazing way that I can call him the author of India." She was on the podium, expressing an interjection for me while the audience was giving big round of applause**. *"Very soon he will be the biggest selling English language novelist in India's history*—** I hope so!" She spoke and once more the people broke into rapturous noise of clapping.

How would I be feeling?

# 50

Seldom, a haze of **Whats** and **Hows** play a hazardous hide and seek with the worst moment of our life. In that, whoever and however hits the nails on the head, that gets success how wonderfully. I, hit big phenomenon personality, the most loved author of India—who had been twirled around by the time of ups and downs fumigating all and who had fledged and proved ownself fully—had the ins and outs of. The dint of sweat and continuity and the quality of self-confidence play how amazing role in life, and all these, how become the reason for surprise, I had encountered that too.

However critical, the incidents were enacted or took place in my life or hemmed me, but now I was on my track, my novel got published, enough wealth now— a special thank for *Bhaa ji*. Now, I was that what I usually would yearned for; was the heart of India. And this all happened not long before; just one year ago I was nothing but now......

But now, I was glad. I had made up leeway. Today I had my own reputation, my own luxuries, a car and a big comfortable palace— Lunar Lot.

And this all could come true because of Amit. As a God sent, he helped me in my necessity; saved me by a hair's breadth of being a meal of death, during the terrible night of hailstorm. He showed me these halcyon days of life, actually. Otherwise, what I was, nothing. He sheltered me, a sort of toss pot stranger, a cold sweated new kid on the block of Bombay; he was really very great.

"So, what do you think about Mani7ha?" He looked at me as he slurped a few drops of tea. May be any particularity towards the topic, but I thought he just wanted to make the communication.

At the time, we both were on the roof of our Lunar Lot. It was a top notch arbor, a topmost torso of the palace to what I always would call *Dream world.* It was the greatest true imagination on any roof all over the world. Awesome! Really, awesome!

It was a flowery moonlit night. Every end of the sky was swathed by its fresh coolness. Stars were twinkling hither and thither. The great fabulous moon was loquaciously jeering at me totting my all desires and dreams high up.

A gentle swing that I was swinging on, was flying in the zephyr, over an artificial zigzag brook, trickling by the margin of foe fountain, continued an artificial stony hill swathed with orbuts and shrubs from.

The brook was filled with swimming shoads of different sorts of fish. Many more showy stones were located in it.

There were all sorts of flowers, lush green grass, wanted fillers along–all the *Lunar Lot* was stuffed with enchanting smell and spellbounding beauty.

"Mani7ha, who?" I rolled my eyes, pretended as if I was really new to this name. Actually, I alluded like this just to delve into bottom of any Mephistophelian mean, in his mind.

"Your girlfriend or who . . . . .?" He replied back at once totally surprised with the sort of strange answer from me.

"Oh, that . . ............" I left the swing and moved towards the core of my *Dream World.* "What's special in her? Now, there are many of her sisters; whupping reply for her in charm and blazing ness– bomb shell!"

"Man, I understand, today you have money. But don't be lost in it so much. Money is not to any one. And I think a person should not forget his roots, however high he may fly because whenever he falls it holds him!"

"So, you say that she is earth for me?"

"No! I say she is everything for you!"

"Really, I don't know . . . . . ." I said watching the lighting high way, swarmed with rocketing motors and people, during an universal flash of moon light.

"How, would you know?" He remarked almost annoyed, "Mind has been corrupt......"

"*Amit bhaiya,* you too....!" I said, trying to put my hand on his shoulders.

"Don't touch me!" He cried with high voltage anger and threw my hand away. "Like this, any day you will forget me, too."

Now, I could not stop myself; I laughed and laughed and laughed till my stomach ached. I wanted to tease him some more but he came in actual acting with a poem, before I had thought anything else. He recited—

*"Butterua, love is true*
*The most holy thing on earth*
*It is. God does it.*
*By love this all world;*
*And in world we all are—*
*So, it is for all!*
*All success in it!*
*All colours in it!*
*I say, it is blue and green*
*It turns a stone into water*
*And a wild in to a cow*
*It is God;*
*And more in some extent.*
*Bless you! Her love true!*
*And no selfishness*
*God listens; if one in it."*

"Oh, poet..........", I laughed once more as he completed all the poem. "Don't be serious, I was just teasing you; peeping into your soul!" I explained while putting my cup on the edge of the little wall, around my *'Dream World.'*

A little later, he got some cool, but still suspicious about my words. He was continuously looking at me.

"Brother, I love her; she is mine......!" I said as I encircled his waist with my arms and hung my all weight on it. "She is the most amazing girl in the world; even *Rati*, the Goddess of beauty is no one before her looks! I'm absolutely nuts about her!"

"And still you haven't thought anything for that poor girl!" He said trying to use his energy on the circle of my arms around him.

For some time, I was in deep silence, but soon came out with action; I left him and moved towards the tiproaring fountain what was the soul of that all imagination on the roof. The drops were springing up, dancing in the zephyr and falling down with a great noise and were producing many more ripples and spashes.

You know, I always loved larking by swinging, watching the scraggy beauty of ripples and splashes and the traffic, leaning on the lowest wall, walking arms folded narrowly on the margin of the brook, talking to moon and ownself, teasing the fish, going on the hill and touching the faux silty soils. But here, now I was serious and did nothing. I went to the pew, near the hill just to sit on, alone—now I own self felt no energy in me.

"Any way, good you *Mr. Butterua!"* He came upto me when we came down stairs; put his cup down and unfolded a white paper. "There is a letter for you!!"

"From *Mani7ha*?" I became excited as if all the energy of the world dropped in me. All it encapsulated was I was still enamored with *Mani7ha*, an enchantress with the whole enchilada, all I needed was. "Bless you!" Today you have shown you are my friend, the best one. I love you. I love you very much . . . . . . ! I was completely emotional; snatched the letter from his hands. And then I lifted him and started bouncing him.

"Put me down! Hey, leave me; put me down!" He cried almost laughing.

I asked myself not to waste my energy in that sort of silly act; I threw him down. "What is this?" I stared at him as I went through all the letter; was angry on this kind of joke.

He smiled "Read again; this is the letter from her college. They are inviting you as the chief guest." He said, "Hundred percent she will be there. And you can meet her..."

"Yaar, it has been long time since I saw her innocent face! Don't know how would she be, now?" I said and fell in emotions once more while we both were in car, going for her college—I sat beside him and he was driving the limousine.

He smiled at me. The chief guest of any college was speaking like this!

# 51

I was completely in her dream. *I saw she was sitting alone, on a pew, in a garden–looked almost feeling the sort of pain. Are you alright? I asked. No! She replied, trying to ignore me and trying to lord it over me. May, I press your forehead? I kept silent for a while and then dared to speak. No, it's not your right she said rudely; stood up and then started stepping ahead. What? I enlarged my eyebrows with surprise. Here, at this, she turned with her all body, dropped her eyes and then held them again. I tell you there was an enchanting morn on her pliant face and that was that I had a predilection for. Nothing! She spoke and ran back towards me. Now we both were one.*

At the time, my limousine stopped, giving a sudden shock.

"What happened?" I, a lazy bozo in dream, woke up.

He didn't speak, but I could see everything, after rubbing my eyes; three young men stood there before the car. I tell you I felt a lot of fear in side the car.

I couldn't feel even, that my body guards were there before them. They tried to remove them from the front.

"You bloody servant of two coins!" one of those three, cried and pushed one of my body guards as he tried to employ some force. "I would beat you, your honcho along."

I could listen them. But I couldn't dare to go out. I really got scared of.

Actually, Pharat was there, that too with all team.

My father would say whenever you find any bull in your way; try to save yourself rather than to face him. Because that is a wild and you . . . . . ., I thought it over and silently slipped out from there—while they all were on with threats of violence.

However, I reached the programme, with out any bodyguard, nor any particular impression. It looked as if I was not a chief guest of any college, but was a criminal trying to escape from the police.

"Actually they are coming!" I pleaded on my own worming my way through the crowd as I noticed some worry on the face of welcomers. "We should take a join; they would come!" I made hurry to enter as if any marriage of faulted people is done.

*Prof. Gobajia* held the podium as we all entered and took our seats. He gave a warm welcome to me.

On being called in, I cut the ribbon and the programme was started.

Crumbs! There was a fairy with some other girls, playing a melodious song Baharon Phool Beresoa, Mera Meha Voob Aya Hai—a nice dance, along.

I smiled at the selection of that song by that cunning girl; yes, my Mani7ha was there! She was dancing before my eyes and I was the chief guest of the programme—guess, my dream came true!

Now, every little thing that was being done by her on the stage increased my heart beats with every passing moment. For some time, I forgot I'm any chief guest. I forgot I was any great author. I forgot the sort of repo I had. I tell you I forgot everything. The spell of hers was dancing on my head.

Slowly-slowly, as I had a trip down memory lane, I got lost in my old days, retrospectively remembering, every little incident that took place at my college—the incident when she offered me handshake and I got disappeared, the incident of loo, the incident of lab, the incident of class when she wrote I think now you won't let me be alive, the incident she fought with me at my ignorance, the incident when we did it, the incident when we reached her field and she praised my poetry, the incident of cinema when she beat that unknown girl, the incident of shrine and the incident when at the last time, I kissed her and sang a song just to persuade her.

Ha! Don't know what motivated me; what happened, I stood up from my seat. Don't know when I climbed the stairs and went upto her. And, don't know when I amorously wrapped her in my arms—needless to describe the violence.

"Sorry!" I whispered and herded my lips away from the pond of my malmsey. Music got over a long time before and don't know how long it has been since we both were on. Any way, now the podium was empty and we both looked not more than the prize idiots.

She clutched her red bordered *lehenga* and then moved away behind the curtain, with a lot of shyness.

Now, I was alone on the stage. I looked at every corner of the audience, with my quick sight. And, I could see, they all were shocked as if I had murdered someone.

I caught the lectern. "Sorry, I'm really very sorry!" I dropped down my tongue; couldn't, speak much any more. It was as though I had become tongue-tied. I looked at everyone and mimed them to be seated. "Yea, I'm really very sorry for the nuisance, I created here! Please...; actually, there I have something to tell you. Please. ..." I said with a sudden tingle of excitement and paused to see their reactions.

Now, there was a hotch-potch of amorphous conversation. I saw all the people were discussing each other in haggling manner.

"Of course, it's a thundering shock for you that my sort of author, the heart of India does this cheap deed. But there is something what you don't know, exactly. I explain you everything and hope you would understand me; please. . !" I continued, "The girl, you saw just before, is the reason behind my existence, my girlfriend, loving me madly; we have studied together in 12th." I was announcing the part of my life, decorously but with declamatory tongue.

All the people were in a fix; looked deducing something–something from the crypt clue, I gave.

"That is *Pharat*, that is *Udit*. And that is *Sindhi*." I introduced them with my fellow friends while all the people moved with their eyes on them. "They all are my classmates, my friends the best ones. We all have crisped our college days together in all respect." I expatiated on my college life and then moved to the particular subject as the crow flies; I threw narrated all incidents of my past.

Now, there was a dead silence when I came to an end of my whole *Ramayana. Prof. Gabajia,* the principal of that institute stood up with an ovation and then rest of the crowd responded with wild applause.

Here, let me tell you it was that what I ever wanted to see in my life; I was happy to don't—know—how—much degree.

"Please, please be seated!" I flattered my hands, eye lashes along at the people as I noticed them hotting up and angled for their further step.

My throat got dried. And, I nudged some one, down the stage to arrange for me a glass of water. "You know I would be a topper in anytime. To be an *IITian* would be the dream of my life. I used to sleep and used to wake up with this dream; I was of its at all you can say. But . . . ., I couldn't be such an arsey to sit with you. I tell you today, when I have everything but believe me, I always feel I'm a kind of flat broke either. Here I always long to be a part of this great institute but I know better it is that what can be never." I picked a glass up from the tray he carried. I halted my words for the time being as I got some drops of water into my dried throat. "I tell you I love you to much. And in future, if I'm able to spend the last drop of my blood for you, be sure I would pay it." I flapped, hot dogging the true feeling of my heart.

The audience was silent enough to hear my mild voice.

"Here, I say something; please, listen . . . . . .!" I said and recited the following lines—

*One who hath—*

*The tsunami of sweat*

*One who can tow*

*The everything, or owt*

*With uneven breaths*

*Who is a swaim strutting?*

*In exploding clouds*

*To impossible who's hooting*

*A dangerous rain*

*Without clouds who is*

*Who is an inferno*

*On the frozen, I miss!*

*I love, I die*

*I wanna always see*

*A dog with a belt*

*I can be. . . . !*

I was exulted in my speech and the audience was all eyes; was hounding my every word. I can say people were exhaustively mine, having an eyeful of my exuberance.

"Dear friends! I don't say you should not have fun. I don't say you should not mooch around. And I also don't say you should not have vodka on the top of the insti roof at night or in viva. I don't say this also that you should be a book worm always. But there is something, what I would like to say." I held my breath; mouthed a few obscenities at the muddling face of the audience and then moved off. "Here, I ask you not be loafer always. Be serious also. Be worried also. Because here you have come just to study; just to make your future, not to juice the pleasure from your present. It's not any cinema or any mall. For all other activities, rest of life is there. Any way, if you don't care for your future, your future would start caring of you. So, please don't follow the primrose path." I threw a bigoted speech.

I happened to catch a glimpse of prof. *Gabajia* in the crowd. He looked fullnod and with the glimmer of a respecful smile in his eyes.

I paused for the water again and then started from a fresh point, "Many people suggest eat, drink and be merry; the life is very short. Here, I gloss over it." I gave a brake to my tongue and chanted the last sentence, glibly. "I understand that our life is very short. But it is up to us that we want to remain alive forever, or want to die with our body. Dear friends, there was Edison. He got died long past ago but he is still alive among us. Why? Because he took his life to his heart, and he performed it!"

I held my voice and craned around to get a better view of the audience. I noted people were almost a palpable sense of an acceptance. "Watch it guys, watch it. This is IIT, not some silly regional College. You are *IITians* means the best engineers of the country. You are supposed to be the best in all over the world. The whole country has so many expectations from you, you know?" I relaxed but ran amok with my tongue in the next moment, almost vociferously "You must think, you are like the soldier on the border of our country. And, if a soldier forgets his duty; starts thinking about the pleasure then what of country— you know better!"

All the students were silent, almost serious. It was a pin drop silence there.

A silence in true sense!

I chased around the table of all speech and then finally come out with an excitement high, "Hey guys, I haven't come here just to bore you; cheer up! Just, cheer up!" A sort of smile covered my face as I felt the pleasure of the further sentence — I was going to put it out. "You are students; and, to a student there is no need to tell how to suck eggs. . . . !" I vocalized with the sort of channels, smiling.

Audience got mad; this was the time of unlimited ovation, a wild round of applause!

# 52

No, any unusual occurrences, all function passed delightfully. At last, the Principal, Prof *Gavajia* gave me a keepsake and then I return.

They came upto my car just to see me off. Any way, I received a lot of respect there.

"Hey, Butterua....!" Some one cried as I bent down to step into the car; I could hear it.

A strange surprise, an old man was there—I turned my head. I kept on goggling at him—he was sharply stepping ahead towards me. I figured out and tried to recognize him—my bloody pop he was!

"Butterua, I've come here just to take you; let's go back." "He gave a strangulated squawk as he neared me.

"Where?" I went google – eyed.

"To your place, or where?" He made a sharp dialogue. "You left home; you know how much I was worried for you."

"Eh? I don't understand what are you speaking this all?" I shrugged smiling and looking at other people, standing there. "And, who are you I don't clock!"

"I'm your ***Amma's Khasam!"*** He remained silent for sometime but soon came out with a slang answer. "Now, something occurred, you rich bloke?"

I got dumb founded, of course with no word. I actually had a lot of guilty secret. Believe me, I was too ashamed to face any one. I couldn't pose my head even.

All people were surprised at this but they didn't dare to put across me any further query. I also didn't speak anything.

"What happened? Should I tell you any thing else? Should I tell you how often I had to hump your mother just for you? Should I tell you . . .?" He kept on barking offensively, a sort of bloody cheap man!

I controlled over it. "Hey, start the car. I don't have time to waste; don't wanna talk to such a shameless man!" I said sitting into my car.

"Don't show attitude. You are the blood of this curmudgeonly shameless old man. Today, whatever you are, you are because of me.!"

"Oh, you did this much for me and I didn't realize even!" I passed a commenting smile, almost lambasting him.

Here, he looked in the ocean of humiliation; couldn't collect the courage to speak.

Soon, I curbed my cult and caught some coolness. "Study; study is not on the periphery of our life. It is important! And you didn't care it. . . ." I bleated and my voice got imbued with the sort of emotions like ***King Khan.***

***"Circumstances; beta, circumstances are the most powerful thing! Situations and events insist a person...."*** He remarked intellectually, in a logical way. "Any way, if I hadn't done so with you, you wouldn't have become so high positioned!"

My lips curved in a smile and then I started laughing. I laughed and laughed and laughed. "Today I've come here, so credit goes to you, yea! Where were you when I was weeping for my books? Where were you when I was on footpaths with no food, a fourteen days hungry boy?" I cried and cried, "I could have died, you know . . . . . !"

"Did I ask you to leave the house?"

"Circumstances; *papa ji,* circumstances are the most powerful thing! Situations and events insist a person . . . . !" I remarked back.

He was silent now.

"Let's go!" I nudged towards *Amit* and he started the car.

"*Butterua . . . .!*" Suddenly *Mani7ha* cried and appeared before me piercing the all crowd, "One second, *Butterua!*"

"What?" I whispered as she caught her breath.

"Butterua, I love you, a blind beloved of yours. But listen, I can't love that man who has no respect for his father." She shocked me.

"Hun?"

"Yea, I would forget that I had ever loved you!"

Now, I was muddled. I was unable to speak even. I only kept on looking at her.

"Don't look; I won't go. Do."

The cunning old man, my pop came forward; thought a right time of taking an undue advantage of the situation. He put his hand on my shoulder—

"A potter beats the clay;

Makes it carton—

No claim, he is in it.

Don't abuse your teacher—

If he beats;

No selfishness of his.

He punishes, and you touch the sky.

We leave a baby—

To let him put his new steps

He falls and cries;

And walks reason by—

We can't' be his enemy!

Here, a fly out of milk you were.

And so much pain, so many tears for you

But note! Good for you that!

If I hadn't done so

You would have reached here never!"

Now, I had no blink in my eyes; was so much angry from inside. I was exhaustively silent but my staring eyes were continuously fixed at him all the time.

"Butterua, you must think at least. He is your . . . . !" *Pharat* also had sympathy for him; came forward in his favour.

"Shut up!" I blared to brush him aside while he couldn't complete his all sentence even. "It's none of your business; don't poke your nose!"

"Quite so!" He waved his head while I asked *Amit* to be ready to leave the place.

Here, Amit also got corrupt. He also ignored me and kept standing as if a perfect statue.

However, everyone tried to change my mood but of no avail; I astringently made them shut up.

*"Butterua,* don't be so cruel. Have heart. He is your creator after all!" He lectured me when I asked him one last time to go.

I got irritated. "What do you think I can't drive; I can! Just see, I can; I can drive and more better than you .....!" I murmured and sat in to the car. I started it and went forward with a high gear, throwing a puff of pollution behind it.

I reached my ***Lunar Lot*** alone, without *Amit* without any of body guard. Note, there I remained without any sympathy, a stone hearted cruel boy. You know what I actually did; I reached there where they all wanted to send–yea, it was my way to my place. I put myself in my old house while before them. As they found me there, they got mad with pleasure.

And then, an emotional scene of any Indian movie there!

# EPILOGUE

Whatsoever, now bad time had gone and we all were happy at all. Time passed. And now, I had become a man of the world. It was the first night of my marriage; you know first night..........

"May, I come in?" I knocked at the door of my bridal room.

"It's open, come in." A very sweet voice endowed with spell pierced my ears and I looked to be turned into stone by an enchantment of its.

Very calmly, I reached in. I latched the door from inside and placed myself on the bed before the most beautiful lady of the world; yes, Mani7ha she was!

I reached out my hands to remove her veil. And I did so.

"My first night gift?" She smiled and then smiled with her eyes; an astute beyond sexy chick!

"You don't shy?" I also smiled and took out key to scooty from the pocket of my sherawani.

It bucked her up that she received a scooty from me – actually, scooty was the thing which she loved the most.

"You have carried that?"

"That what?"

"Beer. . . ."

"You really don't shy!"

"Why should I? You are not new to me. Or should I tell you the size of your that . . . ?" She laughed with her right hand making its way towards my, you-know-what?

"Shut up, Mani7ha! Have some shame!" I caught hold her hand. "I'm your husband, now!"

"So, now you won't do anything like that?" She laughed mellifluously again. ".... Means our love won't result a baby; I wouldn't be the mother of my Indian cricket team!"

Blood started flowing through my veins to activate those testosterones and I could feel the twitch in my Fannies, as she continued speaking like this. I tell you here I had to work hard to control my feelings; I bit my lips.

There was the morning on her face and I wanted to gaze at that forever.

"I'm looking beautiful?" She asked when she found me lost in any world.

I didn't speak but nodded in expression and then, I started putting her all jewellery off from her.

"Hey, what are you doing this?" She moaned in delight when I tried to snatch her tippet.

"I'm in mood!" I gently pushed at her shoulders to make her lie back on the bed and came ownself on her while I had removed almost all clothes.

"You ever missed me?" She asked a childish question while I was a hungry dog around her neck with my tongue.

Oyvey! Now, tell her; tell her how I passed my time without her. "Right now, don't ask anything. I'm in mood!" I said while my hands were under her bra, lecherously cupping her breasts.

"Butterua, I've heard usually you men give a lot of importance to the sex. How you managed it in my absence?" She asked me while I was going to undo the hook behind her brassiere; actually, I wanted her completely with no barriers between us.

"Many of your sisters were there . . . . . !" I said just to tease her.

"What?"

"But I tried only two or three, not more." I teased her even more.

"Get down! Get down, just leave me!" She said and pushed me away.

"What happened?" I said laughing.

"Nothing, get lost. . . ." She cried and then started hitting me with pillows, with bangles and with every thing she could find in her hand at the time. "You bloody loafer, here I was always praying for you. And there you were juicing many other chicks!"

She wrapped her all clothes and I could do nothing except watching the whole play. "Sorry!" I caught my ears as I noticed her anger high.

"Put your sorry here, in my......" She broke into sudden cry and then into smile.

"Hooo............ you use slang?" I laughed goggling at her and closing my mouth with my hands as a sign of what- are-you-saying sort of shame. I also tried to grope, "Mani7ha, you .....!"

"Be away." she pushed me again, "And please, don't put my holy name on your dirty tongue."

"Jaan, I'm in mood!" I said lazily.

"So what should I do? Go, many of my sisters are there." She threw a put-down and didn't listen anything further.

Well, the matter was not going to be cooked now. But the heart couldn't agree with it; I tried again. "If I carry a glass of beer, then. . . ." I spoke stupidly, a no use dialogue.

"Am I asking you for . . . . . ?"

"No but I can if you allow."

"Don't act smart; and go from here. I feel sleepy. . . ." She yanked and pretended to fall asleep.

I was dumfounded, but was next to her, bloody shyless "So come in my arms; you would be comforted." I said and a sort of smile came across my face.

"Shut up!" She cried, loud enough to fall on the floor of my face.

For the next some minutes, no communication occurred; the situation proved me a fool. "At least, you can talk to me, or not?" I spoke out when she kept pretending of sleep and didn't speak to me, excitement to the nth. "It's good, there is my wife and I can't even touch her—that to during first night." I murmured and got down the bed just to sleep on the floor.

She didn't speak but kept on smiling hiding her face which was enough to tease me.

"It's a good cleverness if you don't wanna have a relation with someone, ignore him at all. For some time he would beat his head and then..." I continued speaking grotesquely, really amusing creature or any comic cartoon. I was wrapped in blanket—almost.

"Don't murmur, or get out of the room if you can't; I'm getting disturbed." She said almost with teasing smile.

"Tease me! Tease me, you bloody cock teaser— tease me! But be sure, you won't get even hell; committing a great sin!" I cried, getting mad in annoyance.

And then, I got sleep; about her don't know.

At night, I suddenly found somebody leaning on me, and then some hair strands on my face. A little later, I felt someone juicing my lips. Was I in any dream?

"You . . . . . ?" I suddenly broke into cry; Mani7ha there was, that too in reality, not in dream.

"Don't cry! I'm in mood!" She cooed and pushed me down insistently as I tried to be active.

And then, she did something that I had to carry her up to the bed. Now, she was mine at all.

"I've heard we get a son, if we do it in morn." She said with almost delirious expression on her face as I went up to her cleavage with my panting tongue.

"It is?" I said excitedly. And then don't ask . . . . .